ROBERT GORDON SPROUL

Photograph by g. Paul Bishop

TWENTY-EIGHT YEARS
IN THE LIFE OF A
UNIVERSITY PRESIDENT

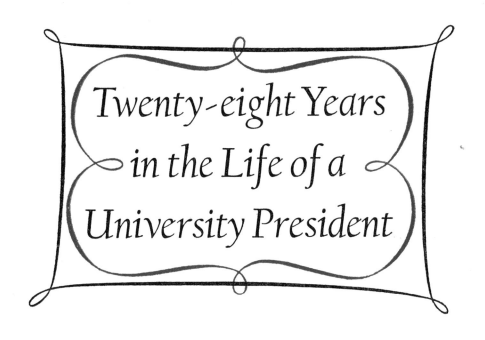

Twenty-eight Years in the Life of a University President

BY GEORGE A. PETTITT

FOREWORD BY CLARK KERR

UNIVERSITY OF CALIFORNIA
1966

Foreword

During the administration of President Benjamin Ide Wheeler, the University of California became a university in fact as well as in name; during the administration of Robert Gordon Sproul, it became one of the most eminent universities in the nation.

"Bob" Sproul worked actively in, and for, the University of California from 1909, when he entered as a freshman student, to 1958, when he exchanged the title of President for that of President Emeritus. For only a short time during all those years was his close connection with his alma mater interrupted—the year following his graduation, when he worked for the City of Oakland. He came back the next year as a member of the University's administrative staff. Later he became Comptroller, subsequently Vice-President, and in 1930 President of the University.

He saw enrollments rise, during his presidency, from 20,000 to more than 45,000. Three undergraduate liberal arts colleges were started—at Santa Barbara, Davis and Riverside. Faculty membership in the National Academy of Sciences grew from 18 to 59. The number of Nobel Laureates on the faculty rose from zero to six. In an authoritative study of the quality of graduate departments, Berkeley stood ninth in 1925, second in 1957; UCLA did not even place in 1925 since it did not grant the Ph.D. until 1938. In 1957 it stood in fourteenth place.

For twenty-eight years, the triumphs and the agonies of the University belonged to him, more than to anyone else. And the triumphs were far greater than the agonies, as the rise of the University to eminence bears unmistakable witness.

Foreword

In the present volume, one of President Sproul's long time associates, Dr. George A. Pettitt, has chronicled the achievements, the problems, and many of the sometimes amusing, sometimes frustrating, and sometimes gratifying daily incidents that went to make up the impressive total of Robert Gordon Sproul's career.

The concluding chapter presents selections and excerpts from President Sproul's large accumulation of public addresses. I do not know whether to be reassured or discouraged by the fact that a number of the problems to which he addressed himself in these speeches are still with us, still under active discussion in California higher education today. In any case, reading them is an instructive experience.

Throughout his career, President Sproul was privileged to have the unfailing sympathy and help of Ida Amelia Sproul, his charming and gracious wife who shared with him both the triumphs and the agonies of the presidential years. This book is issued in tribute to her as well as to him; I am sure that their many friends and admirers will enjoy reading about them in these pages.

CLARK KERR

The editor acknowledges with gratitude the assistance rendered by Miss May B. Dornin, History Consultant, and Mr. Robert S. Johnson, Assistant to the Vice-President of the University, in checking the accuracy of various sections of this work, and at the same time takes personal responsibility for any errors which have been overlooked in spite of their help and that of others who read the manuscript.

GEORGE A. PETTITT

Contents

TWENTY-EIGHT YEARS
IN THE LIFE OF A
UNIVERSITY PRESIDENT

I

Background for a President

Most students of higher education seem to agree that the success of a college or university board of trustees can best be measured by its wisdom in choosing a president—along with faith and trust in its own choice, willingness to allow the president to work out the educational destiny of the institution in full partnership with the faculty, and the determination to provide necessary financial support. It is the responsibility of the board to choose between alternatives, but if board members begin initiating alternatives, there is great danger that they will end up proving only that a camel is a horse put together by a committee.

The University of California has been more fortunate than the average state university in this regard, probably because of the powers assured to the Regents of the University by the state constitution, the long terms of those appointed to the Board, the importance of the position, and the care that governors of the state have almost invariably shown in the selection of appointees. There are many opinions as to the proper length of term for an appointed member of a board of trustees in higher education, but it seems to be clear that the sixteen-year-term of appointed Regents of the University of California, as long as any in the United States, has given this institution a greater advantage of experience and degree of continuity than is normally enjoyed elsewhere. In the last 60 years this has resulted, among other things, in the choice of two presidents who survived the vicissitudes of office for twenty years or longer: Benjamin Ide Wheeler, from 1899 to 1919; and Robert Gordon Sproul, from 1930 to 1958.

In 1943, Iowa State College Press published a "Manual for Trustees of Colleges and Universities," prepared by President Emeritus Raymond M. Hughes, which went through three editions in its first eight years. This volume devotes several chapters to a better definition of the areas in which trustees of a college or university should exercise authority directly and of those areas in which authority should be delegated to a chief executive officer, the president, or to the faculty. Selection of a president is classed as one of the most difficult and frequently recurring responsibilities of a board of trustees, among other reasons because of the tendency to select candidates of established reputation and advanced age who have to be replaced very shortly after they have reorganized the administration and achieved some measure of a pattern of effective operation.

President Hughes suggests that the age range for presidential candidates should be from 35 to 52 years, and that items to be considered should include marriage and children, church relations, education and degrees, publications if any, educational and administrative experience, financial experience, speaking ability, personality in relation to staff unity, and student good will. President Hughes also reminds trustees that consideration should first be given to members of the staff of their own institution. This procedure, they are cautioned, requires some correction of qualifying data; there is always more complete information on the faults of a local candidate than on those of candidates from a distance. The second source to which trustees are advised to look is alumni of the college or university; if any of these meet the necessary qualifications they will bring to the position a pre-existing loyalty.

Background for a President

The first edition of President Hughes' book did not come (
presses until fourteen years after Robert Gordon Sproul was (
eleventh President of the University of California, but the Reg
the University could scarcely have followed the formula more
if they had had the volume in front of them on the June after
1929 when they voted on a successor to President William
Campbell, who had announced his intention to retire at the
the following academic year.

Robert G. Sproul, the first of two sons, was born in San F
on May 22, 1891, to Robert and Sarah Elizabeth (Moore) S
attended James Lick Grammar School, where he won hon
graduation, and Mission High School, where he took the
course, if not by personal preference then in deference to pare
His father had been a school teacher in Lanarkshire, Scotla
he emigrated to the New World in 1887, and his mother th
anyone with a voice like his would make an excellent la'

In those days relatively few graduates of high schools
college. Young Robert, however, in addition to having the
a father who had taught school and a mother who was an
typesetter in the printing business, was stimulated by
Mission High who had been trained at the University (
Among them a young Latin teacher named Monroe E.
later to become a Professor of Latin at Berkeley and to s
former student as Vice-President of the University.

In determining his pursuits young Robert was un
fluenced by the fact that extra money to meet the amb
a teenager cannot always be found in the pocketbook
beginning a new career as an accountant for the San
He sold newspapers as a youngster and worked as a
surveying crew for about a year between high school a
lation at the University in 1909. Later, during summ
sold aluminum ware from door to door and also solic
on commission, for the "Frosh Bible," an orientation
students published by the University YMCA. His
people was deepened by his experience in selling ute

3

tive housewives during a period when rumors still flew that whole families had been poisoned by aluminum stewpans. And it is not strange that he spent a year with a surveying crew and chose a major in civil engineering at college, for he had experienced the San Francisco fire and earthquake and knew that the world needed rebuilding.

Robert Sproul gave up the profession of engineering after one year as an efficiency engineer for the Civil Service Board of the City of Oakland, where the most important thing that happened to him was a meeting with a young lady named Ida Amelia Wittschen, who became Mrs. Robert Gordon Sproul on September 6, 1916. After he resigned his position with the City of Oakland young Sproul accepted a new position as cashier for the University of California, and it was just five weeks after he received his first raise in pay from $125 a month to $200 that he and Miss Wittschen decided to meet at the altar. With bread still selling at five cents a loaf this was an ample salary on which to get married and start a family. It was, moreover, a relatively munificent sum for a young man just two years out of college. It gave promise that he might have a successful career. Undoubtedly he was subconsciously encouraged, also, by the fact that his new job was important enough to require a $20,000 bond, an astronomical sum which made up for the small size of his first desk.

Robert Sproul has always taken pride in his Scottish ancestry and in the fact that his middle name, Gordon, honors General Charles G. "Chinese" Gordon, British Governor of the Sudan, who lost his life in 1885 in a revolt led by the Mohammedan leader Mahdi at Khartoum. But being a Scot who missed being born in Scotland by about four years and honoring a British General whose head was carried through the streets of Khartoum on a spear did not make young Robert dour or downcast. As a student in the College of Engineering at Berkeley he departed from tradition for engineers to the extent of joining a fraternity, Abracadabra; going out for track and winning his Big "C" as a two-miler; and, because of his height, allowing himself to be drafted as Drum Major for the Marching Band. In addition, he made his debut in politics by winning election to the presidency of the junior class and of the University YMCA.

4

Background for a President

Human beings are classified as gregarious animals, and in this regard Robert Sproul is as human as anyone. He likes people and this liking has been reciprocated by practically everybody he has ever met. Warmth of personality is not assumed to be an innate characteristic of the Scottish people, but Robert Sproul's father made up for this by the wisdom with which he chose his son's mother. Sarah Elizabeth Moore had come to California from New York in 1874, thirteen years before the senior Robert Sproul. She made the migration with her parents in what was still the supposedly most comfortable manner—by sailing ship to the Isthmus of Panama, and again by ship from Panama north. They met, in a traditional manner for those days, while attending services at the United Presbyterian Church. It was Sarah Sproul who passed on the sparkle of personality and the arte-sian laugh that have so richly endowed Bob Sproul. With these, came what we so often describe as the "common touch," the intuitive reaction that leaves no one ill at ease. Anyone who met President Sproul and received his hearty handshake came away feeling that in some mysterious way he had started a friendship; and if he chanced to meet him again the odds were high that he would be greeted by his first name and come away convinced that the friendship had, in an equally miraculous way, grown and matured.

Circumstances, of course, played their part in giving young Robert Sproul an opportunity to put his mind and personality to work. As a lowly cashier for the University he had unlimited room for a future but no certainty as to what might fill it. However, a discerning superior officer, the late Ralph P. Merritt, at that time Comptroller, seemed to sense the possibilities of Bob Sproul. This was a period of growth and expansion in higher education. A bond issue for new buildings had been passed in 1914, and plans were under way for the completion of the Doe Library Building and the construction of Benjamin Ide Wheeler Hall, destined to be two of the finest and largest buildings ever to grace the campus. Robert Sproul was at the moment not much impressed with his opportunity. His job was a second choice; the military forces had excluded him because of an occasional bout with asthma.

Within a few weeks after Robert Sproul's assignment to a desk in California Hall the world had entered another of its periodic eras of chaos. On June 28, 1914, Archduke Francis Ferdinand, heir to the Austrian throne, and his wife, the Duchess of Hohenberg, were assassinated in Sarajevo, by a Bosnian Serb terrorist, Gavrillo Prinzip. Various events well known to all followed thereafter, and in the spring of 1917 they reached out to touch the life of Robert Sproul. Comptroller Merritt was called upon by Governor William D. Stephens to develop a draft registration program, and shortly afterwards was appointed Food Administrator for the state. This made it essential to appoint an acting assistant to the Comptroller; so in June, 1917, Robert Sproul, having just turned 26, found himself sitting with the Regents to make recommendations and answer questions concerning the business affairs of an institution with which he had been affiliated as an employee for only three years. A few months later he had the additional title and duties of Acting Secretary of the Regents conferred upon him as a result of the departure of Victor H. Henderson, on leave for the duration.

Although this set of circumstances may convey the impression Robert G. Sproul began his advance to leadership of the University of California because he happened to be standing in the right place at the right moment with a rabbit's foot in his pocket, a study of the facts necessitates a different conclusion. True it is that he was offered an opportunity to try on his "boss's shoes" at a phenomenally early age. In fact he was asked to fill two pairs of shoes belonging to men who carried heavy responsibilities and who left for other duties before the new wearer had time to ask so much as where they kept the polish and the extra laces. But he managed to live up to the responsibility. Advice on how the jobs had been run during the relative calm of earlier years would not have helped much in the period of confusion that followed.

The Regents took the formal action of offering all of the resources of the University to the Federal Government for the war emergency. President Benjamin Ide Wheeler accepted an appointment as Chairman of the State Committee on Resources and Food Supply. The

College of Agriculture faculty and Farm Advisors were devoting their energies to increasing production on all farms in the state. And within a few weeks a University service flag was unfurled from the top of the Campanile with 2,200 stars affixed to it. As the regular faculty and students departed, military instruction moved in. On the same day that Robert Sproul first sat with the Regents, the War Department established a School of Military Aeronautics on the Berkeley campus in which 500 students would shortly enroll. The suggestion that fraternity houses be taken over for teaching and housing proved impractical, so temporary structures had to be built for classrooms, laboratories, and housing. The first American Field Ambulance Corps had already been organized and had left for France. Three additional units were in process of formation. Hospital Unit 30 was organized and departed with 23 members of the Medical School faculty. In answer to needs of the U. S. Shipping Board, special courses for volunteers were organized in navigation and nautical astronomy. Appearances changed, too, when old North Hall was torn down except for the basement floor, which President Wheeler characterized as a "pathetic fragment" left to house student activities and a store.

There were so few regular students of the male sex left on campus that the intercollegiate athletic program fell to pieces, and Benjamin Ide Wheeler was constrained to inform Governor Stephens: "With the continuance of the war it is inevitable that competition between universities and colleges will steadily shrink away toward the vanishing point. This may yield us a valuable opportunity of observing just how essential to the well-being of the college community these sports may be. . . . In these latter years the intercollegiate athletes have come to be no more than a saving remnant of the student body, a group of highly trained specialists who go down like gladiators into the dust of the arena, while Rome looks on and howls."

To add to these local uncertainties the bells for Sather Tower, cast in England, had started their long voyage on the high seas and were in imminent danger of being sent to the bottom of the Atlantic Ocean by German submarines. They arrived, safely and prophetically, on Columbus Day, 1917.

7

Despite all of these earth-shaking events, which did little to ease the problems of an apprentice in business administration trying to carry the load of two experienced men, the Regents of the University apparently saw enough of Robert Sproul's work in this first year to convince them that he was conducting himself very well indeed for a young fellow who knew little about the way the University had operated previously and less about what was in store for the future. As of July 1, 1918, he was instructed to drop the "Acting" qualification from his titles and to designate himself as Assistant Comptroller, Assistant Secretary of the Regents, and Assistant Land Agent. The war and its aftermath seemed to create unprecedented problems and commensurate opportunities.

By the time the Armistice was signed, the University service flag carried 3,500 stars; some 5,500 men had been given intensive training for war service; and 533 women had received special training as nurses, chauffeurs, and auto-mechanics. The War Department desired to make the Student Army Training Corps a permanent operation, and in the fall of 1918 the new Assistant Comptroller was asked to find some way of financing the necessary barracks. He came up with a plan involving a loan of $200,000 from the Regents that he would repay out of the one dollar per day per man subsistence that the Federal Government offered. This required that each man be housed and fed for 70 cents leaving 30 cents for debt amortization. The Regents listened to their 27-year-old investment counselor and authorized him to proceed. The plan worked, in spite of the fact that in the fall of 1918 before anyone could move into the five barracks constructed in three weeks, influenza struck. The barracks were converted into hospitals and accommodated at one time 500 sick students as well as more than 500 women students busily stitching up gauze masks.

In the midst of all this, the demands of southern California for a more reasonable share of educational service from the allegedly State-wide University had to be met. In 1917 a Los Angeles headquarters for University Extension was established, and plans were made for a University Summer Session to open in 1918 in the only quarters available, the new plant of the Los Angeles High School. The President announced: "It is the desire of the University to meet in every possible way the educational demands made upon it by the southern part of the state."

As a result of his weathering of these and countless other emergencies, the Regents expressed their complete confidence in Robert Sproul by naming him Curator of the University in 1920. He was thus given the key to and complete control over locked stores of grain alcohol, whiskey, and other distilled spirits, to be released, of course, solely for such scholarly and humanitarian purposes as preserving specimens, making essential chemical compounds, and treating the sick and injured in the University Hospital. After giving him a six-months trial in this post of ultimate responsibility, the Regents, on October 1, 1920, officially deleted the qualification "Assistant" from his titles, making him Comptroller, Secretary of the Regents, and Land Agent, thereby demonstrating that they were satisfied that he could not only carry the work of two men in an emergency but could continue to do so indefinitely. A little later, when the Regents were precipitated into commerce, temporarily, as a result of gifts, he took on the collateral duties of Manager of the Bear Gulch Water Company and a director of the Perry Lumber Company.

Although there is nothing in the record to confirm a direct relationship, it is probable that the decision of the Regents to appoint Robert Sproul at the age of 29 as Comptroller, Secretary of the Regents, and Land Agent, was influenced by the efforts of others to lure him away from higher education. In March of 1920 the Regents accepted a formal resignation from Ralph P. Merritt, who had previously been absent on leave, but said they were not contemplating an immediate replacement. In June, 1920, newspapers throughout the state carried an announcement that the Directors of the California Prune and Apricot Growers' Association had voted to offer the position of General Manager to Robert G. Sproul, succeeding H. G. Coykendall. Several papers carried the additional information that the salary being offered was $25,000 a year, about five times what Sproul was being paid at the University.

Sproul did not hesitate; he declined the offer with an expression of appreciation for the compliment that had been paid to him. Four months later the Regents appointed him as successor to Ralph P. Merritt. The wisdom of their choice was confirmed by events that occurred in Sacramento with the opening of the 1921 session of the legislature. One was an organized effort by an economy bloc of legislators, backed up by representatives of large tax-paying industries, to reduce the budget of the University; and the other was an equally well-organized effort to change University policies relative to instruction and research in agriculture, or to remove the Land Grant College from the jurisdiction of the Regents and establish a separate College of Agriculture.

The battle over the budget was given special point by an unsuccessful effort that the Regents had made in 1919 to establish a special mill tax earmarked for University support and thus eliminate the biennial controversies with the legislature over the content and amount of the University budget. But the major issue was the post-World War I recession and the demand for a decrease in state expenditures generally. The newly appointed Comptroller found himself in a three-cornered fight, with an economy bloc in one corner, an agricultural bloc in the second, and he alone in the third. From the viewpoint of the newspapers it was a wonderful session, and they carried round by round accounts. It began in January and was still in progress three months later. Edward G. Hamilton, representing the Hearst papers, said: "In the matter of the University, young Robert G. Sproul, the fair-haired Comptroller of that institution was too much for those who attempted to bait him, and he won general admiration for the way he handled himself and his cause."

Ad B. Schuster, representative of the Oakland Tribune added: "The fling at figures between R. G. Sproul, comptroller of the University, and Clyde L. Seavey, member of the State Board of Control and ace among the administration tax experts is setting the capital by the ears." Schuster went on to explain that Sproul was standing off alone all questions raised by legislators and by a whole "corps of trained statisticians."

Another press representative said: "Bob Sproul, youthful controller of the University of California, established a unique record yesterday when he appeared before the Senate, sitting as a committee of the whole . . . three stenographers, one after another, curled up and quit cold under the youthful controller's verbal drumfire. Bob not only jettisoned an imposing cargo of grammar, but from memory unfurled a bewildering array of figures that completely flabbergasted his Senatorial auditors and left them gasping like stranded salmon."

Simultaneously there was taking place a far more serious and far-reaching struggle over the future of the University as a Land Grant Institution with agriculture as one of its major subjects of instruction and research. This movement was not suddenly conceived, but traced its origin back to the founding of the University, and involved the basic American credo that education is the magic process through which prosperity and better welfare are built. Many farmers in the state felt that the magic touch of education had wrought too few miracles in their lives and in those of their sons and daughters, and that the fault lay in intrusting instruction and research in agriculture to an institution that idealized classical scholarship and dealt primarily in theory and abstractions. Some had thought this for more than half a century, and their point of view gained many followers when war markets and war prices collapsed shortly after the farmers had extended themselves to the limit to bring more land into cultivation and increase production per acre. One can learn to live with a long period of marginal return, but it is difficult to slip quietly back into it after a brief taste of prosperity. Farmers on the west side of the Central Valley, who had plunged into rice on governmental urging, found little solace in the fact that they could drive down to the bank in a Cadillac in quest of a mortgage extension.

The University's concern after World War I with the discontent of agricultural interests was not without logical reason. The discontent had been building up for years and involved a number of universities throughout the country. The seed was sown more than half a century before, when Senator Justin S. Morrill of Vermont, son and grandson of village blacksmiths, finally succeeded in obtaining Congressional approval for the Land Grant College Act, signed by President

Abraham Lincoln on July 2, 1862. Today this farsighted statute is recognized as one of the most important pieces of educational legislation in the history of the Nation. It provided for a grant of 30,000 acres of public land for each state senator and representative, for the purpose of endowing, supporting, and maintaining at least one college in each state where the leading object would be to teach such branches of learning as were related to agriculture and the mechanic arts, without excluding other scientific and classical subjects, and with the requirement that military training be offered.

When the State of California, in 1866, moved to establish a College of Agriculture and Mechanic Arts, it seems clear that the chief motivation was a desire to take advantage of the generous offer of the Morrill Land Grant Act before it expired, rather than any conviction that a College of Agriculture and Mechanic Arts was the greatest need of the state. Governor Frederick F. Low, in his message to the legislature in December 1865, said: "To secure this magnificent grant it is necessary that the required steps be taken by the present Legislature, else it will be forfeited. . . . Should the national endowment be lost to the children of our State by reason of our neglect, the merited censure of coming generations would be cast upon the memory of those whose duty it is to act at this time." The Governor further suggested that the institution be of broad base; but the most forceful and enthusiastic supporters of immediate action were the agricultural and mining interests; and, as a result a College of Agricultural, Mining, and Mechanical Arts was chartered three months later.

The first methodical criticism of this action came from Professor Benjamin Silliman of Yale who was invited West to give the commencement address of 1867 at the Christian but nonsectarian College of California in Oakland. He pointed out that the plan adopted by the legislature would result in neither a university nor an adequate college. Governor Low remarked, also, that except for its lack of adequate money the College of California was a very fine institution, and that the state, which presumably would have the money for a college, lacked what the College of California had: scholarship, organization, enthusiasm, and reputation. Out of this came an agreement that the

Trustees of the College of California would deed to the state all of its property in the event that the legislature rescinded its action of the previous year and chartered a University of California, in accord with the mandate of the Constitution of 1849. Thus it came about that the University of California was chartered on March 23, 1868, uniting an earlier, privately established liberal arts college and a short-lived state college of agricultural, mining, and mechanical arts.

Although the Organic Act of the University provided that the President of the State Agricultural Society should be an ex-officio Regent of the University, and certain agricultural motifs were incorporated into the facade of South Hall, it became clear from the first that much of what farmers considered important for the education of their sons and daughters could be learned elsewhere than at a college, and there was as yet no solid foundation of scientific knowledge concerning agriculture that a college might impart. The problems of the University of California during those early years, in finding something appropriate to do for agriculture and at the same time in avoiding subjects normally taught in a trade school, may seem inconsequential now, but at that time they were of serious import.

Research results have a cumulative value, and as the body of scientific knowledge applicable to agriculture began to grow, it became easier for the University to prove its usefulness. It demonstrated the value of selective breeding of both animals and plants, developed means of rating soils and areas for agricultural purposes, established standards of land maintenance and cultivation practice, created higher producing and disease-resistant crops, raised the average level of egg production per hen, of butterfat production per cow, and of meat production per animal, while beginning the endless search for chemical, biological, or other means of saving crops from disease and parasites. At the same time it developed new farm machines and systems of farm management and farm product marketing.

Although this record of achievement (laying the foundation for an increase in California farm receipts from less than five hundred million dollars in 1930 to more than three billion dollars in 1960) was appreciated, it did not help much to satisfy the fundamental desire of many farmers for a college open to all their children—one that would give them preparation and prestige for a successful life without diverting them from the idea of living on the land and being farmers. In 1919, with considerable reluctance, the University agreed to offer at Davis a three-year, nondegree program of practical instruction open to any youngster who had finished grammar school or even had the equivalent thereof. But this didn't solve the problem of making farming attractive to young people. As the years went by more young people from the cities enrolled in the nondegree curriculum and many farm-born youths took the regular scientific course and went into agriculturally related occupations, rather than farming *per se*.

This was the background of the crisis that arose in the fall of 1920 and spring of 1921, when the neophyte in legislative matters, Robert Sproul, began his first year in Sacramento as responsible representative of the Regents and the President. Agricultural interests were organized in force and were determined to seek a solution to their multitudinous problems by moving the College of Agriculture out of what they considered to be its ivory tower, and bringing it back to the good earth. Many of them felt that the Regents and the Academic Senate just needed a drastic shaking-up. Some were convinced that the *status quo* had to be shattered with an axe, separating the Land Grant College from the University of California, and putting it under some other institution (Stanford was mentioned once) or creating a new organization to control it, made up of men who worked with their hands on the land.

Every kind of criticism was leveled at the University of California and its College of Agriculture. The division of instruction and research between Berkeley and Davis was said to be inefficient and costly.

With the exception of the president of the State Agricultural Society, serving ex-officio, it was pointed out, no member of the Board of Regents knew anything about agriculture. If agriculture in the State of California were ever to be stabilized and rural life to come into its own, there needed to be a college run by a board trained and interested in rural problems—a college with one home in the center of a great farm, offering the traditional American four years of instruction. The contention of the University that agriculture would be better served by establishing less technical farm-practice instruction at junior colleges throughout the rural areas of the state was considered to be diversionary and unsound. Some said too many members of the University staff had been imported from other parts of the United States and had not been brought up or trained in California agriculture.

To head off what appeared to be a stampede that would end with legislation all might later regret, Robert Sproul lent his support to those members of the legislature who believed there should be a committee review before any action was taken. So, in January, 1921, the state legislature, by concurrent resolution, authorized a joint Agricultural Legislative Committee of three assemblymen and three senators, "to investigate the present status" of the College of Agriculture and its Farm School. The Committee visited Berkeley and Davis, and on February 25, 1921, held a public meeting in the Assembly Chamber at Sacramento where any who desired could speak. Many did, repeating the criticisms already cited and adding others.

It was the conviction of Robert Sproul that any action taken at the moment would be influenced more by heat than by light. Although he did not pretend to be an expert on the subject, the new Comptroller felt certain that the discontent of California agriculture was not an isolated phenomenon attributable to some local situation, but rather reflected a national problem associated with fundamental changes in the economy of the United States.

Acting on this appraisal of the situation, he repeated over and over again to those involved at Sacramento, that a matter as important as the future of the College of Agriculture and the University of California would justify longer study than could be given to it during the inevitable turmoil of a legislative session. When he was sure that he had at least a few members of the Agricultural Legislative Committee alerted to the need for a cautious approach, he wrote to the chairman, Senator Johnson, with the suggestion that the Committee would be doing the state and education a great service if it recommended the establishing of a commission to study the matter thoroughly, not only within the state but in other states as well. To emphasize the widsom of this approach he pointed out several errors and misconceptions in the preliminary draft of a report that the Committee had already begun to prepare. He further suggested that there should be nothing in the action of the Committee that seemed to prejudge the questions to be presented to the proposed commission.

It was a great relief to the University family when the Agricultural Legislative Committee accepted this suggestion and recommended that the legislature request the governor of the state to appoint a Special Commission on Agricultural Education.

The University of California was certain it was doing as good a job in agriculture, if not better than any other Land Grant College in the country, and that study by a commission should reveal this fact. As Dr. Edwin C. Voorhies pointed out in March, 1921, there really was no basis for the charge that graduates in agriculture usually left the industry. He sent out a questionnaire to 673 graduates of the College of Agriculture and received 464 replies. Of those who replied, 135 were operating farms, 36 were managing large agricultural enterprises, 49 were in agricultural processing or distributing businesses, 133 were teaching agriculture or related subjects in high schools or colleges, or were with the United States Department of Agriculture, or serving on Boards of Agricultural Commissioners. Less than one-fourth, 111 individuals, had gone into work not directly related to agriculture.

The next problem, as the Comptroller saw it, was to make certain that all pertinent information that might be of value to the commission concerning the University of California College of Agriculture was made available and given consideration. He asked various friends to call to the attention of Governor William D. Stephens that there was in the original recommendation of the Legislative Agricultural Committee a suggestion that representatives of the University be named on the commission, and he made known to the Governor that he would be happy to serve if the Governor desired to appoint him. In response to the point that representatives of the University would be "interested parties" and might find it more difficult to reach an impartial decision, Robert Sproul wrote in July of 1921 that he freely acknowledged this but would like to know where any man could be found who was sufficiently versed in agriculture or agricultural education, sufficiently active in the state to serve effectively on the commission, and not affiliated with interested organizations. "Who would find it easy to be impartial?"

As a consequence, the list of appointees named by Governor Stephens to the commission, read as follows: Sheridan W. Baker, W. S. Guilford, J. James Hollister, Elwood Mead, Sam J. Mortland, G. Harold Powell, and Robert G. Sproul.

The commission went about its work in a businesslike way, investigating the University of California College of Agriculture, and then making a similar study of other colleges of agriculture, both those affiliated with universities and those operated as independent Land Grant Colleges in Montana, Minnesota, Wisconsin, and New York.

While still traveling with the commission, Comptroller Sproul wrote: "The difficulty arises from the general dissatisfaction of farmers with the present economic situation and the class consciousness that has been developed among them through the Farm Bloc, the Farm Bureau, and other agricultural movements of the last few years.

"Everywhere we go among the agricultural professors and dirt farmers we hear talk of an agrarian culture to be developed through universities or colleges and other agencies dominated by farmers; of the need for a civilization based on rural life which cannot be attained through institutions of higher learning moulded and directed by the professional and business interests which are held to be not only nonagricultural, but antiagricultural. I tell you these things not because I consider the fight a lost one by any means, but in order that you may understand the very grave difficulties of the situation. Pray for me."

As the commission wound up its long and arduous investigation it became more and more apparent that the facts substantiated the analysis of the situation that member Sproul had been reiterating at every appropriate opportunity, and it began to appear that the final report would not be too unfavorable to the position that the University of California had taken. It was also clear, however, to Comptroller Sproul that the University of California needed to make important changes in its methods of operating, notably as regards its efforts to concentrate agricultural research at Berkeley on a campus where land available for plant growing was becoming more scarce each year.

As early as March, 1921, the Finance Committee of the Regents moved to determine what could be done at Davis to make it a real center of university-level work. At the moment it was chiefly engaged in nondegree instruction at the high school level. The Attorney for the Regents expressed his legal opinion that the Regents could move to raise it from a high school to a junior college level, but they would be obligated under the enabling act of 1905 to continue short courses open to all, and to offer general instruction in farm practice.

In the fall of 1922 when the report of the commission was imminent, Sproul became convinced that definite action toward the acquiring of land at Berkeley would be important in determining the attitude of the commission and of the farmers of the state. At one point he wrote to Jack Struble, Assistant Comptroller, instructing him to find 1,000 or even 2,000 acres of land that might be acquired within about 15 minutes of the Berkeley campus, in San Pablo Valley, or elsewhere. In September, 1922, he wrote to Charles Keeler, Secretary of the Berkeley Chamber of Commerce, pointing out that it was entirely possible that the College of Agriculture would be moved out of Berkeley, not inconceivably to southern California; this would mean a loss to the community of one-third of the University budget, involving a payroll and miscellaneous expenditures of $2,000,000 a year. He added that the decision on this matter would possibly hinge on whether more land for agricultural purposes could be found in Berkeley, and this in turn, considering the prohibitive price of land, might depend on whether the San Francisco Bay Area was sufficiently interested to make the land available.

There was no hesitation on the part of the members of the Chamber of Commerce in responding to this call for help. Bob Sproul was not just an official of the University about whom they had read in the newspapers. He was a friend and fellow worker in community affairs who had, among other things, been elected to the presidency of the Berkeley Rotary Club at the age of 28. Chamber President Roy O.

Track meet held at Stanford in 1911. Sophomore Robert Gordon Sproul is third from right in the starting line.

Nearing the end of the mile run, young Sproul (right) in a tie lead.

Inauguration Day, October 22, 1930. President Sproul is congratulated by his predecessor, William Wallace Campbell.

Regent Chester Rowell presents the key to the University to President
Sproul following his inauguration, October 22, 1930.

President Sproul stands with Governor James Rolph after officiating at his first Commencement as President, May, 1931.

President Sproul in 1937 with Dr. Earle R. Hedrick, newly appointed Vice-President and Provost of UCLA.

*Students demonstrate outside President's House on campus in 1939
to urge President Sproul to stay at the University. He had been
offered the presidency of a bank at three times his University salary.*

Father and son, Commencement, 1942. Bob, Jr. graduates and is commissioned second lieutenant in the U.S. Navy.

Singing All Hail *with Governor Earl Warren at a University Meeting, 1947. Banners in the background again beg the President to stay at the University and forego a more lucrative appointment.*

The President and Mrs. Sproul are hosts to visiting President and Mrs. James B. Conant, September, 1947.

President and Mrs. Sproul meet Secretary of State George C.
Marshall as he arrives to deliver the Charter Day Address,
March, 1948. (Official U.S. Navy Photograph)

*Prime Minister Nehru and his sister, Madame Pandit, address a
University Meeting, October, 1949.*

President Sproul officiates at the dedication of Alumni House, 1954.

*A quiet evening for President and Mrs. Sproul in the library
of the President's House on campus.*

*An Alumni reception, 1955, to celebrate President Sproul's
twenty-five years in office. Sarah Elizabeth Sproul, the President's mother,
is standing at the left.*

Among the many gifts President Sproul received at the celebration
of his twenty-five years in office, the one that brought the
heartiest laugh was the drum major's baton, presented in memory
of the President's undergraduate days as a drum major.

President Sproul's
last Commencement in office.
He retired shortly thereafter,
June 30, 1958.

Long wrote back promptly that they had organized a fund-raising campaign and were ready to start when Bob gave the word. Subsequently, the effort to raise money expanded, and $50,000 was subscribed by businesses and individuals both in San Francisco and the East Bay. When it became apparent that a fund of about this amount would be raised, Sproul used it as an incentive for the legislature to match it, and Chapter 311, Statutes of 1923, appropriated $50,000 for land purchase and greenhouses in Berkeley, contingent upon private gifts in equal amount. In reporting the success of this program to the Agriculture Committee of the Regents in March, 1924, Comptroller Sproul said he wanted it understood that success in raising the funds was attributable to others, notably the Dean of Agriculture and Dr. Elwood Mead, because he, Sproul, had been in the East most of the time. Two months later President William Wallace Campbell corrected this statement by pointing out that thanks for the fund raising belonged to all three, the *Comptroller,* the Dean of Agriculture, and Dr. Mead.

Along with other members of the commission, Sproul made his contributions to the commission's final report, and the arguments that he presented were not weakened by the evidence of University of California intention to meet past criticism. The final report supported what member Sproul had long contended: "The disappointment of California at the comparatively small enrollment in its agricultural college is shared by every state we visited, no matter what the type of institution in it. The more the commission studied this problem the more it was convinced that the problem of increasing enrollment in agricultural colleges and keeping boys on the farm is not to be solved by changes in curriculum, equipment, or method, but by the betterment of the social and economic conditions of rural life."

The commission stressed the point that there were really two types of institution and two types of education needed to meet the demands of agriculture: one of them emphasizing science and the economics of agriculture and carried on in close connection with the broad research resources of a university, the other emphasizing the day to day business practices and skills used in operating a farm—skills that could more beneficially be provided through expansion of junior college offerings at strategic places in the state.

Finally, the commission recommended that the College of Agriculture be continued as a part of the University of California, and that support and encouragement be given to the development of the Davis campus.

For Robert Sproul this first experience as a responsible representative of the University in Sacramento was an intensive postgraduate course in a new kind of engineering—human engineering—too much like learning to swim by falling off the end of a pier to be pleasant, but nevertheless highly educational. One could hazard the opinion that through this early involvement in the task of assuring the University's continuance as a Land Grant institution, Robert Sproul not only took the first major step toward election to the presidency less than a decade later, but also confirmed and deepened certain personality attributes and an administrative *modus operandi* that made it possible for him to weather the handicap of being the first nonacademic president in the history of the institution, and to serve longer than any other president, in fact, longer than all but a few presidents have served in the history of American higher education.

On the personality side there was his interest in people and his delight in friends. From the start of his career with the University he seemed to operate on the anthropologically sound principle that there are no really significant problems in the world except those that involve people and no really lasting solutions to problems to be found without the help of people of good will and friendly purpose. One exercises foresight by knowing people and making friends among them before problems arise or solutions are needed. If this is not always possible it is still good judgment to get to know the people involved in a problem before one tries to analyze the issue. During those hectic first months in Sacramento, Sproul turned instinctively toward the people who might be involved, the leaders in the agricultural industry of the state. His purpose was not alone to discover whether the voices he heard in Sacramento reflected the thinking of all, but also to understand better what lay behind the obvious. He met and talked to many agricultural leaders, and the experience was so mutually satisfactory that there grew out of it an annual meeting, sponsored by Dr. George P. Clements, Chairman of the Agricultural Committee of the Los Angeles Chamber of Commerce, held in an isolated retreat near Palm Springs, the Andreas Canyon Club.

Dr. Clements was the epitome of good will and friendly purpose. He left a medical practice in Nebraska to come to Los Angeles because of a lung ailment that threatened to cut short his existence, and then lived to a ripe old age on vitamins extracted from good deeds—deeds directed toward everybody he met, including the Indians of the area as well as farmers of the state. He, too, believed that people who know each other well and understand the goals of other groups and their plans for achieving these goals will automatically adjust so as to avoid head-on collisions and will more willingly listen to alternative programs. At regular intervals he brought together groups of agricultural, educational, and other leaders in Andreas Canyon, many of them bringing their own sleeping bags, for a kind of campout and fireside discussion of the problems of the state and nation, away from all distractions of telephones, radio, and current newspapers. In such a group as this Robert Sproul was completely at home. He could debate with the best, cap every story with another, add volume to every song, and leave behind him a conviction that the "eggheads" at the University were not so bad after all.

This deep-rooted faith in the reasonableness of the majority of people was demonstrably effective in Sproul's career. Even more important was the related conviction that the major threat to California education, intensified by the size of the state, its heterogeneous population, and the widely different ecological environments from north to south and east to west, was the tendency for local interests to override the general welfare of the state through political action. Robert Sproul came to look upon the orderly process of responsible study on a statewide basis, initiated in 1921 to prevent a disastrous schism in agricultural education, as the state's best hope for wise development of higher education. As will be related in the next chapter, his constant championing of this approach led to the Report of the Carnegie Foundation for the Advancement of Teaching in 1932; the short-lived but exceedingly important State Council for Educational Planning and Coordination, in 1933; the Liaison Committee of the Regents and the State Board of Education, in 1945; the Report of a Survey of the Needs of California in Higher Education in 1948; the Restudy of the Needs of California in Higher Education, in 1955; the Study of the Need for Additional Centers of Public Higher Education in California, in 1957; and laid the foundation for the present organization of leadership in higher education under the Regents of the University of California, the Trustees of the State Colleges, and the Coordinating Council for Higher Education. The United Nations, faltering and uncertain as the organization may still be, could not have come into existence at all without the experience that was gained through the League of Nations. So it is in the field of higher education in California. How well the new Board of Trustees of the State Colleges and the Coordinating Council on Higher Education will work is not possible to predict with accuracy. But it is possible to say that if a league-minded man had not been directing the destinies of the University of California for 28 years, we would not have achieved even this much.

All of this was undreamed of, either by Robert Sproul or anyone else, when the State Commission on Agricultural Education rendered its report in 1923. However, it is not without significance that the Regents of the University, on recommendation of President W. W. Campbell, appointed Robert Sproul Vice-President of the University in charge of finance and business as of July 1, 1925, sharing with Walter Morris Hart, Vice-President of the University for academic and scholastic matters, the honor of being first to hold this title. Unquestionably, the part that the Comptroller played in the crisis of 1921–23 and in subsequent representation of the University at Sacramento was an important consideration.

During his career with the University of California, Sproul was engaged in a multitude of public services resulting as much from his inability to deny calls upon his time from old friends as from his desire to make new friends for the University. He accepted the post of treasurer of the Save the Redwoods League in 1921, in order to work with his friends Newton and Aubrey Drury, and as this is written, 41 years later, he is still treasurer of the Save the Redwoods League. He was one of the organizers with his friend William Herms, of the Mt. Diablo Council of the Boy Scouts of America. He served as head of the local Community Chest and on both the State Board of Social Welfare and the Commission on Revision of the State Constitution of California. After he became president, of course, his name appeared on more organization lists than can be named here, but his early services were a part of this story of the origin and development of a president.

It was in June, 1929, that the Regents of the University, having received notice of President Campbell's intention to retire the following year, decided to take the step, unprecedented in the history of the institution, of naming the Vice-President of the University for finance and business, eleventh president of the University of California. Regents Guy C. Earl, Mortimer Fleishhacker, and James Mills were asked to serve on a committee to wait upon Robert Sproul, inform him of the decision that had been reached, and ascertain whether he would accept the position proffered. He accepted. His letter of acceptance asked for a leave of absence from September, 1929, to March, 1930, in order that he might give undivided thought to administrative and educational matters and in particular widen his acquaintance with the academic world. He also had the foresight to ask that he be relieved of the duties of Comptroller; for on his return there would be a University budget to prepare. He concluded with the statement: "I appreciate deeply this expression of your confidence and regard after fifteen years of close association. Long ago I dedicated my life to the University and I now accept the trust which you have offered me and pray for strength adequate to the great work which a president of the University of California may do."

II

Robert Gordon Sproul as State University President

If one were to select from the last two centuries the most auspicious years for an aspiring young man to embark on a career as president of a major college or university, there is no doubt that the year 1930 would not be on the list. The year 1930 was not a troublemaker; it was the heir to troubles that had been developing throughout the "Roaring Twenties" and that culminated on that fateful Tuesday, October 29, 1929, when the bottom fell out of the New York Stock Market. The difficulties that Robert Sproul faced as a 26-year-old Acting Comptroller at the opening of World War I were minor compared to those he faced as the second-youngest university president in the United States at the opening of history's worst depression. On the first day of panic-selling in the stock market, fifty stocks dropped an average of 40 points each, and from then on the American economy became sicker by the month, with an estimated 10,090,000 workers unemployed by the fall of 1932, and money so scarce and people so frightened that President Franklin D. Roosevelt closed all the banks in the country on the day after his inauguration in 1933.

California was particularly hard hit by the Depression, some said, because so many of its major industries depended on sale of products that the world could get along without if it had to, such as scenery for tourists, motion pictures, canned olives, figs, and dates. Others cited the fact that California had a relatively large number of retired citizens dependent on rapidly dwindling income from investments. Whatever the reasons were, they created difficulties for all money-consuming institutions, especially public institutions of higher education that were without tuition charges, and in which enrollment steadily increased while income went down. This was the era of NIRA, of NRA, of PWA, WPA, and CCC. It was also the era of Upton Sinclair and his EPIC plan to End Poverty in California, for which 879,000 good citizens of California voted; of Dr. Francis Townsend and his plan to end the Depression by giving everyone over sixty a check for $200 a month with the requirement that all of it be spent within three months; and of "Thirty Dollars Every Thursday" with its weekly newspaper *The National Ham and Eggs*. The atmosphere in the state was anything but intellectual.

Again, as in 1921, hard times not only increased the difficulty of securing adequate support for institutions of higher education but also raised a question as to the effectiveness of the existing educational program. Schools, colleges, and universities have been supported generously by the people of the United States because of their basic philosophy that citizens in a self-governing democracy must have some education and that the opportunity to secure as much as can be used with profit is a cornerstone of free enterprise. But American citizens always reserve the right to question the *quid pro quo* when expenditure of tax funds is involved, and the "something" desired from public education is always a better and more prosperous world. This better and more prosperous world was not in evidence for a good many years after the 1929 crash, and it was inevitable that education in general should come within the orbit of public dissatisfaction, and that the State University, as the keystone of the public system, should be regarded as the bull's-eye in the target of criticism. Ordinary citizens complained about local schools, and the local schools passed on the complaint to the University, considering it the great power that prevented them from doing the kind of job they wanted to do. California's troubles of the moment, many thought, could be overcome only by breaking the alleged monopoly of the University of California and establishing a system of regional four-year colleges and regional universities on the foundation of existing junior colleges and teachers' colleges. These proposed colleges would enable young people to live at home while studying, would be open to all who had finished high school, and would provide more practical training. The idea that young people were out of jobs because they hadn't been trained for any specific job was part of the Depression fantasy.

The Depression, of course, did not create all the problems that Robert Gordon Sproul met as he entered on the presidency of the University, but it caused some of the worst of them and intensified others. When the world is sick and wise men are unsure of the cure, self-appointed doctors spring up like mushrooms after the first rain, and the people are ready to listen to any proposal for change.

Bob Sproul was sufficiently well acquainted with the University and with the state to know that he had problems even without a depression. Not all of the Regents of the University were convinced that a professional administrator, and such a young one, was the wisest choice for a position traditionally held by an older man, primarily a scholar, though they finally went along on a unanimous vote. Many members of the faculty, he knew, held reservations on this same point, even though it was generally agreed that aside from not being a trained teacher and researcher, Bob Sproul was as good a leader as one could hope to find. The University of California at Los Angeles, just moving to a new and more adequate site in the Westwood Hills and with assured plans for a beautiful campus, was aware of the reluctance with which the southern branch had been established, and was so conditioned by the condescension, if not open opposition, of some northerners, that it looked on all Berkeley proposals with suspicion. But more important than all of these, was the problem of continued growth of the population and of need for expansion of higher

27

educational facilities, with no agreed-upon plan to assure cooperation and complementary efforts by universities, state teachers' colleges, and junior colleges, private as well as public. Moreover, this same problem posed great difficulties for the integrity and quality of the University itself. Could a university become a multiple-campus institution and expand tremendously in enrollment without losing unity on the one hand or sacrificing excellence on the other. President Sproul made it clear from the first that he was in favor of expanding the University to accommodate all who were qualified to enter, and that he proposed to do this without violence to the standards and ideals of a community of real scholars.

What Bob Sproul brought to these problems, however, was not some unique omniscience of perception—for others recognized the existence of these same problems—but rather a tenacious intent to do something about them, not through fireworks, but through cooperation with reasonable people of good will, and a continuing campaign of public acculturation. He was helped by a voice that carried a hundred yards in a whisper. His ability to stand before an audience and speak apparently extemporaneously on the most complicated topic, with never a moment's hesitation for a word or a figure, in biblical prose with a small touch of Shakespeare, helped considerably to make his causes group causes. Few people knew that getting ready for each of these addresses was an ordeal. His well-chosen words had been written out, perhaps rewritten, then edited, and finally committed to memory, regardless of how little time was available. Without a photographic mind no man could have done it. Robert Sproul had a sense of obligation to an audience, a horror of being dull, and an antipathy against saying anything in public that he hadn't thought through with care and that he couldn't substantiate and stand by later.

In his earlier years with the University, Robert Sproul was on call for an endless variety of local civic enterprises, heading up community chest drives, Christmas seal sales, American Legion funds; serving as a director and executive committee member for the Berkeley Chamber of Commerce; organizing and raising funds for Boy Scout troops, for natural resource conservation projects, etc. It is indicative of the regard in which he was held that the dinner that honored his election to the presidency was sponsored by the combined civic organizations of Alameda County and drew 700 people to the Grand Ball Room of the Hotel Oakland. The closeness and personal nature of this regard was shown when many of these same people participated in a luncheon ceremony of only mock seriousness, to bring him congratulations from President von Hindenburg of Germany, an autographed picture of King George V of Great Britain, and a suggestion that he was really wasting his time as President of the University of California when he could serve the whole Nation by supplying gas for dirigibles. The wives of these members of the Berkeley Rotary Club also arranged a luncheon ceremony on the same day to make known to the world that the only thing that saved Robert Gordon Sproul from being a nonentity was the fact that a wonderful lady, Miss Ida Amelia Wittschen, had earlier condescended to accept his name. She contributed to their marriage partnership a limitless supply of common sense, graciousness, and charm.

As the years went by it became quite clear that Ida Wittschen Sproul was fully deserving of the compliment paid to her by the ladies of the Berkeley Rotary Club. She was the perfect complement to President Bob, performing the duties of a "First Lady" in her own quiet way with a sincerity of purpose that collected friends and respectful admirers almost as numerous as the legion who gave spontaneous allegiance to her husband. She achieved an honor that very few wives of university presidents, if any, have gained. Two years before President Sproul became President Emeritus, the Regents of the University bestowed upon her a Master of Arts degree, *honoris causa*, just as, she confessed, she had reconciled herself to being the only member of the family without a degree from the University of California.

In the spring of 1964 at the dedication of Ida Sproul Hall, a residence hall for women, Mrs. Sproul gave one of the few public addresses she had ever consented to make. All of her life she avoided any other role than that of the wife of a President and the hostess of his home. Her brief remarks at the dedication included an explanation of this. She confessed that she was frightened by the responsibility that had suddenly been thrust upon her when her husband became President, and she was particularly concerned over the possibility that she might have to speak in public. Knowing that Mrs. Benjamin Ide Wheeler had managed to survive years as the wife of a President without being called upon to make speeches she went to her and asked for advice. Mrs. Wheeler assured her that the only way to avoid speech-making was never to start. If one never made a first speech there would never be a second. Then Mrs. Wheeler added that she should not worry about this because one "loud speaker" in the presidential family would be enough. Mrs. Sproul accepted this expert opinion and considered advice. In fact, she went further, and would never let herself be photographed unless she shared the picture with her husband or a group.

People always seemed to know by instinct that the President of the University was not stodgy, even those who had not been privileged to meet him at the annual encampments at Bohemian Grove or to follow his career as a thespian. (His acting career reached its climax at Bohemian Grove but started forty years earlier at Fallen Leaf Lodge when he played the part of Mr. Beanhead, a banker, in a stage rendition of Stephen Leacock's nonsense story, "Tom Latchford, Promoter.") At the same time, people admired him in much the same way that John Gunther found the French people admired Charles de Gaulle. Gunther said of de Gaulle: "He memorizes his speeches, and can talk for an hour on the most difficult matters without departing from his text by a jot or a tittle, and for some inexplicable reason the French admire this—he is called a *cerceau,* a brain."

The Regents of the University set October 22, 1930, as the date of the Inauguration of the Eleventh President of the University. By the time this action was taken he had already survived one of his first great tests, namely a vote of confidence from the faculty of the University. Some of the Regents, probably, and Robert Sproul, certainly, had been concerned over how the faculty would accept the idea of a nonacademic president, even though the man involved had won their respect as a financial and business officer, and was recognized as a good friend and dependable champion of the scholarly point of view in Sacramento. It was to his advantage that there had been a "schol-arly revolution" by the faculty some years before that resulted in a clarification of the areas within which the respective authorities of the President and the Academic Senate should prevail. Essentially aca-demic decisions and a voice in educational policy and budget prepar-ation had been specifically assigned to the voting members of the Academic Senate by revisions in the Standing Orders of the Regents. In other words the day was past when a President (Benjamin Ide Wheeler) could hold the reins so tightly that a professor was subject to censure if he appeared on campus without a hat.

It was also to Robert Sproul's advantage that a sufficient number of years had elapsed for the faculty to recognize that they didn't really need or want all of the administrative participation to which they had successfully laid claim. The image of a president as a distinguished autocrat against whom one had to take defensive measures, had been softened and mellowed by time and experience into an image of some-one to be tolerated as a necessary evil under most circumstances and even welcomed at times. As Professor Emeritus Joel H. Hildebrand has phrased it in recent years, the so-called "faculty revolution" was really not a revolution, but just an attempt to have the President and the Regents understand that if self-government for students was a good thing then the faculty might safely be trusted with a certain amount of it. As one of its first actions the Academic Senate elected the new President of the University Chairman of the Senate.

One of the first internal problems to which President Sproul ad-dressed himself was that of overcoming the antagonism between the Berkeley and Los Angeles campuses. The task was not easy, and never completely successful, but among the outstanding contributions that President Sproul made to the life of the University, one of the top-ranking items is the fact that he kept this open wound from fester-ing and gave time, that great healer, a chance to initiate the process of granulation. To understand the nature of the trouble one has to go back into history and realize that as early as the 1880's violent debates were going on over whether southern California should secede, create a separate state, and thereby free itself forever from what it regarded

31

as the overbearing, self-serving, and self-sanctified attitude of California's "yankees," particularly those around San Francisco Bay.

This old, north versus south squabble moved into the educational world when Regent Edward A. Dickson, an alumnus of Berkeley who had become a resident of Los Angeles, together with Ernest Carroll Moore, President of the Los Angeles State Normal School, succeeded in convincing the Regents of the University, in 1919, that southern California deserved more educational opportunity than was provided by a University whose three campuses, at Berkeley, San Francisco, and Davis, were all 400 or more miles away.

President William Wallace Campbell shared the perturbation of scholars at Berkeley over the pressure from southern California to expand the southern branch faster than the money obtained from the state for that purpose would permit, and with them he was concerned over its lack of a solid university foundation. It was his conviction that the experiment would succeed only if the southern branch divorced itself from the Normal School. He proposed that this be done when the site of the campus was moved from Vermont Avenue to Westwood. The Regents of the University at first agreed with this proposal, and facilities for the new campus were planned without space for the Normal School and its staff and students. But pressure from southern California again developed and in August, 1928, the Regents reversed themselves and voted to move the Normal School to Westwood. In his report for the biennium 1928–1930, President Campbell said that the result of this was to handicap everyone by moving an activity to a campus not planned to accommodate it. He stated quite bluntly, in a report to the Governor of California, that the action of the Regents was taken "in the face of the President's continuous and unalloyed opposition."

This was the situation into which President Sproul moved. He had followed the controversy from the very beginning, for he was a member of the commission appointed by President Wheeler back in 1917 to consider the feasibility of taking over the Los Angeles Normal School. There had never been any question in his mind that southern California needed and would have university facilities, either under the

Regents of the University, or apart from them. Neither was there any question in his mind that between these two choices an institution under the Regents was the best thing for higher education in California. As he saw it, the problem that had developed was not insoluble, provided that the people concerned would work together. His first move after accepting the presidency in 1929, months before his formal accession to office, was to move his headquarters as vice-president, temporarily, to Los Angeles. The immediate purpose was to facilitate the moving of the southern branch from Vermont Avenue to West-wood, characterized as the greatest academic migration since Columbia University moved from 49th Street to 116th Street in New York. But the other reason was to get to know people on the Los Angeles campus better, and to let them know that he had no horns and did not propose to grow any. Even though the Berkeley faculty was by this time in favor of moving Los Angeles ahead in graduate work as well as undergraduate, the old opposition had not been forgotten in the south.

Like those who say there are no good or bad laws, just good or bad people administering them, Sproul continued to think, as he had in the controversy over agriculture in 1921, that getting to know the people who are parties to a controversy is the first, essential step to settlement. Within a few months of his accession to the presidency he went to Los Angeles to welcome students to the campus. This was the first time that a president of the University had taken the trouble to express interest in the campus personally. It may, also, have been the first time that a president was encouraged to do so. And because he had served on the original Southern Branch Commission, and had established temporary headquarters at Los Angeles the previous fall, he was able to say to the students: "I am no stranger here. I am no carpetbagger from the North. I have been a part of this institution since the time when it was first a dream."

This willingness to acknowledge the strained relations then existing and to allude to them humorously, was a spontaneous approach to a problem he meant to solve. As Professor Walton Bean wrote in the *California Monthly,* many years later, "Sproul's sympathy with the problems and needs of the southern campus and his willingness and ability to endure the rigors of constant travel in order to study them at firsthand played an important part in his selection and in his success as President of the University of California. For many years he spent about half of his time at Berkeley, about a third in Los Angeles, and the rest in transit, leaving Vice-President Monroe E. Deutsch in charge on the Berkeley campus. After the retirement of Provost Ernest Carroll Moore in 1936, Sproul and his family transferred their main residence to Los Angeles for a year. One purpose of his travels, he once told a reporter, was that of 'making my person the visible symbol of the unity of the University.' But his contribution was far more than merely symbolic."

As Professor Bean further explains, there was about President Sproul's regime an aura of dedication to a chosen purpose. He had indicated this earlier when he turned down the general managership of the Prune and Apricot Growers' Association at five times his salary of the moment. His general attitude toward his job, perhaps vaguely comparable to that of one who had taken vows in a monastic order, was confirmed at intervals by his refusal of the presidency of a bank, his refusal to accept the presidency of Columbia University, and his discouraging of various suggestions that he run for governor of California, or for the United States Senate. In the field of national politics his most active participation involved support for an old friend; this led to his service as a delegate to the Republican National Convention in 1948 and as the nominator of Earl Warren as the Republican candidate for the Presidency of the United States. Earl Warren, in Bob Sproul's eyes, was not only a great man but a close and loyal friend of both the University of California and its President for more than twenty-five years. He had also played the clarinet in the same undergraduate band for which Bob Sproul had been drum major.

What President Sproul did to maintain the unity of the University of California during its early years of tribulative experiment with multiple, major campuses, was not only a significant contribution to higher education in California, but also proved to the entire country that this course of development was possible under the right leadership, and that it resulted in a higher standard of performance and achievement than did competition between politically equal but independent institutions. A number of states have since studied the University of California under President Sproul and subsequently moved in the direction of a single authority over public institutions of higher education.

As already noted, the Donahoe Act of 1960, and subsequent legislation establishing the state colleges of California as an integrated system under a single Board of Trustees, and the creation of a Coordinating Council for all higher education in California, were partly a result of President Sproul's continuing efforts over a twenty-eight year period to bring reason and order into the state's great array of colleges and universities, private as well as public—even though the final result, reached through compromise, is not, perhaps, the one that he would have advocated. More will be said about this later.

The text of President Sproul's faith as regards the University of California and higher education was laid out clearly and forcefully in the inaugural address that he delivered in October 1930. He said therein,

> Fundamentally, if the history of public education in this country means anything, there must be but one state university, and by this I mean not only one institution which is called the State University, but only one state-supported institution in the field of higher education—there must not be so-called colleges or universities at every crossroad or even at every county seat. In no state which has followed in higher education a program of distribution of state institutions and state resources has there been general satisfaction with the result; the counsel of experts is positive and unanimous against dividing the effort of the state in this field. Every year that goes by adds force and confirmation to the report of Henry S. Pritchett at a time when he was president of the Carnegie Foundation, that "the greatest weaknesses in the maintenance of good standards by the state universities have been exhibited in those states where the state institutions of higher learning are conducted in two or more colleges instead of being united into a single institution. In such cases it has almost inevitably happened that unwise competition has sprung up demoralizing alike to the institutions themselves and to the public school system. Duplicate courses, low standards of admission, and log-rolling with the legislature are the natural outcome.
>
> It is true the University has never been in this state the only public institution

35

giving work beyond the high school. Almost synchronously with the College of California, a normal school system was initiated in San Francisco to train at public expense the teachers for the public schools. The growth of the first school in that system was slow on account of the general indifference of the school authorities and hostility on the part of teachers. It was kept alive by the enthusiasm and activity of John A. Swett, superintendent of public instruction, and was moved in 1871 to San Jose, where it has been every since. From time to time thereafter the legislature established seven other normal schools at various points in the state, in certain cases in response to political pressure rather than educational needs, with results which should be a warning to those disposed to follow a similar course with reference to university work. In 1921 the normal schools were changed into teachers' colleges, and since then they have been gradually expanded from two-year institutions to four-year colleges, granting the A.B. degree . . .

Another educational activity which has developed in the field which was formerly occupied by the University alone is the junior college. In 1907 a law was passed authorizing the high school board of any high school district "to prescribe postgraduate courses of study for the graduates of such high schools." Fresno high school was the first to take advantage of this law in 1910, and by 1914 there were ten of these "upward extensions of the high school," with a combined enrollment of about 700 students. The law of 1917 recognized the junior college as an integral part of the secondary school system of the state and made financial provision for it on the same basis as for high schools. Subsequent legislation has brought the junior college to a position of assured permanence in California, and last year some 20,000 students enrolled in its thirty-four centers, more or less. Any plans for the development of higher education in California must take into account the junior college, and we are pleased that this should be so . . .

The attempt of our public school system should not be to have one broad highway on a grade so easy that it never can scale the heights, and so designed as to force all to travel the same road all the way once they have made a beginning; rather it should provide a number of highways of varying grades leading to many useful careers and open, every one of them, to all whose talents and desires make it seem probable that they may come thereby to a happy and successful life. One function of the schools all along the line should be to discover those who have the capacity and will to make good use of further training, and of what kind . . .

. . . the University of California occupies a proud but not altogether comfortable position. It suffers the inevitable penalty of leadership: envy, denial, and detraction. On the one hand it is criticized for being too aristocratic, on the other, for being too democratic. There are those who maintain that it sets its standards on an unreasonable plane; that it should admit every high school grad-uate. That, we believe, would be a fatal blow to the quality of education by the state and to the careers and happiness of great numbers of young men and young women. Surely it is not aristocratic to insist that students who come to us should have such training as will make their success in the University probable, and such basic grounding in various subjects as will open up a wide range of pos-sible specializations . . .

On the other hand, we are criticized for being too democratic, for admitting and keeping too many, on the theory that the efficiency and value of a university are determined by its selective and eliminating processes; that the fewer it admits and the more it weeds out, the better it is. My standard is an altogether different one; for I believe that, with proper organization and ideas, with intelli-gent standards of admission and graduation, with enlightened and progressive methods of education, a very large number of students may receive an excellent education on a single campus, and that to the delimitations here implied there is no need to add the further delimitation of a numerically restricted enroll-ment . . .

The above statements of policy and personal conviction, as well as a number of others made in the same address, stood up very well over the years and proved to be just as applicable, fundamentally, in 1958 as they were in 1930. Sproul continued, from first to last, to support the thesis that if we were to have three kinds of post-high school educational institutions, operating under separate authorities, they should offer a variety of educational opportunities for a variety of human talents; and each should try to do its own job well, rather than let civic pride or any other irrelevant motive push all into the pattern of the State University. He continued to maintain that numbers of stu-dents at the University, *per se*, were no threat to the standards of education if the quality of the students, the faculty, and teaching facilities remained high. President Wallace Sterling of Stanford, years later, attempted to poke friendly fun at President Sproul by stating that any herdsman knew there was a limit to the effective size of a sheepfold or a corral. If it took in the whole outdoors the animals would not even be aware they were in it, and the herders wouldn't be able to distinguish by behavior those who were inside from those on the outside. President Sproul ignored the chance to point out that President Sterling was operating a physically larger corral for a campus at Palo Alto than any in use by the University of California. He did point out, however, that during his term in office the number of students at the University of California increased from 18,689 to 46,786, and at the same time its reputation as a center of higher education continued to deepen, broaden, and spread around the world.

As the ardent champion of Land Grant colleges and universities, he also continued to reiterate the statement he made at his inaugural, "We cannot accept the dictum of certain self-styled 'prestige' institutions, that a state university must be content to operate on a lower plane for a less gifted group of the population; nor are we convinced that, because the state universities derive their support from taxes, they reside any less in 'the sphere of liberty' than those institutions that derive their support from benefactions of the generous, who are, also, sometimes, the wise."

But when President Sproul delivered his inaugural address in 1930, he was not thinking primarily of Stanford but rather was concerned over the future of higher education as it might be determined in Sacramento under Depression-stimulated unrest and dissatisfaction. The legislative year 1931 bid fair to be a repetition of 1921 on a much grander scale. Agriculture, with considerable justification, was still unhappy. The industry had never really recovered from the post-World War I recession, and was in worse position financially than the rest of the American economy to survive a depression. But others were also unhappy, and as pointed out earlier, any failure to move forward each year to a better and more propserous world, inevitably leads to demands for change in the educational system. Some state teachers' college communities were for immediate broadening of these institutions so that young people could have the advantage of a university-type training without the expense of leaving home or the difficulty of meeting University of California entrance requirements. Some junior college communities wanted immediately to expand their schools into four-year institutions for the same reasons; they also wanted the state to bear a greater share of their building costs and operating expenses.

It became clear in the fall of 1930 that concerted moves to establish regional four-year colleges and universities would be one of the major activities at the 1931 session of the legislature. When the session opened, bills were introduced to convert the Sacramento Junior College into a four-year institution, and to expand Fresno State Teachers' College and San Diego State Teachers' College into general colleges. But simultaneously President Sproul moved, as he had in 1921, to avoid a crucial decision on the higher educational future of the state by political debate under the hectic pressures of a legislative session. He had long since dispatched Vice-President Deutsch to New York to discuss the crisis with President Henry Suzzallo of the Carnegie Foundation for the Advancement of Teaching, and to ask whether the Foundation would take responsibility for an impartial survey of higher education and contribute to the cost of it, if the California State Legislature were to ask for such a survey and provide up to half of the money needed. Vice-President Deutsch was an able emissary and succeeded in persuading Dr. Suzzallo that the question being raised in California was fundamental to the future of public higher educa-tion throughout the United States. If educational problems were to be settled by political debate and local community political pressure, it could be disastrous not just for California but for the Nation.

With the cooperation of the Carnegie Foundation assured in the event it should be requested, legislative cooperation was secured in the introducing of a bill requesting the governor of the state to have a survey made and providing an appropriation for the state's share of the expense. It was President Sproul's strong conviction still, that reasonable men of good will would acknowledge the wisdom of defer-ring drastic changes in the higher education program until all the pertinent facts were assembled, until a study had been made by authorities in the field, and until some guidance could be secured from recommendations based on the study. The Regents of the University supported the President in this stand, and unanimously authorized a public statement against precipitate action on the regional four-year college issue. Shortly thereafter, both houses of the legislature also supported this approach, and Governor James Rolph, on request of the legislature, impowered the Carnegie Foundation to proceed.

President Sproul and other representatives of the University presented their case to the Carnegie Foundation, as did representatives of the junior colleges, the state teachers' colleges, and the State Department of Education. But over the course of the next two years this battle to prevent the immediate establishment of new and costly institutions of higher education became complicated by the fact that the state could not find money enough to continue the current level of support for institutions already established. The state was obliged to inform all agencies that it might not be able to meet appropriations made by the legislature of 1931, and requested that all expenditures be cut insofar as commitments already made would permit. President Sproul found himself in the delicate position of asking the faculty to take a voluntary cut in salary not very long after its members had given him the vote of confidence described in earlier pages. The faculty decision on this matter was a second vote of confidence, and it was given cheerfully and generously. A total of $300,000 from salary savings was refunded to the state—a sum that the state eventually decided it would not be equitable to accept, in view of complications in other agencies; so the volunteers were reimbursed, and asked instead to take a scaled decrease in salaries beginning with the fiscal year 1933–34. Incidentally, President Sproul marked himself down for the heaviest cut of all, and as a result found himself carrying the burdens of the presidency for a number of years at less money than he had earned when he became Vice-President in 1925.

The Carnegie Foundation Report, when submitted, was not completely acceptable to the University of California though the Regents were willing to go along with it in principle. It was not acceptable at all to the forces seeking to establish independent regional four-year colleges because it recommended that there be no further expansion of senior college facilities until it was demonstrated that existing facilities had reached the saturation point and the finances of the state were more prosperous. The report went much farther than this and much farther than the Regents were prepared at the moment to accept, by recommending that all higher education be placed under one authority, The Regents of the University of California.

So President Sproul found himself faced with the doubly difficult task of defending the report in principle though not in detail, and at the same time fighting to save the University from budgetary disaster for the biennium 1933–35. His position was made no easier by the continued attacks of regional college proponents who were also facing budget cuts and saw fit to inform their local communities that the cuts were being forced by the overly large demands of President Sproul and the University of California. Enrollment at the University had gained eight per cent during the biennium 1931–33, and it was clear that there would be less money available in 1933–35, than in 1931–33. This fact had to be accepted, but neither the Regents nor the President were willing to sit quietly by and allow panic to destroy the institution. In his effort to carry information to all citizens of the state, President Sproul spoke everywhere. Oddly enough, many citizens were for adding local regional colleges to the state's burden but at the same time against giving existing institutions enough money to take care of the students already enrolled.

It was natural for President Sproul to carry his problems to the people. In 1921 he had expressed the thought that the University and the College of Agriculture would have been better off if the farmers of the state had been kept more fully and continually aware of the services being rendered on their behalf. Again in 1931 and 1933 he devoted himself to getting the facts out and to making the people aware of the University and of its services and problems. As early as 1923 he had persuaded President Campbell to establish an Office of Public Information or a News Service, and by 1925 had brought in as manager, Harold Ellis, who had represented the McClatchy Newspapers at all of the deliberations of the Commission on Agricultural Education. To the efforts of the University News Service he added the more effective stimulus of his own speaking ability. He made the educational problems of California and the budget of the University his chief topics at Charter anniversary gatherings of more than 500 alumni in March of 1931 and March of 1932; met with alumni leaders at two conferences, and addressed the first conference of alumnae and alumni wives ever held, with 500 in attendance, for the specific purpose of aiding Robert Sibley in establishing a regional organization

of the California Alumni Association. In connection with the Tenth
Traveling Conference of the Agricultural Extension Service he addressed farm leaders from 42 counties and followed it up with talks
at the Thirteenth Annual Convention of the California Farm Bureau
Federation and the Annual Encampment of 4-H Clubs. In August,
1932, for the first time in his life, and with frankly admitted "stage
fright," he went on the radio to ask for the support of all friends of
higher education. He pointed out that the University of California
could well be destroyed if the state followed out its expressed intention to cut the budget from its then current level of $17,035,891,
down to $12,000,000 for the biennium 1933–35.

In his radio talks and other addresses President Sproul said the
University was willing to reduce salaries, to leave staff vacancies
unfilled, to crowd students into existing buildings and postpone
repairs, to take on heavier teaching schedules, to reduce its purchases
of books and supplies, and search out every economy, but it could not
continue to provide service for an increasing enrollment under the
hysterical program proposed by the state. He further warned that this
year of crisis was not the time to wipe out research. He followed up
this point in his message to the governor by stating: "there have been
better points in history at which to call a halt than the year 1932.
Endlessly going over old lessons is a narcotic to progress. Progress is
always the product of fresh thinking, and much of it thinking which,
to practical men, bears the semblance of dreaming. That is the trouble
with practical men; they are so busy practicing the mistakes of their
predecessors that they fail to see the possibilities of more intelligent
methods arising out of that inevitable change which is the one unchanging law of Nature."

These were dark days. The budget for 1933–1935 was finally settled
on a compromise with a decrease of 19 per cent in operating funds and
25 per cent over-all including elimination of funds for the building
program then in progress. President Sproul referred to the fact that
the University was kept going solely by the steadfast loyalty, zeal,
and continued productivity of its faculty.

It was quite evident, also, that pressure would continue to set up or expand various regional colleges that might benefit a few specific localities, but would further imperil the financial future of higher education in general. The Carnegie Foundation Report had been effective in stimulating widespread discussion, and in counteracting the public willingness to act in haste even if it meant repenting later. Efforts were under way to discredit the report and to bury it as quickly as possible. President Sproul requested and obtained the cooperation of Vierling Kersey, Superintendent of Public Instruction, in calling together a joint committee on problems in higher education to review the recommendations of the report and determine whether agreement could be reached regarding them. Out of this committee came a recommendation that in the opinion of President Sproul was most important to the future of higher education: that the legislature establish a permanent State Council for Educational Planning and Coordination and that no action to extend junior colleges or expand state teachers' colleges should be taken until the proposed State Council could study the matter. Senate Bill #566 was introduced to authorize the creation of the State Council, and was eventually passed, and signed by the Governor of California on June 10, 1933. Two weeks later President Sproul pressed the State Superintendent of Public Instruction to agree on the nine people who should be appointed to the new State Council. By October 30 the State Superintendent had agreed on eight of the nine members but was still weighing two names. However, by November 14 agreement had been reached and the Regents approved on their part a membership consisting of Vierling Kersey, Robert G. Sproul, Chester H. Rowell, Allen T. Archer, Will C. Wood, Gurney Newlin, Charles Albert Adams, Miss Annie Florence Brown, and Mrs. William J. Hayes.

With this much gained, President Sproul fought continuously to persuade the Regents, the State Board of Education, and the legislature, to take no action that would substantially change the nature of any institution of education above the high school, or affect its relations with other institutions, until the matter had been submitted to the State Council on Educational Planning and Coordination for study and recommendation. The Regents recognized the importance of this, but it was a never-ending, up-hill struggle to persuade all advocates of change in this or that educational institution to discuss and defend proposals over a conference table before moving to put them into effect by unilateral fiat or political decision. Furthermore, the State Council suffered under the handicap of being largely an advisory and recommending body without power to implement its findings, or even to hold its own members to policies that they had agreed to support in open conference.

The State Council was comparable to a League of Nations in the educational field, holding insufficient authority to be effective, and weakened by lack of support from those who looked on it as a potential threat to their own sovereignty and private plans. Nevertheless, it constituted a step toward rational, orderly consideration of California's higher educational problems. Its first published report, issued in 1934, was a milestone in the history of American higher education, for it represented one of the first efforts by any state to define and correlate the functions of its various educational institutions above the high school level through the instrumentality of a representative council of institutional and public representatives authorized by the legislature and the governor. This report, of less than seven pages, pocket-size, provided a plan of development for higher education, but could offer it only as a suggestion. The limitations of the Council were made clear in the opening paragraph.

"The State Council on Educational Planning and Coordination, after studying for many months the major problems affecting the relationships between the schools of the public school system and the University of California, presents jointly to the State Board of Education and The Regents of the University of California, through the Superintendent of Public Instruction and the President of the University of California, the following statement of basic principles and of the respective functions and programs of the junior college, the teachers' college, and the University, and urges that each of these boards give consideration to this statement in so far as it concerns the institutions under its jurisdiction."

By 1935 President Sproul was casting about for additional methods of promoting cooperative and joint consideration of the state's higher education program. In October of that year he prepared a tentative statement for the benefit of the Regents and others which frankly summarized the situation as follows:

> Forty-seven public institutions are today at work in the field of higher education, of which the University of California was at one time the exclusive tenant, and each of these institutions is pursuing its own program with little or no regard for what the others are doing. . . . We have urged always, and we urge again, that there be educational planning rather than political log-rolling. The question before us is: what positive, constructive program of higher education can be launched that will discourage the dissipation of the state's resources for higher education, check the retardation of the work of existing institutions, and forestall mediocrity in advanced study and research?
>
> I am quite sure that conflicts and duplication of work in institutions of higher education, authorized and maintained by the state, cannot be eliminated unless there is somewhere an authority which has power to specify the particular function or functions of each type of institution. This authority would need to have jurisdiction over all state institutions maintaining work above the junior college level, including adult education.

Pressure upon the legislature to make various changes relative to the function and purposes of publicly supported colleges, at the instigation of interested local groups, became very strong again at the opening of the 1939 legislative session, and it was only with great difficulty that leaders in the legislature, acting on a suggestion from President Sproul, were able to win support for deferral of immediate action and for recognition of the State Council on Educational Planning and Coordination as the appropriate body to study the various proposals and to make recommendations at the next session. Among the questions at issue were whether the University of California should develop a new campus in Santa Barbara County or in Fresno County, and whether California Polytechnic Institute at San Luis Obispo should become a four-year college granting the bachelor degree. The legislature finally acted by amending a bill to create a branch of the University at Fresno into a request for a study by the State Council on Educational Planning and Coordination.

Indicative of the then prevailing situation, on April 6, 1940, before the State Council on Educational Planning and Coordination had completed its work, the State Board of Education voted to grant the request of the California Polytechnic Institute for four-year, degree status, even though the State Superintendent of Public Instruction had assured the State Director of Finance and the University of California that to the best of his knowledge this matter was not on the agenda of the meeting of the Board scheduled to open on April 5, 1940. President Sproul reported this discouraging, independent action to the State Council on April 15, as follows: "It was the understanding of the President of the University and the Superintendent of Public Instruction that no action would be taken until the Council could review the problem. For reasons not made public the State Board of Education overlooked this understanding and took action a week ago. . . . The Council may wish to review this matter for the purpose of weighing the advisability of suggesting emendations to the State Board's action."

California, of course, was not alone in having problems of higher education precipitated by competition between independently administered colleges and universities. The 69th Annual Report of the Board of Trustees of Ohio State University, June 30, 1939, contained the statement: "The conclusion is inescapable and must be frankly faced by all concerned that the State of Ohio cannot and should not embark upon the impossible purpose to build five equally large, highly specialized and all-equivalent universities worthy of comparison with the single, outstanding state universities in surrounding states."

The Council on Educational Planning and Coordination struggled valiantly to discharge its responsibilities even though it had no funds for a working staff and insufficient time for thorough study. The best it could do by the legislative session of 1941 was to present a progress report and request extension of time and appropriations of funds.

This progress report said in part: "The State Council has reached the conclusion that neither the interests of taxpayers and parents, nor the interests of young people seeking an education, can be protected if major changes in the educational system are to be made without concurrence of at least a majority of the educators and public leaders concerned with education. Such concurrence cannot be sought or obtained until there has been some agreement on the future educational policies of the state, with due regard to population trends and economic limitations, and until a proper procedure has been set up for cooperative planning by the state as a whole." This was the last official act of this first Council for Educational Planning and Coordination. It was unable to accomplish the full purpose for which it was established in 1933 and revivified in 1939, but it, too, played an important part in ground clearing for later moves toward rational planning.

In the meantime, pressure on the legislature and on the Regents to develop new four-year general colleges began to grow, and leading citizens of the Santa Barbara area, particularly its legislative representative, were active in pressing for transfer of Santa Barbara State College to the Regents in accord with the precedent set at Los Angeles more than twenty years earlier. The Regents were not at all certain that additional campuses of the University should be provided while the United States was at war, and enrollments on existing campuses were dropping sharply. In 1943, in an attempt to discourage local ambition and political maneuvers, the Regents took action to make known that as a matter of policy they were opposed to taking over any state college anywhere. Despite this, Santa Barbara continued its efforts, and in 1944 the legislature passed a bill transferring Santa Barbara State College to the Regents of the University and they, after extended study of alternatives, agreed to accept the transfer.

It was generally agreed that this was not an educationally desirable method of forcing the development of the University of California in one geographical area or another, and possibly was an unconstitutional action by the state legislature. President Sproul was still persistently intent on getting people to sit down together and work out educational problems. The following January, in an effort to bring out some new ideas he called a conference attended by Vice-President Monroe E. Deutsch, Dr. Joel Hildebrand, Dr. George Adams, Dr. Frank Freeman, and Dr. George Louderback. He asked two alumni leaders to sit in with them, Ralph T. Fisher, 1901, president of the California

Alumni Association, 1936–1937, and Joseph Loeb, 1905, attorney in Los Angeles and member of the State Board of Education. Many proposals were made but the general consensus was in favor of further efforts to establish a committee, perhaps along the lines of the moribund State Council on Educational Planning and Coordination, but certainly one jointly appointed by the Regents of the University and the State Board of Education, to which problems of concern to both boards could be submitted for full and open discussion. As a consequence of this meeting President Sproul proposed to the Regents of the University just four days later, that they pass a resolution:

> That the State Council of Educational Planning and Coordination (or a liaison committee of the State Board of Education and The Regents of the University of California) be permitted to continue its present efforts to perfect a plan of coordination, with the assistance of state educational agencies, which will provide a permanent basis for the economical and adequate development of all education.
>
> That sufficient funds be appropriated by the State Legislature to defray necessary expenses for technical and clerical assistance, travel and incidentals . . .
>
> That any major changes in the organization of the public educational system of the State of California, including changes in status of institutions (for example: 1. the taking over of State Colleges by the University, 2. the conversion of Junior Colleges into four-year colleges granting the bachelor's degree, and 3. the conversion of State Colleges from undergraduate colleges to institutions of university grade giving graduate work) await the submission of the final report of the State Council on Educational Planning and Coordination (or a liaison committee of the State Board of Education and The Regents of the University of California).
>
> Also, that the Chairman of the Board be authorized to appoint a committee of three, including the President of the University, to meet with a similar committee of the State Board of Education to bring about joint endorsement and support by the two Boards of such plans for the coordination of education in California as may be approved, to promote public understanding of these plans, and to secure their acceptance by the voters of the state, when necessary, at the earliest possible moment.

President Sproul presented this resolution to the Regents with a statement that in his opinion it was vital and urgent that it be passed. He pointed out to them the dangers of a continuing situation in which they could be pushed by local pressure from a policy against taking over state colleges, adopted in March of 1943, to the contrary policy in

October of the same year, and without opportunity for conference with the State Board of Education. When the matter came to vote, all of the Regents present, except one who asked to be excused, supported the proposal made by President Sproul.

Word of this action was conveyed to Mr. Loeb for presentation to the State Board of Education, but no action was taken by that body until after the close of the 1945 session of the state legislature; this again left the University of California alone in its efforts to defer basic legislation until it could be studied from an educational point of view. It was able to do this because it had made a proposal for joint consideration of such problems to the State Board and the Regents, and Comptroller James H. Corley gave assurance that the University would do everything in its power to promote cooperative action.

The importance of the Liaison Committee of four representatives of the State Board of Education and four representatives of the Regents had its first confirmation in 1947 when another rash of bills representing local community or individual institution interests erupted in Sacramento. Among them was a bill to establish a Stanislaus Polytechnic School, another establishing a Stanislaus State College, one creating a Mt. Shasta State College, one a Los Angeles State College, one a Sacramento State College, one to start a School of Agriculture at Fresno, and another to change the name and function of California Polytechnic. Again it was President Sproul's contention that no action should be taken until the proposals had been considered and the need for them weighed. The fact that a Liaison Committee of the State Board and the Regents had been established in 1945 and still could be revived helped to gain support for A.B. 2273, introduced by Assemblyman Francis Dunn, Jr., which authorized the State Board of Education and the Regents to make a joint survey of the organization of publicly supported higher education and of the need for additional publicly supported facilities. Reciprocally, the placing of responsibility on the State Board of Education and the Regents gave stimulus and strength to the Liaison Committee. The appointment of the survey team made cooperation essential. From this date the Committee developed into an effective instrument for the promotion of over-all planning.

The survey was under the direction of a committee of three men: Dr. Monroe E. Deutsch, Provost and Vice-President Emeritus; Dr. Aubrey A. Douglass, Associate State Superintendent of Public Instruction; and Dr. George D. Strayer, formerly Director of the Institute of Educational Research, Columbia University. This study, for the first time, brought together population statistics and projections which indicated the general magnitude of the needs of the state for higher education, and identified the areas in which the need was greatest. The reception accorded to it was better than that received by the Carnegie Foundation Report of 1932, but those who could find in it no support for their own plans were, as usual, most conscientious in suggesting shelves where it might be stored and forgotten; and most people were not ready to face up to the facts of state growth and contemplate seriously the costs entailed in providing higher education facilities and services.

However, this report, "The Survey of the Needs of California in Higher Education" was another milestone in the history of higher education, for it indicated how much factual information could be accumulated to help in making wise decisions on educational expansion, and it alerted the state to the magnitude of the problems ahead. In addition, it recommended the continuation of the Liaison Committee and an annual state appropriation to support a full-time technical staff for research on educational problems and the preparation of background material. The state legislature, however, was not yet convinced that it should spend money on further studies, and at first turned down a direct request for an appropriation and then deleted requests for such funds from the University of California budget and the State Board of Education budget. However, in 1951 it saw the light, and from that time on provided support for the Liaison Committee and its full-time technical staff, under the direction of Dr. T. C. Holy, retired Director of the Bureau of Educational Research, Ohio State University, who brought to the task a world of experience and limitless energy.

As a consequence, when the next wave of uncoordinated proposals for expansion of education institutions began to mount in 1953, the

Liaison Committee was in a position to propose to the Sub-Committee on Education of the Assembly Ways and Means Committee that the first step should be to study what had happened to the state since the Strayer report of 1947 was completed, and to up-date its statistical data. Moreover, the Sub-Committee on Education was in a position to recognize the importance of this move and to recommend to the legislature that the Liaison Committee of the Regents and State Board of Education be authorized to conduct such a study. By this time, too, the population research staff of the State Director of Finance was turning out predictions of population growth that made it clear that planning for expansion was essential.

This most detailed of all surveys, titled: "A Restudy of the Needs of California in Higher Education," was undertaken by a task force headed by Dr. T. R. McConnell, formerly Chancellor of the University of Buffalo, Dr. H. H. Semans of the California State Department of Education, and a relatively large staff of technical aides. The report of the task force made many recommendations, but none was more important to the future stability of higher education than that which advocated putting all state colleges under a new board with wide enough powers and strong enough authority to make them an integral and organized part of the state's system of higher education. In furtherance of this and other recommendations of the restudy report, the state legislature of 1959 passed Assembly Concurrent Resolution 88, which requested the Liaison Committee of the State Board of Education and the Regents of the University, to prepare a Master Plan for the development, expansion and integration of higher education in the state. That Master Plan was prepared, unanimously approved in principle at a joint meeting of the Regents and the State Board of Education, December 18, 1959, and accepted by the state legislature as a guide for policy-setting legislation at its 1960 session. The key bill was S.B. 33, designated as the Donahoe Higher Education Act, in honor of the late Assemblywoman Dorothy M. Donahoe of Bakersfield, who had started the legislative machinery in the previous session. Senate Bill 33 established a new board, the Trustees of the State College System; created an advisory body to the Trustees and the

Regents of the University under the title of the Coordinating Council for Higher Education; and set the basic policies for determination of primary functions to be served by the University, the state colleges, and the junior colleges. It is too early to know how well this integration program will work, but given a determination on the part of all concerned to see that it works, the people of California may look forward to more rational and orderly development of higher education.

Although the final achievement of a state-established plan of coordination for higher education came two years after Robert Sproul retired from the presidency of the University, it was clearly a step related to and developing out of those in which he had been centrally involved over a period of some three decades. As the idea of coordination took hold, more and more people made greater and greater contributions toward this end, but no individual was more persistently and continuously involved over a longer period of time than Robert Sproul. He outlined the problems caused by independent educational developments in his inaugural address of 1930, expressed his intention to work for improvement, and then proceeded to do so with undiminished determination. The part that he played in this evolution is without question one of the major and most lasting of all the services he rendered both to the University of California and to all higher education in the state.

The preceding account of major steps in the progress toward rational planning of higher education in California is, of course, no more than an outline. Among the important contributing movements supported and encouraged by President Sproul that limitations of space have caused to be left out, mention should be made, at least, of the Committee on Affiliations with Secondary Schools, the Junior College Conference, the Committee on Coordination with State Colleges, and the California Committee for the Study of Secondary and Collegiate Education. The maintenance of a university of high standards with consistently enforced subject and grade requirements for admission and continuation, inevitably tends to develop resentment in those who believe they are adversely affected, and if there is also a feeling that some of the requirements are just arbitrary decisions by scholars who fail to appreciate the problems of other schools, trouble eventually results. In this as in all other areas President Sproul was convinced that the only effective antidote was understanding to be gained through discussion and conference. If the people involved knew each other, problems had a tendency to shrink or at least to order themselves so that the real issues came to the surface and could be met on a rational basis.

III

The President and
The Faculty

President Robert G. Sproul opened his inaugural address on October 22, 1930, with the following words:

> This great gathering representative of the State of California, increases the pleasure, but it cannot make me feel more deeply the seriousness of the task with which I have been entrusted. No man who, through more than twenty years, has felt himself a part of the life of the University—as undergraduate student, as alumnus, as administrative officer—could come to its presidency without some realization of its fine traditions, its noble character, its extraordinary prospects; without some awe of its heavy responsibilities and some humbleness before its mighty opportunities; without a sense of high and holy obligation to give all that within him lies of devotion and ability to maintain for this University its acknowledged place as one of the notable institutions of the world.
>
> Not only is this occasion in itself momentous; it is made more so for me by the fact that it is the first time I have been inaugurated as a university president, and being less assured of my wisdom than those who have had theirs passed upon by time and academic experts, I approach this test as a freshman does his first examination, having prepared for it by a comprehensive review of the authorities; in this case by a careful reading of the words of the great and near great in some twenty institutions throughout the country as expressed in their inaugural addresses.

The President and the Faculty

In the preceding chapter attention was given to President Sproul's ideas as to the place which the University of California should maintain in the higher educational program of the state, and as to the variety of opportunities that all institutions, working cooperatively, should provide for young people of different interests and talents. Farther on in his inaugural address he turned to the question of maintaining and improving the quality of the services rendered by the University and broached a subject that continued to plague him for 28 years.

> The educational activities of a university must be examined in the light of their directive concepts. University education, even today, is influenced by the tradition of the middle ages, by the idea of academic discipline and of authoritative instruction. That tradition met with difficulties in the nineteenth century under the impact of the natural and social sciences, and in the twentieth century it is facing the problem of marked increase in the number of subjects to be investigated and taught, and in a consequent questionable specialization of instruction. The difficulties arising from these impacts have resulted in various systems of electives, of majors and minors, and in suggestions for improving instruction, such as granting privileges to superior students. But these difficulties of the present situation in American education have not, as yet, provoked what is most urgently needed—a careful, scientific study of the whole problem, the prosecution of inquiries which will lead to new knowledge in the field of university education.
>
> That university man is rare indeed who would claim that the present system of higher education is adequate; yet we adhere to it because it is easier than to make a radical change. . . . Why should we not look on education as a problem for experimentation just as we so look on a problem in physics or astronomy? Why, when we recognize the importance of theories and experimentation in every other field, should we accept, with such complaisance, our present system of education? The reason is that most of us either give no thought to the theory underlying the system of education we support, or think of education as an exception to the rule that every subject must rest on some cardinal theory.
>
> Such theories and investigations have been left in the universities almost entirely to departments of education, which for all the contumely that has been heaped upon their heads have been more progressive than other departments, for they have been making an honest, sincere study of a problem baffling in its complexity. . . . But they cannot solve the problems alone. In the first place we will not let them, and in the second place, they are too much involved with the problems of the elementary and secondary school systems to see the problems of

higher education clearly and to see them whole. What we need is men outside of departments of education, as well as in, who will think not in terms of their department but in terms of the university, and who will follow the scientific method in education as they do in their own subjects, never thinking of advancing theories without painstaking, well-grounded study, and never thinking of putting these theories into practice without controlled experimentation. That attitude of mind toward education, as toward every other phase of university life, I hope to cultivate and encourage during my presidency, through the whole faculty if possible—if not, then through the assistant professors, who will be the University for which I shall take credit or receive blame when my course is run. If they will take me seriously when I say these things, and will jolt themselves out of the ruts that have been worn smooth and deep by their predecessors, we can together, in the next few years, change the entire aspect of education in this University.

President Sproul went on to give in more detail what he thought might be the direction in which improvement should be sought.

The information that appears in textbooks . . . should be merely of secondary importance in university life, and should be gained by students incidentally as part of the equipment for that independent thinking which should be their main object. . . . It seems to me that if research is the great adventure we believe it to be we cannot introduce good students to its inspiring difficulties too soon. The interest aroused by such an early introduction would make better students of all who are capable of being students at all. . . .

Conversely, the products of such a system would do much to bring to an end the incessant debate between teaching and research, because men trained under such a system would know that you cannot keep the two apart, that while one man may elect to teach and another to investigate, the teacher must keep abreast of his subject and the investigator must transmit what he has learned. Research is merely a search for knowledge, and no man belongs on a university faculty who is not engaged in that search.

But this does not mean to me that all faculty men must be productive scholars in the narrow sense of the term. There will always be some good men who are primarily investigators, and some extraordinary men who are both. . . .

Under present conditions we have the strange anomaly of teachers being judged not on their ability to teach but on their research output, and investigators being forced to devote valuable time to teaching that might be given to advancing the frontiers of knowledge. As a result men who might be good teachers if they were encouraged by the hope of future advancement are drifting about in laboratories with a couple of test tubes in their hands making themselves useless in a most arduous and time-consuming way, while men who might be good investigators are wearing out their patience and the students in a vain effort to expound and to inspire large classes. . . .

Moreover, both teachers and investigators should be recognized far more liberally in a financial way than they now are. As things are, very few of the best college graduates can be persuaded to undertake a scholarly career because they feel quite properly, that a man is foolish to enter even a pleasant field where the laborer is held to be not worthy of his hire.

When President Sproul spoke of the anomaly of teachers being judged solely on their research output and commented so forcefully on the need for constant restudy of traditional practices, he was not offering himself as public defender for those who ascribed their failure to obtain or hold a University appointment to noninterest in teaching by a closed corporation of research monomaniacs. Rather he was expressing the personal concern of a practical-minded engineer and experienced administrator over the responsibility for recruitment and evaluation of men and women with a talent for which there are no clear specifications. It seemed plausible to suppose that a talent recognized as the touchstone that motivates and inspires youth, as the catalyst that makes the civilization of today out of the civilization of yesterday and the civilization of tomorrow out of both, should be identifiable while it is still a corm, or seed, or spore. It was not enough to judge the wonder of the bloom, after the fact, by counting the seeds it had scattered, or the number that germinated vigorously in the next generation; and then hastening to express appreciation to the cultivator thereof with a geriatrical honorary degree.

Every university president, of course, must meet this problem and solve it in one way or another, if he wishes to succeed at his job, and the institution he guides is to benefit by his ministrations. The fact that President Sproul held his position for twenty-eight years, and that his University steadily continued to develop into and stand confirmed as a center of higher education known and respected throughout the world, would appear to indicate that his solution of the teaching-talent problem was a good one. As far as a bystander can judge, the basis of his success was common sense applied with uncommon persistence. He indicated by his actions and statements on countless occasions that in his opinion talent for teaching was not necessarily assured by deep knowledge and highly developed creative ability, although a talent for teaching without deep knowledge and some creative ability was of little use to a major university.

As an undergraduate, and for the first six years of his employment at Berkeley, Robert Sproul worked under and served with President Benjamin Ide Wheeler, who placed a high value on interpretation and synthesis of knowledge. In his inaugural address in 1899, Wheeler said "the first thing must be that the University of California calls to its aid the best talent in teaching and in methods of instruction that the world affords. Men must be taken, without reference to locality or origin, for what they are as exponents and interpreters of what is highest in the civilized life of man."

The fruitfulness of President Wheeler's approach to the recruitment of faculty is indicated by the fact that he stayed in office for twenty years and the University grew and prospered despite the aura of benevolent autocracy that surrounded him. The average great scholar has great difficulty in meeting the lay public's conception of what a scholar should be, and President Wheeler seemed to sense the need for scholars with a personality which lived in the memories of all who heard them, as symbols of the University—among them such men as Henry Morse Stephens and Charles Mills Gayley.

The University of California went through a period of change during the regime of President and General David P. Barrows, and that of Astronomer-President William Wallace Campbell, which followed. Dr. Campbell was inclined to think of ability to lecture as one of the less important attributes of a scholar. In his last biennial report to the governor of the state, for the years 1928–30, he expressed the conviction that the best way to improve education at the university level would be to drop the idea of lecture courses as the principal teaching staple. He suggested that a first step in the right direction would be to reduce the number of lectures given by all faculty members, and the number of lecture course units taken by all students, by one third, while at the same time bringing about a vast increase in the amount of required reading and writing. Probably most university teachers would agree that more active participation by students in the educational process would be highly desirable. But a vast increase in the amount of individual—as opposed to group—effort by students would require an equally vast increase in the number of faculty members required to counsel them, and guide and criticize their efforts.

President Sproul, in some ways, seemed to combine the old and the new. He was an engineer who had enjoyed the study of Latin. He was enough of an artist on the speaker's rostrum to appreciate what Wheeler had been striving for, enough of an administrator to share General Barrow's respect for the logistics of the situation, and enough of a scholar to understand that the scientific mind and the creative mind are fundamental to a modern university. His first task was one of preparation to meet the inevitable fact that in scholarly potential, as in everything else, one gets just about what he is prepared to pay for. If he were to meet the competition of other major universities for outstanding scholars, he had to overcome the then prevailing provincial attitude in California that a reasonably fair salary range was one just above that of other public institutions such as the state colleges, the junior colleges, and the high schools, or one about equal to that paid by local private institutions.

In his first major address after accepting the presidency, delivered before the Commonwealth Club of San Francisco on July 25, 1930, Sproul pointed out that: "the maximum salary for a professor has increased very little for many years, and the average at California, $5,200, is far below that of other institutions with which we must compete for the very limited supply of first-class men. . . . If the stream of our civilization is not to be dried up at the source, we must pay salaries in education that will attract first-class men in competition with business and other professions."

His philosophy was that the University of California had to meet the competition of the best universities in the United States and that salary levels in the local market were irrelevant. Over the course of years he had studies made of salary levels in universities and colleges throughout the country. His primary concern was with such institutions as Harvard, Yale, Princeton, Columbia, Chicago, and Michigan. But he backed up the argument with data on salary levels at Michigan State, Wisconsin, Minnesota, Ohio State, Illinois, Indiana, Purdue, Iowa, Washington, and Oregon. The Regents of the University were quite willing to agree that they must move toward comparability in salaries with other leading institutions of higher education if they expected to get a reasonable share of the best men, particularly at the peak of their careers and at the top of the salary range. However, it was a long and arduous struggle to get agreement from the officers of the state and from the legislature that the University was operating in a labor market national in scope. The Depression, of course, put limitations on all programs involving increased expenditure by the state, regardless of their intrinsic merits. But, in addition, there was a feeling that one should not go out of the state to recruit more teachers as long as there were native Californians out of a job who might be able to teach; that it was preposterous to say California could not produce and train teachers equal to the best to be obtained anywhere, and that any teacher on the East Coast smart enough to be worth having would not need to be lured to California by a higher salary. Nevertheless, the principle was finally accepted, and it laid the foundation for the further strengthening of the University, and most important of all, for its successful expansion in campuses and enrollment without sacrifice of steady growth in quality.

Associated with the problem of salary levels was the equally important one of providing library resources, laboratory facilities, and ancillary equipment, equal to those at longer-established universities in other parts of the country. This was particularly important in the development of additional campuses at Los Angeles and Santa Barbara, though it applied to Berkeley and the older campuses as well. Productive scholars with a consuming interest in the pursuit of new knowledge, or better understanding of the old, are not at all interested in burying themselves in some isolated spot away from library resources or research laboratories, and distant from other scholars working in the same or closely related fields, even though the salaries they are offered may be very attractive.

The President and the Faculty

An indication of the reputation that President Sproul earned in his fight to raise the level of support for the University in spite of tradition and the Depression, can be gained from comments by newspaper editors. On March 8, 12, and 14 of 1935, the McClatchy chain ran an editorial statement in the *Sacramento Bee*, the *Modesto Bee*, and the *Fresno Bee and Republican*, that said in part "As a university comptroller he achieved a reputation second to none for engaging favorably the ears of members of the Senate and the Assembly . . . if the exigencies of the present situation do not permit his personal appearance in Sacramento, Sproul's fertile mind is not without ideas as to reaching the desired objective. For he now is inspiring a massed assault on the economizers in the present legislature. . . . Are not the legislators able enough and honest enough to consider the needs of the University on their own merits?" The writer of the editorial went on to make clear that he was getting tired of watching Sproul build up the University of California while the educational ambitions of other public institutions were being throttled.

The stimulus for this protest, apparently, was a series of talks by President Sproul throughout the state and on the radio, on the general subject of "The High Cost of Cheap Education," in which he spoke of Governor Frank Merriam's provision for the University as "niggardly," and a "Ghandi Diet," which put the University of California about on a par with Folsom and San Quentin. However, there were other activities involved, including articles in alumni magazines, and a suggestion to all students wanting to help that they write to their parents and friends on the need for more state support. During the month of January, 1935, President and Mrs. Sproul moved to Los Angeles and attended nine different social affairs that were widely publicized on the society pages; at the same time his statements about the bright future of the University of California at Los Angeles, providing budget difficulties could be overcome, were receiving attention on other pages. Back of this special effort in the south, of course, was the general reluctance of Los Angeles to consider the University of California at Los Angeles as part of a statewide system. Two or three years earlier the *Los Angeles Examiner* had confined the space given to the President of the University to a taciturn comment that Dr. and Mrs. Robert Sproul were visiting the southland from Berkeley where the former was President of the University.

The year 1935 was a significant one in the history of higher education in California. Although President Sproul was unable to move Governor Frank Merriam on the matter of a more realistic provision for the University in his budget recommendation to the legislature, he was able to get a special supplementary appropriation of $1,455,000 from the senate and assembly, and then to seek and obtain Governor Merriam's reluctant approval for $1,000,000 of this amount on the last day before it would have been pocket-vetoed. This success in breaking through the inertia of the Depression started the steady climb toward equality of scholarly opportunity in California relative to other major universities. This is not to imply that the University of California had not attracted outstanding faculty members in earlier years, but rather that it was now placed in a position to attract more of them, and to survive a period of major expansion of campuses and enrollment without sacrificing internal development. One of the incidental and unforeseen results of this campaign was its effect upon other institutions of higher education in the state. As the University of California brought itself into line with universities on the eastern seaboard and the Great Lakes area, private colleges and universities in California found themselves facing an inexorable pressure to follow suit, and state colleges found themselves presented with a strong argument for commensurate increases. In effect, the level of higher education in the whole of the state was moved upward. In order to avoid open opposition from private institutions, President Sproul had to agree not to use whatever salary advantage the University of California might from time to time enjoy, for indiscriminate raiding of the best men from private colleges and universities in the state. And at the same time he had to give assurance to the American Association of University Professors that he would not enter into any secret compacts that would arbitrarily protect existing budgets at private institutions by eliminating the normal influence of supply and demand and interinstitutional competition on salary levels and chances for advancement. As usual, President Sproul sought for the most reasonable course between Scylla and Charybdis, recognizing that it was to the advantage of the whole state to import outstanding scholars from other areas, and equally to the advantage of the state to see that opportunities for advancement were preserved after these scholars arrived.

In 1930–31, when Robert Sproul began his administration of the University of California, it was already a large institution with 19,626 students, a plant valued at $40,631,000, a library of 1,035,181 volumes, state appropriations of $8,057,054, and total annual income amounting to $12,710,122. In the year 1956–57, the last one for which he saw the accounts closed in the fall, enrollments had increased to 45,303, the value of the plant had increased almost seven times to $274,853,000, the library resources had increased to 3,997,245 volumes, state appropriations had increased approximately nine times to $72,878,665, and total income, including Federal grants and contracts for research, had mounted to $209,009,875. In addition, endowment funds, which represent the venture capital and quality insurance for a state university, had increased from $16,696,000 to $86,207,000. To a considerable extent, of course, these increases represented the growth of the State of California, the growing national interest in university research, the dedication of the Regents to the building of endowment funds, and a considerable drop in the value of the dollar. But even with ample allowance for these factors the residual gain in economic and related academic strength was impressive.

At the December, 1942, meeting of the Regents, presaging the 75th charter anniversary, President Sproul reported to the Regents on the development of the University in the following words:

> From time to time, in recent years, I have presented to the Board various evidences from disinterested authorities which confirm my own conviction that the University of California has been developing in quality as well as growing in size.
>
> The first important evidence of this type, based upon an impartial survey of all American universities, was made public by the American Council on Education in 1934. In a previous national survey by the American Council on Education, completed about a decade earlier, the University of California had been ranked tenth in eminence in the country. Ten years later, in a study based on the findings of 2,034 of the leading scholars of the United States, the Council found that the

University of California rated as either distinguished or adequate in thirty-one different fields of knowledge, a record not exceeded by any other university. In distinguished departments alone, it rated second only to Harvard University.

Subsequent studies by such men as Walter Crosby Eells, Lawrence Foster, and others, based primarily on the surveys made by the American Council on Education, but including other criteria of eminence as well, invariably placed the University of California among the first four or five universities in America. . . .

Two years ago, in 1940, Kunkel and Prentice made a statistical study correlating the persons whose names had been added to *Who's Who in America* for the decade 1930–1940, with the universities, if any, that had contributed to their education. These investigators came to the conclusion that, in these years so recently passed, only one university had surpassed the University of California in the number of alumni winning sufficient eminence to be included in the current *Who's Who.* In a similar study, records of the Guggenheim Foundation indicate that the University of California leads all other universities in the number of Guggenheim Fellowships won since the Foundation was established in 1925.

Statistics on the relative size of leading libraries in the country have long been available, but the first comprehensive study of the relative *quality* of libraries has just been completed by the Board of Resources of American Libraries, appointed by the American Library Association. The Board approached the problem by asking 500 leading scholars to list the most important book collections of which they had knowledge in seventy-five specified fields. With this information the Board made a careful comparison of the relative depth and breadth of various libraries. Compilation of the results reveals that the University of California Library has "eminent" book collections in 54 of the 75 fields. Of greatest significance, however, is the fact that there are only two libraries of any description in the United States which exceed this record, namely, Harvard University Library and the Library of Congress.

. . . In releasing this comparative information, however, the American Library Association has issued a warning which it hopes will be kept in mind by all library administrators. That warning is in the form of a reminder that no library can remain eminent unless it is constantly augmented through judicious purchases.

President Sproul paid tribute to faculty advisory committees in accounting for the high status of the University Library, and Associate Professor Walton E. Bean, some ten years later said: "He might have added that he had often used his contingent funds, or exerted himself to find other special funds, to make special purchases which his faculty recommended."

The President and the Faculty

All of this is concerned with the financing and equipping of the University for competition in securing a reasonable share of the best teachers of the country. There still remained the basic problem of selecting teachers for first appointment, for retention, and for advancement in rank. The approach to this problem had already been established by the faculty in the so-called "faculty revolution" at the end of President Wheeler's regime and was reflected in a provision of the Standing Orders of the Regents as follows: "The President shall recommend to the Board appointments, promotions, demotions, and dismissals of the officers and employees of the University. Whenever any such action shall affect a professorial or equivalent position, such action shall be taken only after the President shall have consulted with a properly constituted advisory committee of the Academic Senate."

At no time did President Sproul consider this standing order as a definition of the area of appointments in which he was required to seek faculty advice. Rather he regarded it as laying down a general principle that he ought to follow on every occasion whether technically required to do so or not. His efforts were directed toward the improvement of what he felt to be the best possible procedure that he, as chief administrative officer, could choose. The Academic Senate, by resolution first adopted in 1920, and revised in 1939 and 1947, established a procedure that the President might follow in accord with the Standing Orders of the Regents. This procedure involved consultation with the teaching department concerned, on every appointment at the rank of instructor, assistant professor, associate professor, or professor; and consultation with the Academic Senate Committee on Budget and Interdepartmental Relations on all appointments above that of instructor. This Academic Senate resolution further provided that the Committee on Budget and Interdepartmental Relations might at its discretion nominate a special faculty committee to be appointed by the President to review the qualifications of individuals under consideration for appointments or promotions to the assistant professor level, and to make a confidential, written report. For all appointments or promotions at the tenure rank of associate professor or professor the committee is given no choice, but is *required* to nominate a committee of faculty members to report confidentially, in writing, to the President through the Committee on Budget and Interdepartmental Relations.

As this evaluation system operated under President Sproul, all recommendations for appointment, promotion, or merit increases in salary had to originate with the chairmen of the departments concerned. Those involving assistant, associate, or full professorships were referred by him to the Academic Senate Committee for further recommendation and for special review committee consideration. This meant that a young man or woman starting as an instructor had to demonstrate his or her ability and industry as a creative scholar and teacher to the satisfaction of older colleagues at the end of the first two years, or find employment elsewhere. If the individual did surmount this hurdle, he advanced to the rank of assistant professor, and during a further trial period of no more than six years, he was subject to at least two review committee reports by his peers; these ended either with his being helped to find a position in some less exacting institution or with a recommendation for advancement to the rank of associate professor. Although this latter rank carries tenure, contingent on satisfactory service, further advancement to the rank of professor depends again on a detailed review of demonstrated abilities and achievements by a confidential committee of the candidates' colleagues. Intervening reviews may occur in the event that the individual is recommended for merit increases in salary. As a documentary basis for all such reviews the faculty member concerned is expected to keep up-to-date and to file in the Office of the President, a bio-bibliographical record on work accomplished, special services rendered, and on creative achievements, as evidenced by publication or artistic or professional production.

Although the President of the University is not obliged to abide by the faculty recommendation, his own recommendation to the Regents, whatever it may be, is made on the basis of a more extensive accumulation of factual information about the faculty member under consideration. Without question, this painstaking and time-consuming process is of vital assistance to the President and an extremely important safeguard of faculty quality. It is particularly effective in appraising the intellectual quality of the candidate for appointment or advancement, his industry and productiveness, his public services, and his contributions to the work of the University. It is a process appropriate to appointment of a man as a member of a community of scholars charged with a high degree of responsibility for self-governance, and for maintaining academic standards in such matters as student relations, admission requirements, courses and curricula to be offered, and requirements for degrees at the various levels.

Needless to say, this generally effective appointment and promotion system meets its greatest difficulty in appraising teaching ability. As President Sproul indicated in his inaugural address, he found a tendency to appraise men for tangible achievements in research or other scholarly and professional pursuits, and to assume an equal capacity in teaching unless there were complaints on record to the contrary. It was also true, when President Sproul took office, that the written reports of review committees varied a great deal in thoroughness, depending upon the previous experience of committee members, their appreciation of relevant detail, the energy of the chairman, and the time that was available. Then there was a tendency for committees to try for a unanimous opinion or to submit a majority report without giving great detail on any minority point of view that might develop.

Although President Sproul could and did reject review committee reports that seemed inadequate and return them to the Committee on Budget and Interdepartmental Relations with a request for a second review by the same Committee or by a new one, his major emphasis was on more detailed briefing of review committees before they began their task. Over the course of years, on his urging, the letters of appointment to committee members grew steadily longer and more specific. By 1943 he was convinced that there had to be some formal directive or regulation that would serve the dual purpose of guiding review committees and apprising all members of the staff of the kind and quality of services for which they were subject to evaluation for promotion. By 1953 this guide had grown into a 1,200 word document entitled "Instructions to Appointment and Promotion Committees." In this, as in every other document of importance, President Sproul relied on faculty aid and consultation over principles involved.

The instructions opened with the statement that "The quality of the faculty of the University of California is maintained primarily through objective and thorough appraisal, by competent faculty members, of each candidate for appointment or promotion. Responsibility for this appraisal falls largely upon the review committees nominated by the Committee on Budget and Interdepartmental Relations and appointed by the President or by the local chief administrative officer."

Whereas earlier letters of instruction to review committees had listed teaching ability as a secondary object of inquiry, the 1953 instructions placed it first and went into detail on criteria as follows: "Teaching is a primary activity of the University. It comprehends not only lecturing, but the broad range of faculty-student relationships whereby education is imparted. Routine performance is not ground for appointment or advancement; effective teaching is, and it has many manifestations. The committee should consider such points as the following: the candidate's command of his subject; his continous growth in the scholarship of his field; his ability to organize his material and to present it with force and logic; his capacity to awaken in students an awareness of the relationship of his subject to other fields of knowledge; his grasp of general objectives; the spirit and enthusiasm which vitalize his learning and teaching; his ability to arouse curiosity in beginning students and to stimulate advanced students to creative work; his personal attributes as they affect his teaching and his students; the extent and skill of his participation in the general guidance and advising of students; his contribution to student welfare through service on student-faculty committees and as an adviser to student organizations. The committee should clearly indicate the sources of evidence on which its appraisal of teaching competence has been based. In those exceptional cases where no such evidence is available, the candidate's potentialities as a teacher may be indicated in closely analogous activities."

The President and the Faculty

As one reviews President Sproul's efforts to emphasize teaching ability it seems clear that he started with the conviction that teaching was a talent of some scholars and not of others, and that granted the individual possessed high intellectual capacity, and great depth and breadth of knowledge constantly augmented by reading, he could in many fields be a distinguished teacher on the undergraduate level without engaging in research or developing a long list of publications. It seemed to him that concentration on the production of liberally educated young men and women might be a very worthy enterprise that neither required nor left time for other kinds of creative work. It also seemed to him that teachers who were particularly useful at the undergraduate level might be lost to the University if retention and promotion at all levels depended primarily on criteria most essential at the graduate level. He spent much time thinking about additional ways of detecting teachers of high ability whose concentration on students and reading in their fields prevented them from making major, personal contributions to knowledge. One of the obvious possibilities, to which his thinking returned constantly, was that of systematically gathering judgments from students or former students as to the relative stimulus and benefit received from the professors under whom they had studied. He knew from meticulous reading of hundreds of review committee reports on teachers that opinions of selected, mature students, gathered informally from casual conversations, played a part in the process of evaluation, but he was not certain that this approach was used consistently or that it carried appropriate weight in crucial cases. The production of successful candidates for a bachelor of arts or bachelor of science degree did not seem to be recognized widely as an individual creative activity. It was more of a group enterprise. Only when a student went on for graduate work did an individual member of the faculty seem to feel that some personal credit could be claimed for a creative achievement. To the extent that this attitude prevailed, it helped to explain the reluctance of faculty members to be judged by undergraduate students at large, even though they made a point of seeking undergraduate reactions to teaching efforts on an informal basis.

The President and the Faculty

On every appropriate occasion President Sproul sought to encourage review committees and individual faculty members to make full use of student opinions in identifying and giving due recognition to teaching talent. If anything, this feeling deepened with the years as his own children entered the University of California: Marion in 1934, Robert Gordon, Jr., in 1938, and John in 1941. The mere fact that the president of a university trustfully sent his three children to the same institution or, to put it more accurately, that the three children of a president of a university decided they could survive the notoriety indicated that the Sproul family members were reasonably well-blessed with equanimity. As a consequence President Sproul was often able to support his contention that student opinion could be very enlightening, by causally mentioning that he learned more about teaching in ten minutes at the dinner table than he did from half a dozen faculty reports.

But student reaction to teacher performance is akin to children's reactions to parental authority. A parent may seek criticism from his son, but resent having his son egged on by a neighbor. Faculty members encounter all degrees of maturity and judgment in undergraduate students, and they are uncertain about the dependability of any appraisal from a small number of students particularly if a third party obtains it by passing out questionnaires. This uncertainty was naturally intensified by the Depression. Unemployment, breadlines, men selling apples in the street were disillusioning experiences even for the firmest believers in self-government, free enterprise, and the American way of life. Young people who tended to find grounds for disillusionment under the best of conditions were understandably discouraged by the general pessimism, and astonished by the apologies of their elders for the sorry state of the economy, and by requests for help in making a newer and braver world. Such exhortations to youth were most pointedly directed at students in universities throughout the country, in commencement addresses and at other times. And university students, in accepting the challenge, usually began by seeking to improve the universities they were attending, while waiting for graduation and a chance at the larger world.

The President and the Faculty

At the University of California various efforts were made by students to express their opinions concerning courses, curricula, and members of the faculty. These efforts assumed an organized form in 1938. On November 18 of that year the Student Welfare Council of the Associated Students sent a letter to Vice-President Monroe E. Deutsch informing him of the availability of students for help in the difficult task of improving teaching, and calling particular attention to an idea for a "student reaction sheet"; the latter had been worked out by a student under the guidance of a member of the faculty. The young lady who was chairman of the Welfare Council at the time assured Vice-President Deutsch: "The plan is in no way directed towards student control over or dictation to faculty members."

The key to the plan proposed was "The Schneider-Cleland Reaction Sheet." Its purpose was to make available to all students wanting to express an opinion about a faculty member a kind of questionnaire with an eighty-point scale on which the professor might be graded as regards courtesy and consideration for students, tolerance for student viewpoints, clarity in presenting subject matter, and success in stimulating intellectual curiosity.

Despite a noticeable antipathy on the part of the faculty toward this offer of "trial by public shotgun," the faculty member involved in setting up the plan was so convinced of the helpfulness of organized student opinion-polling that he began a one-man crusade to gather and publish student ratings of his colleagues as teachers in particular courses. As a result, student opinion-polling became less popular on campus and student reactions were regarded as on a level with the opinions of William Jennings Bryan expressed some years earlier during the trial of John T. Scopes at Dayton, Tennessee, on the charge of teaching evolution. President Sproul and Vice-President Deutsch found themselves caught between two fires, with one member of the faculty suggesting that the administration support a student opinion-poll of some kind, and other members of the faculty demanding that their crusading colleague be disciplined for disturbing the academic peace. President Sproul reminded the faculty that this was a matter clearly assigned to the Academic Senate under the Standing Orders of the Regents, and as a result, on March 17, 1941, the Academic Senate approved a resolution as follows: "That the unauthorized issuance by members of the Faculty to students of questionnaires for the collection of data as to the professional competence of other members of the faculty, or the unauthorized publication by members of the Faculty of such material, is a violation of Faculty Privilege against which all members of the Faculty have a right to be protected."

President Sproul was aware that the controversy over student opinions on teaching at Berkeley was not unique, and that it constituted just one example of hundreds of similar discussions and controversies throughout the United States, precipitated by Depression-bred iconoclasm. On October 30, 1939, following an extended conference with presidents and deans of American colleges and universities at Columbia, Missouri, he wrote a longhand letter to Vice-President Deutsch which ran in part as follows: "Having just listened to a stimulating discussion of the status of teaching in the American university, I am jotting down some of the things I heard about the proposal which I have discussed with you from time to time, but without much encouragement. There was general agreement, among both the deans and the presidents, that we should explore the possibilities of student appraisal of teachers. The point was made that students are going to appraise anyway, and publish their appraisals, as they have already done in many cases. Would it not be wise then to direct their efforts along constructive lines?" He then cited the methods being used to meet the same problem at Massachusetts Institute of Technology, by President Ruthven of Michigan, and by President Dodds of Princeton.

In an effort to meet the objection that many students may not come to appreciate the benefit they have received from a given course of instruction until years after, he allocated money from his contingency fund for a survey of alumni opinion. For purposes of the survey a random selection was made of 550 members of the Class of 1929, at that time just ten years out of college. The selection was restricted to those who had earned a degree in the twenty-three most often selected majors out of the forty to fifty then offered at Berkeley. Each was asked to name the three most memorable teachers under whom he or she had studied, and 352 of the 550 replied; this represented 64 per cent of those asked, a rather high return for a single inquiry without follow-up. The results indicated both a wide diversity of opinion as to who the most memorable teachers were, and a good opinion of a relatively high percentage of the total faculty involved. Some 249 different teachers were mentioned from once to more than ten times each. In general the teachers picked were those who had also been recognized under the University's review committee procedure. In fact only one of the teachers mentioned ten times or more had not advanced to the full professorship by 1939–40, and this was, perhaps, partly because the teacher concerned was a woman in one of the less academic departments. However, the fact that the judgement of alumni ten years out of college did support the findings of review committees, *ex post facto*, lent support to the theory that student opinion, properly qualified, could be of help in identifying good teachers.

In the months that followed, President Sproul continued to raise the question of better methods of early evaluation of teaching ability. In answer to one query he received the following assurance from the Committee on Budget and Interdepartmental Relations: "The Budget Committee recognizes that determination of teaching ability should be useful not only in judging fitness for promotion or retention, but, more important, for the improvement of teaching."

With this comment as a fulcrum he promptly turned his attention to the chairmen of departments throughout the University and asked them to give him prompt replies to two questions: 1) "What means are at present being used by your department to determine the teaching ability of its members, especially the younger men?" 2) "Can you suggest improvements in those methods?"

The response to these questions was impressive. Every department of more than a few faculty members held one or more formal or informal conferences, and the reports received were of such length that they could have been used as the foundation for a book on the subject of "Prospecting for University Teachers." Many different criteria of evaluation were in use. Departments concerned with the graphic or plastic arts explained that every judgment of student work was in part a judgment of the teachers under whom the students had studied. There was general agreement that no single standard of teaching excellence could be depended upon, for a major university needs men who are at their best in lectures before large audiences, and also those who blossom into imaginative guides only under the stimulus of a few advanced students working at a high level. It needs some teachers who are patient but exacting drill masters on fundamentals, and others who ride hard to reach an inspiration point and leave the students to go back and pick up the dull details later, hopefully with a little more perspective and discrimination than they had at the start. It was pointed out that the number of students attracted voluntarily to a given course is not a dependable measure of the teaching ability of the man in charge, because experience demonstrates that student choices of program at the lower division or undergraduate level are often based on extraneous reasons. Class visiting by other faculty members was also considered to be a doubtful procedure, because one lecture doesn't make a course any more than one bird makes a Spring, and the presence of a faculty visitor creates an abnormal situation which might give a totally false impression. What the departments stressed most were such things as the breadth and depth of a man's knowledge; his lucidity, as evidenced in faculty conferences and seminars; his enthusiasm for the subject he teaches and the students he is teaching; comments made by students during informal and extended conversations; the adequacy of course outlines, reading lists, and supplementary teaching materials that the instructor has developed; the quality of examination questions he devises; his general conscientiousness in meeting his assigned tasks, including office hours for student visits.

Despite this highly informative survey, President Sproul did not relax. Having stirred up discussion at the departmental level he began making inquiries as to whether the Academic Senate should appoint a special committee to make a continuing survey of ways and means of measuring and encouraging teaching ability, with particular reference to establishing procedures for accumulation of facts from students or otherwise. Although he received no encouragement in this direction he made up his mind to appoint an administrative committee of his own and asked Dr. Gerald E. Marsh in Public Speaking to serve as chairman. Inasmuch as it was the first committee of its kind it is interesting to note the membership: George P. Adams, philosophy; W. H. Alexander, Latin; L. M. K. Boelter, engineering; Stanley B. Freeborn, entomology; Frank N. Freeman, educational psychology; and S. F. Light, zoology.

By this time it began to be clear to some of those close to President Sproul that his interest was not specifically aimed at the identification of some particular kind of man, with a special talent for teaching, say *Homo Paedogogicus;* his concern was with the development of an environment in which all staff members, regardless of their initial capacity for teaching, would be encouraged to develop and improve it. As World War II came closer and national interest in the support of basic research and development increased at a geometric rate, the competition for faculty time and energy became exceedingly keen, particularly in the physical sciences, engineering, and health-related fields. With literally scores of public and private agencies offering unheard of sums of money to demonstrate the importance of more and better research, it was essential to maintain the importance of more and better teaching in positive and dynamic ways. Without question the constantly reiterated position of the President of the University was a most significant influence in maintaining some degree of balance during a period of almost revolutionary change. If a faculty constantly can be reminded of the primary consideration given to teaching by its president, and if it can be stimulated into continuing discussion, good teaching should flourish by a process of natural selection within an ecological niche where teaching talent contributes to survival.

The first committee on teaching evaluation, and particularly its chairman, continued to work for a number of years in developing and distributing carefully thought out reaction sheets that faculty members could have for the asking as an aid in ascertaining student views on the success of their personal teaching procedures.

By 1943, however, President Sproul was thinking of additional ways of getting faculty consideration of teaching and other problems with particular reference to the University situation when World War II ended. He wrote to Dean E. T. Grether, Dean Gordon S. Watkins, and Dean C. B. Hutchison:

> In the course of the past several months I have been giving considerable thought to the questions: What is the University going to do after the War? Shall we be prepared for the hordes of students which some authorities predict will invade the campus? What shall we do if State appropriations for University support are drastically reduced, as they well may be in a period of economic crisis after the War? Will the University of California be ready to maintain its place as a leader in higher education in this country?
>
> May I, therefore, encourage you and your colleagues to constitute yourselves a committee on postwar planning, and to present to me, as soon as you conveniently can, such recommendations proceeding from your thinking as may require action by the President or the Regents, including recommendations which will make it possible to operate a school of high quality with support less than normal in prewar years, if such should prove to be necessary?

The response to these inquiries, and others made shortly thereafter by letter or by discussion with individual staff members, served to emphasize the importance of stimulating and integrating constructive thought about the future of the University during a possible period of fundamental readjustment, as well as the desirability of bringing as many members of the faculty into the process as could be arranged. It occurred to President Sproul that it might be beneficial from many points of view to plan a conference of selected faculty members from all campuses, to hold the conference under conditions that would minimize interruptions—by students, research and office staffs, telephone calls, and even wives and families—and to devote two or three consecutive days to serious discussion. In some respects his thought anticipated what business, industry, and government were later to call a "brain-storming session," but it was something more than this, for it visualized a series of sessions on various problem areas, each to be introduced by a written report prepared in advance; and it recognized a long-term as well as immediate benefit to be realized, through the information and orientation that participants would carry away from the conference.

Behind this idea, undoubtedly, was President Sproul's experience in overcoming the disruptions of World War I and his feeling that the end of World War II could well present an even greater problem. But in addition there were other considerations: the continuing and basic responsibility to further promote team spirit and cooperation between campuses; the desirability of assessing, before re-establishing, traditional practices that had been discontinued or altered to meet wartime exigencies; and, finally, the need to pick up again promptly the subject of quality in teaching.

To work out the details of this post-war conference President Sproul called in Professor Joel H. Hildebrand, partly because he was recognized as a great teacher in addition to being a member of the Academic Senate Advisory Committee to the President; partly because of his versatility as evidenced by his chemical warfare service, his photography, and his success in teaching the President of the University how to extend the distance between his *sitzmarken* on the ski slopes of the Sierra Nevada; and, finally, because he had previously developed another of the President's ideas as first chairman of an Administrative Educational Policy Committee, which later became permanent as a standing committee of the Academic Senate. Professor Hildebrand, however, insists that his success with the University Post-war Conference arrangements derived from none of the above qualifications, but rather from his foresight in demanding the services of a young assistant professor to do all the work that might be involved—a young fellow named Frank L. Kidner, who subsequently became Director of the Bureau of Business and Economic Research and then Dean of Educational Relations.

It was decided to hold the first All-University Faculty Conference at Davis, over the weekend of November 3 to 5, 1944, when students were absent and the faculty representatives could be herded into one Residence Hall and kept there until critical and creative possibilities had been exhausted. To assure that this would happen planners even made special arrangements to get around the wartime shortage of cigarettes and to supply each delegate with enough to keep him going through three days, including evening sessions. No one could leave on the excuse of just going over to Sacramento for a package of cigarettes.

The President and the Faculty

President Sproul had made clear in his preliminary outline that he wanted to choose the delegates to the conference personally, and that he did not intend to invite anyone because of the position he held, or because of his ability to justify the *status quo* either logically or rhetorically. The last thing he had in mind was to produce an oversized meeting of an academic committee so charged with traditional responsibility that it could not entertain a new idea less than twenty-one years old. What he did have in mind was a town meeting where participants could, without legislative authority, propose ideas and leave them to stand on their merits for subsequent dissection by established academic and administrative courts.

This was a novel approach in the academic world, and when the last day of the session was over the faculty members went home feeling as if they had taken part in an academic bonfire rally, full of enthusiasm for the years ahead and with more team spirit than they had ever enjoyed. President Sproul had not thought, to use a favorite undergraduate phrase, that he might be "establishing a tradition," but he soon found that he *had* accomplished this culturally impossible feat. He was flooded with inquiries as to when the next conference would be scheduled, and with suggestions for discussion subjects that simply took it for granted that there would be another conference. One important result of the first and subsequent conferences was to clear up misapprehensions among the campuses. As a member of the Los Angeles faculty remarked after the first conference: "We all used to think that the Berkeley faculty disagreed with everything we tried to do at Los Angeles because they were prejudiced against us. Now I know they just like to disagree and they disagree among themselves more than they ever do with us." Consequently, a second general conference was programmed on "The Relation of the University to the State," during the interregnum between the fall and spring semesters, February 9, 10, and 11, 1947, and by unanimous vote of this and subsequent conferences the practice was continued annually. The thirteenth annual conference was held on April 2, 3, and 4, 1958, just prior to President Sproul's retirement. Among the subjects considered over the years, were the following: "How Can the Educational Effectiveness

79

of the University be Improved?" "The University of California in the Next Ten Years," "Problems and Opportunities of the Large University," "The Graduate Academic Function of the University," "The Function of the Upper Division of the University," "The Faculty and Educational Policies of the University," "How to Appraise the Value of the University to Society," "The University of California Student, 1945–1965," "The Role of the University in Higher Education in California," "Quality of Education in Relation to Numbers," and for President Sproul's last year in office, "The University of California: Retrospect and Prospect."

This device for bringing together faculty members of a multicampus institution, and for side-tracking for three days all matters of protocol and academic routine, proved to be a most successful and productive means of bringing out new ideas and subjecting them to representative judgment. Resolutions passed at these conferences have no force until they have been considered and approved by appropriate academic and administrative bodies, perhaps the Regents, but they assure that the ideas will be considered, and have as a matter of record initiated many significant changes in objectives, organization and procedural regulations. Dr. Clark Kerr, as a member of the faculty, and as Chancellor of the Berkeley campus, attended the fourth, seventh, eighth and thirteenth of these All-University Faculty Conferences, and when he in turn became President of the University, the practice of holding them continued. Incidentally, the same idea was adopted by other universities, and the published proceedings of these conferences have been in demand throughout the country.

In opening the Second Conference in 1947, President Sproul said,

> I do not need to remind you that there are 40,800 students in the University this semester, 55 per cent of whom are veterans. We, along with others, are busy with the task of overcoming the wartime educational deficit of the nation, of balancing the educational books for a college generation of many million men which has been away to war. Here at the University we are determined that this process shall be so administered that the years of the current present and the immediate future shall be fruitful ones for the veterans. . . . But we are also looking farther ahead and wondering what is in store for us after the period of demobilization has ended.

The President and the Faculty

Then, in a prophetic strain, subsequently proved to be more accurate than the best attempts of the Oracle of Delphi, President Sproul went on to say:

> It is evident, then, that the facilities for post high school education in California will have to be very much enlarged before a stable level is reached. To care for the expected increase, the University, the state college, and probably the junior college systems will have to be expanded either by enlarging present institutions, or by adding new institutions, or by doing both. . . .

> It is in the nature of the State University to reflect the complexion of the State's population. Therefore, exceptional students come to it only in the proportion in which exceptional persons exist in the general community. . . . For the average student—the mass of our students—techniques must be invented which combine the efficiency of mass production with a decent respect for the dignity of the individual. As a part of the University's social responsibility, it is immensely important that these students be suitably educated, for they will do most of the world's work—other than manual labor—take most of the responsibility, and control the bulk of public opinion. This does not mean that average students should be permitted to set the tone of the University. Quite the contrary. The superior student should be sought out, and everything in our power done to aid his rapid progress. No educational crime could be greater than to frustrate or pervert the power of a first-class mind. It is, therefore, both natural and right for a faculty to devote more time and energy to the brilliant student than to the ordinary one. Not to do so, far from being commendable softheartedness, is rather the grossest and most culpable softheadedness.

And, finally, President Sproul brought in the subject to which he continually gave thought:

> Education involves much more than courses of study. It is a process by which an older person draws out and guides a younger. It concerns itself always with human qualities, and it depends upon eagerness of youth to learn, and the capacity of elders to teach. Therefore, on all levels of education, the first essential is to endow the teacher with the respect due to a learned profession, with economic security, and with the continuing opportunity to study to the end that, as he grows older, he may also grow wiser. It is to the professional teachers that democracy entrusts the guidance of its children, and, in the final analysis, for weal or for woe, the conduct of its government. Surely, the State of California cannot rest content with less than the best on any level of its educational system.

These All-University Faculty Conferences have served many excellent purposes in the life of an educational institution as large as any in the world with campuses distributed widely through one of the largest states in the Union. But among these purposes none was closer to Robert Sproul's personal interest than the promoting and maintaining of a high level of teaching, and each annual conference offered a most effective means of re-emphasizing the central importance of this goal before approximately 120 teaching staff members. One conference after another brought in the subject of teaching quality. One committee report in the 1948 conference, for example, said: "The effective university professor is of necessity an effective teacher; and, therefore, a record of excellent teaching must be given the recognition it deserves by committees on promotion and by administrative officers. Much more can and should be done, also, to make faculties aware of new instructional methods and techniques; and much more no doubt might be done in the ever-recurring task of initiating young members of the faculty into the methods and aims of the established courses they are required to teach. To emphasize the importance of good teaching, some members of the Committee recommend an annual teaching lecture in recognition of outstanding teaching performance similar to the annual research lecture in recognition of outstanding research work."

This idea of offering special recognition to good teachers, of course, had been central in President Sproul's thinking from the time he accepted the presidency in 1930, and faculty support for it was important. The problem again, was to devise a plan which would define good teaching in sufficiently specific and meaningful terms to permit a panel or committee to make selections, and also provide some means of bringing candidates to the attention of the committee. Efforts of other universities in the United States to achieve this same purpose were followed with great interest. The University of Chicago, with the financial sponsorship of one of its alumni, had established a series of annual $1,000 prizes for excellence in teaching in 1938; this came to President Sproul's attention in 1947 through Chicago's Alumni Bulletin. He promptly introduced this as a subject for discussion at his Administrative Advisory Conference, and with the encouragement of that group appointed a faculty committee to recommend a plan for the University of California. The chairman of the committee was Professor E. W. Strong, later to be Chancellor of the University of California, Berkeley.

The deliberations of the Special Committee on Recognition of Superior Teaching immediately encountered two areas of rather strong disagreement: 1) on the adequacy of available means of judging good teaching; and 2) on the usefulness of alumni or student opinions if gathered by questionnaire. Further consideration by the Administrative Advisory Committee led to the suggestion that the problem be turned back to the chairmen of departments for recommendation. When this proposal was submitted to the Committees on Budget and Interdeparmental Relations they in turn pointed out the need for caution in setting up a special system of rewarding good teaching with its implication that promotion in rank and periodic salary increases were a reward for something else. Consequently, President Sproul, as an interim measure, sent a directive to all departmental chairmen reiterating that recognition of superior teaching was a primary responsibility of departmental chairmen; it was their duty actively to seek evaluations of all staff members. The directive then went on to say: "It is equally the responsibility of department chairmen to improve standards of teaching especially among the new and younger members of the department by encouraging critical self-examination of methods. In this respect, it should be recognized that student opinion questionnaires may be useful to individual staff members. In addition, individual staff members should be encouraged to invite colleagues to visit their lectures for the purpose of giving them helpful advice and suggestions for the improvement of their teaching."

Then in 1953 the Carnegie Institute of Technology announced an award in recognition of superior teaching from the Carnegie Corporation for the purpose of financing study-leaves of six months on full salary with traveling expenses, and President Sproul again started a chain of inquiries as to the desirability of such a program at the University of California. Simultaneously, Chancellor Clark Kerr introduced the subject of "quality in teaching" at his advisory administrative council. A member of the faculty, widely recognized as one of the most distinguished teachers on the staff, commented that any university instructor could inform himself on how well he was teaching by just looking at the faces of the students in front of him; he suggested that the way to help a teacher who remained dull and uninspiring despite that challenge would be to get him another kind of employment. In his opinion the rewards for good teaching were already multifold.

Nevertheless, in December, 1956, the Academic Senate, Northern Section, adopted a recommendation of the Committee on Procedure and Non-Tenure Appointments, that a faculty committee be appointed to study and report within one year on a program of recognition for distinction in teaching. By the end of 1957, this special committee, under the chairmanship of Professor Mark Schorer, recommended to the Academic Senate that a system of recognizing distinguished teaching (by public citation only) be adopted, and that it be confined to young staff members of less than five years' service who were most in need of encouragement. Nominations of those to be honored could be made with supporting evidence by any member of the faculty who had served more than five years, and final selection of the six young teachers to be honored, one from each of the six divisions of the Northern Section of the Academic Senate, was placed in the hands of special committees of the Representative Assembly of the Academic Senate. The President of the University was designated as the officer to implement the recognition in May of each year.

This program was approved by the Academic Senate, Northern Section, and placed in operation, and President Sproul applauded it. Thus, in his last year as President he saw the implementation of a plan that would alert the faculty to the teaching qualities of younger staff appointees and keep constantly before everyone, in a period of heavy emphasis on research, the primary importance of conscientious and creative attention to teaching excellence. It is characteristic of Robert Sproul that this problem loomed as large in his interests after 28 years as it did in his first year as President, and that in the interim he contributed much to the quality of the faculty by constant efforts to raise salary levels to attract the quality of scholars that the University wanted and needed. At the same time he invariably relied on the judgment of the faculty as to the scholarly quality of new appointees and provided an atmosphere in which good teaching might grow and proliferate along with research.

President Sproul held the confidence of the faculty throughout his presidency even on those occasions when his Scottish caution proved exasperating. Almost invariably he approached decisions with deliberation. He liked to walk around a subject, view it from all angles, and get reactions from both involved and uninvolved people. An additional chapter for "Parkinson's Law" could be produced from a close study of President Sproul's career. Some of the axioms might read as follows: "Exasperation over delay in a decision that proves to be correct dies shortly after the decision is made; but exasperation over a wrong decision, however quickly made, lives on like Methuselah." "The strength of a recommendation for action leads the recommendation forward, but its weaknesses tend to lag behind, and only if time is allowed will they catch up before the decision is made."

The dependability of these guides was fully proved by one significant departure from them in 1949, when he allowed himself to be persuaded that he should support the adoption of a Special Loyalty Oath by the Regents of the University. It was adopted to meet charges by the State Senate Fact-Finding Committee that members of the faculty were permitting their names to be associated with Communist Front Organizations and that not enough care was being taken to enforce the 1940 action of the Academic Senate and the Regents against the employment of Communists. These charges were said to be proved by the case of a teaching assistant, Irving David Fox at Berkeley; a piano player in the department of physical education, Mrs. Miriam Brooks Sherman, at Los Angeles; and the mysterious death of Everitt Hudson, a student at Los Angeles, believed by some to be connected with Communist activities. Before this matter was settled, everybody concerned was up in arms for or against the original action by the Regents, or for or against the subsequent actions taken. But during the entire controversy the faculty went to great lengths to protect the President of the University from being saddled with the responsibility for an action that had been dictated by the temper of the times.

When President Sproul observed his twenty-fifth anniversary in office a few years later, a number of symposia on science were held in his honor, and Professor Joel Hildebrand, a participant in the symposium at Berkeley took occasion to say:

> . . . I have been impressed often by his imagination and his willingness to strike a bold stroke to enhance the greatness of the University, as when, despite his Scotch extraction, he shouldered the expense involved in establishing the Radiation Laboratory and the Virus Laboratory. He would approve an expensive piece of apparatus for our department whenever we could guarantee getting results worth the money. A great university cannot be built without cooperation of a president who understands other values in relation to money values . . .
>
> Professors are hard to please, as they should be, because timid uncritical men cannot train youth for courage and adventure, and the president who retains his intellectual and moral stature under their cold scrutiny is indeed a good one. Many a president has had to take refuge in aloofness and the authority of his position. Not so President Sproul. He is the kind of president who can be called by his first name without loss of dignity. His government by cooperation rather than ukase has fostered a fine sense of loyalty and responsibility. We respect his wisdom as we like his friendly humanity.
>
> I conclude by quoting from a resolution adopted by the Academic Senate at a time when President Sproul had received a call to go to another university. I was the principal author of this resolution and therefore I give it to you as my own opinion, then and now. "You have abundantly earned our confidence. You have demonstrated over the years your appreciation of the high standards of both discovery and teaching upon which the greatness of a university must be built. You have devoted yourself with zeal and success to maintaining the unity, the dignity, the distinction of the University of California. We deeply appreciate the fact that your leadership has been effected by patient, persuasive wisdom rather than by recourse to the formal authority of your office. You have been receptive to constructive criticism. You have treated us as colleagues and have shared the sense of obligation to our common task which has become the genius of this institution. Such a combination of virtues, essential to the distinction of a university, is too rarely found in a university president."*

---

* *Symposium on the Physical and Earth Sciences,* Honoring the Twenty-fifth Presidential Year of Robert Gordon Sproul. Published 1958, University of California Printing Department.

The President and the Faculty

In the same symposium at which Professor Hildebrand made his statement, Professor Perry Byerly pointed out that the University of California was the first institution in the western hemisphere to undertake seismographic study of earthquakes, beginning in 1887, but that up until the advent of President R. G. Sproul it had only three instruments with which to work. Then in the middle 1940's he received a telephone call from President Sproul asking what he could do to broaden and strengthen this important field of research. As a result, over a period of a few years, the number of instruments and stations was increased from three to eleven in California and Oregon, and the instruments were modernized to improve their sensitivity. Professor Ruben Stirton added that in the field of paleontology, both at Berkeley and Los Angeles, the keen foresight and understanding of the administration was basically responsible for the success of the staff in maintaining the leading role of paleontological instruction and research; and Professor William G. Young of the Department of Chemistry at Los Angeles acknowledged that without the personal interest of President R. G. Sproul it would have been impossible to develop a program in chemistry from normal school status to one internationally recognized at the university level in twenty-five years. He added that in one early crisis he had needed four emergency increases in salary to hold men on the staff, and had made great promises as to the future eminence these men would achieve. President Sproul granted the extra money and said he would be happy if one of the four lived up to the promise indicated. With this support all four men went on to do the high quality of work predicted for them.

Professor Dixon Wecter, in another tribute to Robert Sproul at a Faculty Club dinner, summed up general feeling with a paraphrase from Dr. William Butler: "Doubtless God could have made a better President, but doubtless God never did."

IV

Twenty-eight Years of Student Affairs

The ability of a university president to hold the confidence and the loyalty of students is often a primary factor in determining whether he will stay in office long enough to demonstrate such other high abilities as he may have. This is particularly true in large universities which are a part of major metropolitan areas, both because of the wide range of backgrounds from which the students are recruited, and because even minor problems of administration impinge more directly on the general public and are magnified by the public attention which they receive.

Young people entering college are generally minors in the eyes of the law, and the average citizen, forgetting his own actions and attitude at the same age, is appalled by mass demonstrations of youthfulness whether they represent a last fling with departing juvenility or a first essay at action in a sensitive adult area. The cross that youth bears is a wait of approximately 20 years after birth before completing growth and development. Worse yet, this long period is just an average which tradition and the law applies to all whether they are precocious and fully mature several years earlier, or late bloomers who continue their psychical growth and development for several years longer. Explosions during this rather vaguely delimited stage of transition can be avoided only by full understanding on the part of administrators who hold the confidence of the young people involved.

Whether or not explosions develop is often beyond prediction because they may be triggered by inconsequential local questions, by the degree of political or social unrest in the world at large, or even by the state of the weather. The only certain factor is that if an explosion occurs and is not promptly met by the cooperative action of the students and the administration, the president of the institution will be held responsible.

When Robert Gordon Sproul became President of the University he entered upon his duties about as well-prepared for good student relations as anyone could be. Not only was he relatively young to be president of a major university, and therefore not too far removed from his own undergraduate days at the same institution, but he had kept in close touch with students and their interests throughout the intervening years. He had belonged to a fraternity and also served as president of the University YMCA; acted as drum major of the marching band, and performed as two-miler on the track team, establishing a new kind of record, among other things, by winning a race in the rain carrying an umbrella. Later, as cashier and business manager, he got to know students who had financial difficulties, and as a member of the Berkeley Chamber of Commerce and the Rotary Club he was kept aware of how student activities appeared to the local citizen.

Moreover, he attended college and began his career as a member of the University staff under the influence of President Benjamin Ide Wheeler, who initiated the concept of student self-government on the Berkeley campus. Not only was he familiar with President Wheeler's philosophy of student leadership and the administrative practices supporting it, but also he was a firm believer in the same principles, ready to fight to preserve them even when changing conditions and particular circumstances made the championing of this cause both difficult and uncomfortable.

To understand the situation one has to know what President Wheeler's philosophy was. He explained it quite frankly on a number of occasions, notably in his report to the governor of the state for the year 1914–15, and in his commencement address of 1918. There was a system of government operated chiefly by students when he arrived in 1899. As a matter of fact there had been a cooperative store for books and supplies started by students as early as 1883 and as early as 1887 an Associated Students of the College of Letters and Science which exercised control over athletics, field days, and the gymnasium. What President Wheeler added to this administrative organization was a judicial branch, the concept of senior responsibility for student affairs, and a general *esprit de corps*. These concepts and this atmosphere worked very well in the college of less than 1,800 undergraduates that existed in 1899, and continued to operate with reasonable satisfaction for more than 30 years, though the protection that they provided was stretching beyond its elastic limits as the undergraduate student body at Berkeley passed the 16,000 mark in 1930–31.

President Wheeler at no time indicated any abstract concern with the protection of "student rights." What he sought to bring about was a greater sense of personal responsibility among students for their own actions in so far as they impinged upon the welfare of the University as a community of scholars and students, and upon the relations of this community with surrounding towns and cities, or the state and nation. The incident that started him off occurred within a month of his arrival on the Berkeley campus in October, 1899. A student named Jim Whipple received a notice from the faculty on the night before the Big Game with Stanford that he was ineligible to play because of a grade deficiency in one of his courses. Whipple felt that he had a higher duty to discharge as a team member and played in spite of the notice. As fate would have it California trounced Stanford 30–0 on that occasion, and Whipple returned to the campus as a hero in the eyes of the students. The faculty was aware that this created a "most deplorable" disciplinary problem but felt that a defiance of the rules could not be passed over lightly. President Wheeler wisely recognized that whatever was to be done would have to be preceded by consultation with student leaders; so with the consent of the faculty he chose a group of seniors, designated it as the Student Affairs Committee, and requested that the committee review the entire case and recommend what action should be taken. The recommendation proved to be reasonable, was approved by the faculty, and accepted as fair enough by the student body. Whipple was suspended for one term, which meant he could not graduate with his class, a real disappointment in those days; so disappointing in Whipple's case, that he never returned to get his degree.

Encouraged by this experiment, President Wheeler made the Student Affairs Committee a permanent arm of student government and thereafter referred to this body all infractions of the rules of the University by students. He made clear that the legal authority to set penalties remained with the faculty of the University, but that this was a matter secondary in importance to the determination of the guilt or innocence of the accused, and that the acceptance of student-recommended penalties by the faculty would depend solely on how wise and just the decisions were. The keys to the success of the operation, President Wheeler felt, were: 1) that the Student Affairs Committee met and considered cases without any faculty or administrative representative present; 2) that hearings were conducted on an informal basis, as a family council affair, without the administering of oaths or other formal procedures. It was his opinion, after years of experience, that the Student Affairs Committee on a student to student level, was more successful in getting at facts than any faculty group could possibly be, and that from the student's point of view, the prospect of being brought before a tribunal of his peers was just as much of a deterrent to rule infractions as were the penalties that might subsequently be invoked.

President Wheeler recognized, as all presidents must, that it is not possible to persuade students to carry responsibility without sharing authority with them. It was not within his power to surrender to students the disciplining authority that the Regents had specifically assigned to the faculty, but as long as they made decisions that were concurred in by the faculty without amendment, the question of who had final authority need not arise. He took pains to see that the Student Affairs Committee investigated each case thoroughly, that every student found guilty of an offense clearly understood what the offense was, and that such a student accepted the resulting penalty recommendation as reasonably fair. President Wheeler personally interrogated the culprits to make certain of this, explaining to them that they had the right of appeal to the faculty for a hearing if they wished, but that if this was their desire, the President proposed first, to send the case back to the Student Affairs Committee for review. As a result no protested decision came before the faculty, and the authority of the Student Affairs Committee was upheld in the eyes of the student body by the fact that it was never challenged.

There is some implication, however, that questions were raised as to the propriety of seeming to put authority in the hands of students, even in the days when the Berkeley campus still could be administered on a "one big family" plan. President Wheeler felt called upon to defend his policy vigorously in the annual report for 1914–15. He said, "The operation of student self-government in this University has been of such far-reaching advantage to the order of the University community and, what is far more, to the attitude and spirit of the students themselves, that no pains must be spared to devise and recognize a procedure which will insure to the system workableness under the law and avoid any crippling of its freedom and full responsibility."

Of course, even in its heyday, student self-government did not work perfectly. In September, 1902, for example, there occurred a post-rally riot that involved the misappropriation or destruction of so much railroad, streetcar, and private property that threats of civil suits and criminal actions were heard on all sides. The editor of the *San Francisco Examiner* wrote: "The state has been generous with its University. It has been proud of it. A day may come when its citizens will tire of paying taxes for the education of hoodlums."

The Student Affairs Committee, with the newly established principle of senior control to back it up, took leadership in settling the matter, determined the extent of damages, and collected funds from students to pay all verifiable bills. President Wheeler expressed his great regret that such an episode had occurred but regarded its quick settlement as evidence of the value of student self-government. Undoubtedly he recognized that occasional student riots had a long tradition behind them, starting with pitched battles between students and town authorities in the streets of staid Oxford long before Columbus set out to prove that the world was round.

In 1924 President William Wallace Campbell was able to say in his annual report: "I marvel at the high degree of success with which the students govern themselves. They elect their own officers and appoint their own governmental committees. Their Student Affairs Committees sit in judgment upon every reported infraction of the simple and fundamental rules of student conduct, and their verdicts in cases of guilt take the form of recommendations to the President or his representatives for final action. I do not recall that any verdict of the students' committees within the years of my administration has been revised or reversed."

In this same report he made the further comment: "I have been an interested observer of the honor spirit at examination time in the past year. I have no hesitation in expressing the conclusion that this system succeeds at least as well as the monitor system would, and the general effects of the honor system are vastly to be preferred. However, no system, and possibly least of all the honor system, will run itself. Continual vigilance throughout the student body is the price of success, and the results are well worth the effort. The administration gladly cooperates in maintaining the honor system."

There is implied by President Campbell's reference to the need for continual vigilance to keep student self-government, and particularly the honor system, running effectively that some trouble had already been encountered. But certainly by the time that Robert Sproul took over the responsibilities of the presidency in 1930, expanding enrollments had reduced the individual student's importance and diluted his sense of personal responsibility for the student behavior code; correspondingly, the effectiveness of student group-pressure and senior leadership within the campus community were reduced. In 1923, with the dedication of Henry Morse Stephens Memorial Hall as a student union and of the Memorial Stadium for intercollegiate competitions, the Associated Students began to grow into a substantial business enterprise. Within a few years the ASUCLA found itself in the same position, particularly after the move to Westwood in 1929, and the completion of William C. Kerckhoff Hall as a student union and store on the new campus. By 1930 the Associated Students at Berkeley were launched on a decade in which the average annual income was to exceed half a million dollars. The major interest of student leaders swung from senior responsibility for discipline and activities of the Student Affairs Committee to a struggle for financial and general administrative control of the Associated Students through member-ship on student legislative committees. Student prestige was less and less identified with cooperation in maintaining discipline and the honor spirit, and more and more identified with defending the inde-pendence of the Associate Students in the expenditure of funds, the hiring and firing of personnel, and the conduct of extracurricular activ-ities. The concept of "student rights" became an important issue.

The term "student self-government," which President Wheeler had used to describe senior control and the Student Affairs Committee, came to be interpreted by the students as a kind of grant that recog-nized, as our founding fathers so aptly phrased it, "that all men are created equal, [and that] they are endowed by their Creator with cer-tain unalienable Rights." Each new generation of entering students brought with it at least a handful of iconoclasts who felt that "Life, Liberty, and the Pursuit of Happiness" had to be protected by assert-ing the independence of student government. A major point of contro-versy was whether the Regents of the University, through the Presi-dent and his administrative representatives, should have the power to veto student proposals for expenditure of funds. But equally import-ant was the question of whether faculty and alumni representatives on student legislative bodies should have a vote. The fact that this vote could not control student decisions, as they saw it, was beside the point. A matter of principle was involved and also the vote of older heads often threw a wet blanket on student initiative. The students realized that the Regents of the University were legally

95

responsible for any debts the Associated Students might be unable to discharge. They also came to realize that any tax exemptions they might enjoy were dependent upon acknowledgment of the Regents as the ultimate and final authority. Nonetheless they seemed to feel that the Regents ought to find a way to get around these legal problems. None objected to having the President and the Regents hold whatever residuary authority legally might be required. All that they asked was that this residuary authority not be exercised until the students had tried to deal with problems independently.

What this boiled down to was a growing conviction that student government could not be "self-government" unless it included freedom to make mistakes. The students were willing to admit that they might make mistakes; who doesn't make mistakes? The issue, as they saw it, was simply whether one had or didn't have the right to make his own mistakes in his own way. The issue from the point of view of the administration was how to let students enjoy the educational advantate of making their own mistakes and at the same time keep a check on the size of those mistakes. This held particularly true for the student editors of campus newspapers and magazines whose mistakes were made in public print, and who championed the "rights of students" with the added nuance of protecting "freedom of the press," as guaranteed under Article 1 of the Bill of Rights of the constitution of the United States. Just as student political leaders brushed aside the legal responsibilities of the Regents, so the student editors rejected the thought that they might be expected to operate as a house organ for an educational corporation for the sole purpose of gathering and disseminating campus news. They also rejected the claim that student publications belonged to the Associated Students, and that the elected representatives of the Associated Students, as owners and publishers, should have something to say about selection of editors and the establishing of editorial policy. From a practical point of view the editors maintained that the welfare of the students depended on the existence of a free press that could criticize both the government of the Associated Students and the government of the University when necessary. It was their contention that the maintenance of editorial independence was an asset beyond price to the President and the Regents in the discharge of their respective responsibilities, and a protection to students against the arbitrary exercise of power by either their own elected representatives or the Regents of the University and their executive officers. Any other conclusion, from their point of view, would be out of harmony with the spirit of a major university dedicated to the discovery and dissemination of truth, and the freedom of teachers and students to participate in these processes. Even mistakes have their value, from this point of view, for they help prove to the world that the University of California is a place where everybody is free to think his own thoughts, reach his own conclusions, and announce them to the world.

President Sproul made clear on many occasions during his long term in office that he recognized the validity of the student attitude, and that he intended to respect it providing students recognized and respected the responsibility that he shared with them. On those occasions when public and even faculty and student criticism of puerility, poor judgment, or bad taste in student publications flared up dangerously, he made no move to take away the freedom of student editors. He insisted only that the editors carry a notation on the editorial page to the effect that opinions expressed therein were those of the editor or of individuals whose names were signed to the offending articles, and did not represent the opinion of either the University or the student body. Even after twenty years in office, as the heated decade of the 1950's dawned, President Sproul again publicly expressed his personal philosophy: "There is no easily definable middle ground between authoritarian control by the University, and student self-government; one must make his choice, and on the whole, over a period of fifty years, student self-government, with such advice and guidance as could be given informally, has functioned rather well."

It should be pointed out that student problems at the University of California are essentially no different from those at other major public universities, except that the size of the institution, and particularly the possession of two large campuses in metropolitan surroundings, makes them more numerous. Most students don't create problems, because they are too busy with studies and more orthodox activities. But it requires only a few students at any one time to establish a nucleus around which problems accumulate. Sometimes the problems are created by adults off-campus and the students join in for the excitement of it. The years 1935 and 1936 were particularly productive in this regard. On one occasion, President Sproul considered himself most fortunate to secure Secretary of Labor Frances Perkins as Charter Day speaker, until a prominent alumna publicly refused to serve as a hostess because she considered the Secretary of Labor to be "a mere politician." This caused consternation in the administration and led to vitriolic student comments. At about the same time the National Student League, a communist organization, began a nationwide effort to organize peace strikes on college and university campuses, and, because it had active members on the Los Angeles campus as well as at the Los Angeles Junior College and the Pasadena Junior College, it concentrated its California efforts at these places. Handbills were passed out and the "Red Squad" of the local police went into action. The University said it would be glad to approve a peace assembly, but could not tolerate a strike led by an off-campus organization. A group of students thereupon erected a series of fiery crosses on campus and installed a banner which carried the words "Communism will not be tolerated. The Ku Klux Klan rides again." Other students, of course, mobilized a fire brigade to stamp out the fiery crosses and to defend any point of view, regardless of what it might be.

At this opportune moment, U. S. Congressman Hamilton Fish, Jr., who had been investigating Communist activities in colleges and universities, came out with a public statement that listed the University of California as one of the institutions under observation. This led State Assemblyman Frank G. Martin to introduce a bill to drive communism out of public educational institutions. President Sproul pointed out that the legislation proposed would make felons out of the Regents of the University for having books about communism in the campus libraries, and do the same for members of the faculty who carried them to classrooms. While he was in the process of bringing the temperature of those supporting such legislation down to normal, the editors of the *Pelican* at Berkeley were inspired to issue a "Radical Number" lampooning Assemblyman Martin; and eighteen members of the faculty joined in writing a letter of protest against the proposed legislation. In the uproar that followed it was necessary to establish that the *Pelican* was a humor magazine and not a political pamphlet, and to insist that the faculty had a right, as citizens, to express their opposition to repressive legislation, regardless of whether dissenters thought what they said was well-timed or well-stated.

As the months went by, the controversy grew more heated, and the President of the University found himself badgered from both sides. He felt it necessary to make his own position clear. To the students he said:

> The University never has, and hopes it never will stifle freedom of discussion, but there is a difference between liberty and license. The line between liberty that protects the rights of every individual citizen and the license to organize disorder must be sharply drawn.
>
> Disciples of discontent proclaim a program that, if it were realized in action, would deny to all but a particular group the liberties that they talk so much about.
>
> We are compelled in the University, as elsewhere, to listen day by day and almost hour by hour to the enemies of an ordered program under the law, on mimeographed sheets and in fevered conversation. You will hear violent abuse of all who are in authority, rabid appeals to prejudice and hatred, and tireless attempts to stir your worst emotions. Only clear thinking can meet such provocation.
>
> There are among our people grievous fallacies in the generally accepted social theories of democracy, and there are vital defects in our practices of government. But salvation does not lie in the exchange of our liberties for political, intellectual, or spiritual serfdom. It lies in the traditional American concept that liberty under the law is the most enviable possession to which we may aspire. And your obligation here, your prime obligation, perhaps, is to get for yourself the largest possible measure of that boon by learning enough of the history of your country, its institutions, its ideals, to hold the liberty it gives you as a trust, and to use and defend it "with malice toward none; with charity for all."

To the legislature he said: "The President has been constant in his insistence upon loyalty to the constitution and laws of the State and Nation on the part of all connected with the institution. At the same time he has been on the alert to protect academic freedom without which a university cannot live in any real sense."

To organized labor, through the *San Francisco Labor Clarion*, he added: "it is inconceivable to me that any intelligent man should be willing to exchange his status as an American citizen for the intellectual and spiritual stultification which prevail among peoples who have delegated either voluntarily, or under coercion, their lives, liberties, and possibility of happiness, to the State."

He reminded the citizens of the state that "The University is open to all who wish to study and think clearly. We even accept members of the Communist Party, for it is a recognized party in the State of California, and the State is a higher authority than the University."

In the midst of all the controversy he was sustained by the fact that thirty-four members of the state legislature pledged their support to him, and individual citizens occasionally took time to write letters such as that which appeared in the *San Francisco News* on October 7, 1935: "The United States could well afford to have among her citizens more men of the type and caliber of the president of our State University, and would not greatly miss those individuals who stir up the populace for purposes not wholly commendable by pouring more oil on the fire."

When it appeared that legislation of the same regressive type might be introduced in 1936 he again wrote to the legislature: "We are unalterably opposed to those who would change our social system or form of government by force or violence. But in days when men are beset by poverty and insecurity, bitter conflicts of thought are generated, and legislation inevitably reflects the tendency to coerce and prohibit.

"This is not, in our opinion, the way to serve liberty or establish confidence. We must steadfastly set our faces against those who act to destroy peace and order, but we neglect the lessons of history if we attempt to prevent free men from stating their beliefs and from peaceably assembling."

Shortly thereafter he spoke to an assembly of newspaper editors and publishers to remind them that: "This Freedom of the Press is almost as dear to us as it is to you, for academic freedom is its blood kin. If you print the facts we have no quarrel with you, little as we may like them. If our professors speak the truth, you should have no quarrel with them, however disappointing that truth may be to your dearest prejudice."

Meanwhile it was necessary to use his persuasive powers to divert students at Berkeley and Los Angeles from following the lead of the girls of Vassar College in organizing a chapter of the Gold Star Mothers of Future Wars and demanding Federal subsidy of a trip to Europe to see the future burial ground of their future sons; and the lead of the boys of Princeton in organizing a chapter of the Veterans of Future Wars, to collect their veterans' bonuses while they were still alive to enjoy them. But he simultaneously agreed that it was the students' privilege to petition the Regents of the University for the abolition of compulsory military training, if they desired to do so. They did so desire. The argument of the president of the Associated Students at Los Angeles was: "If you agree preparedness prevents war, then Hitler and his legions are the greatest guarantee of peace in the world today."

When the Regents of the University came to the conclusion that they would not abolish compulsory military training, the editors of the *Daily Californian* raised a question as to whether the Regents were performing their duty, for "They showed no consideration for the will of the students whose interests, it is assumed, they serve."

Such lese majesty is frequently more difficult to bear than overt breaking of rules because the perpetrators of it are too old to be taken out to the woodshed and not old enough to be impressed by the importance of prudence. A president who allows himself to be pressured into using a steamroller to control gnats usually ends up more embarrassed than he was in the beginning. On one occasion, some years later, when the editors of the *Daily Bruin* first irritated and then exasperated the student body, the faculty, and the administration, President Sproul explained to all:

> The Regents of the University have laid upon the President the responsibility of governing its students. In turn, he has delegated to them, not the right, but the privilege of organizing for self-government. Such powers as their organizations

101

exercise are by delegation only, and subject always to the approval of the President as head of the University family. Obviously, such a relationship can be maintained only upon the basis of mutual goodwill and cooperation between all members of the family, with the interests of the University as a whole always in mind.

Although, as thus indicated, the jurisdiction of the President extends over all student affairs, throughout my administration I have been extremely reluctant to exercise the so-called "veto power" which remains in my office: and, on the contrary, have been solicitous to extend to the students such freedom of action as they might prove capable of using with intelligence and discretion. It has been my normal practice to observe the autonomy of the student government in the conduct of purely student affairs—that is, in those which do not concern directly or importantly other members of the University family, including alumni as well as faculty and administration. Except in rare cases of extreme delicacy, I have forborne direct mandates and, while giving advice and warning, have nevertheless permitted the students to make their own mistakes when they have chosen to do so.

To anyone who lived through and observed closely the development of student problems from 1930 on, it should be clear that an important factor was a shift in the character of the influence to which student leaders were subjected. In the early years of President Wheeler's regime the rest of the students provided the influence. With a small student enrollment this was quite simple to arrange. As President Wheeler himself said: "It is essential to the plan that it should find certain trustworthy mechanisms for the ascertainment of public opinion and its stimulation to action and defense. For this we have found the Thursday night 'senior singing' good, also the various honor societies, and in matters of more limited range, the fraternities. Best of all, when definite issues are raised, is the mass meeting, with the seniors stating the case."

Under such conditions, when student leaders spoke and acted, or editors wrote, they did so with full knowledge of student opinion, and they were guided by it. They also were better acquainted with faculty and administrative opinion. But by 1930 the student body was roughly 1,000 per cent larger. The campus community had become urbanized, and the individual student acquired a kind of "big city anonymity" and an impersonal relationship to the University. Student singing on

Thursday nights and "town hall" meetings were not only impossible to house, but out of tune with the times. More and more, the influence on leadership came from external sources, and more and more it reflected the problems of the outside world which, to an impatient and idealistic group of young people, all looked as if they needed resolving.

One of the early evidences of a decline in individual concern for University student codes was a call from the Student Affairs Committee, Berkeley, for help in reviving the Honor Spirit. The call was in fact a request that the faculty reinstitute closer supervision over examinations in order to support the committee in its efforts to create and maintain a student opinion that would be intolerant of dishonesty. By 1936, after a study by a Special Committee on Maintenance of Order in Examinations, President Sproul accepted the Student Affairs Committee's recommendation, and in December, 1936, issued a directive making instructors personally responsible again for the conduct of students in examinations. Members of the faculty at Los Angeles, some years later, expressed the opinion that the amount of cheating one might expect was correlated with the social heterogeneity of the student body, and that the honor system normally worked well only in institutions of less than 5,000 students with greater homogeneity of family background. It would be possible, also, to defend the thesis that the increase in number of honor system violations over that attributable to increase in enrollment was a reflection of a change in the strictness of concern over such matters in the populace generally. A college degree, many seemed to feel, was something of value that was being paid for in advance by taxpayers, and a peccadillo or so in the collection of it was not to be condemned too vigorously.

Still later some faculty members raised a question as to why the honor system had been abandoned, to which President Sproul responded that it was not his idea. He added: "The honor system could be re-established at the University, either as a whole, or by schools and colleges, if it could be demonstrated that there were reasonable prospects of success. Those of you who have been long connected with the University will remember that originally student self-government meant student self-discipline, particularly in examinations, and that for a decade or more the so-called 'honor system' worked fairly satisfactorily. Then the system began to break down, due in my judgment to no deterioration in the general character of our students, but to the increase in their number. . . . At any rate, conditions at Berkeley and Los Angeles deteriorated to a point where the students themselves requested the administration to protect them against the 'cheaters,' which it did with some initial reluctance. If any small campus or small school or college should wish to reinstall the 'honor system' I should not object."

The economic depression, starting in 1930, was a breeder of additional discontent, skepticism, cynicism, and antagonism toward established institutions and authorities. At the same time, the world began to go sour. Alfonso XIII of Spain dissolved the dictatorship of Primo de Rivera and thereby initiated a series of events ending in a civil war that aroused the emotions of the world and left every supporter of law, order and constitutional government branded with a "hammer and sickle" because the U.S.S.R., for its own nefarious reasons, chose the same side. In 1932 the Japanese invaded Manchuria and established the puppet state of Manchukuo. In 1933 a man named Schickl-gruber became Chancellor of Germany and withdrew from the League of Nations. A year later Italy refused to arbitrate its Somaliland border problems, and not long thereafter Benito Mussolini shocked the world by invading Ethiopia. England and France capitulated to Germany over the Sudetenland, and the toboggan run which ended in World War II was well under way. On the borders of Mongolia the Communists were fighting the Japanese, who were busy creating a pact with Germany, while Germany completed the circle by entering into a nonaggression pact with Russia. In the United States, there were German Bunds, Italian Blackshirts, the Pro-Nazi and Pro-Japanese Friends of Progress, sporadic revivals of the Ku Klux Klan, and always the ubiquitous Young Communist League, working not only under its own name but through every organization it could establish or strongly infiltrate, including the National Student League, the American Youth Congress, the American Student Union, and others. Compared with the Communists, all other propagandists for foreign ideologies were amateurs. The Communists were dedicated to a cause, the winning of which, in their own minds, was important enough to justify any means.

These were among the outside people who had a purpose in propagandizing university students and who willingly devoted time to it. They established bookstores near college campuses apparently as duck blinds, for they did not appear to sell enough books to pay their rent. Their real work, apparently, was not concerned with selling literature or with efforts directly under the communist banner. Rather it depended on establishing or infiltrating organizations and movements that often were under the leadership of people of high idealism and good reputation who refused to be diverted from what they considered a worthy cause by the fact that a few Communists also supported it. The communist purpose appeared to be the arousing of militant movements among young people through campaigns and protests on behalf of any virtuous cause: better housing, higher wages for students, elimination of religious and racial discrimination, promotion of world peace through opposition to expenditures on national defense, support of strikes by organized labor, etc. One may surmise that they hoped to get young people involved in open opposition to some constituted authority; to have them pushed around by police or civilian anticommunists, and thus to arouse their anger and a conviction that they were being treated unjustly. It is doubtful that these efforts were often successful in gaining converts to communism, but they were very effective in breeding cynical iconoclasts and causing trouble for college administrators, among others.

It was this undercurrent of manipulated student activity that made student problems progressively more difficult to meet in the 1940's and 1950's. Beginning in 1939 with an Assembly Interim Committee to investigate communist infiltration of the State Relief Administration, the California Legislature authorized a continuing series of such committees for the investigation of Un-American Activities, and from time to time the University of California came in for strong criticism because it was unable to build a fence around the institution that would keep all Communists at a safe distance. There is no question that large university campuses are always meccas for "torch carriers" of all descriptions, including Communits, and that a few of them, like drops of red dye in a pitcher of water, impart a pink tinge to both the contents and the container. The Chief Campus Officers at Berkeley and Los Angeles, particularly, as a result of the metropolitan location of these campuses, were periodically under fire, and often felt themselves to be in the position of chicken ranchers condemned because chickens attract hawks, and because it is impossible to get rid of hawks as long as civil liberties are protected for all. The Regents of the University, with the full concurrence of the Academic Senate, adopted a policy against the employment of Communists and denying the use of facilities to them except as bona fide students. But this did not prevent Communists from seeking to stir up trouble among students, nor dissuade citizens from labelling any opinion or action they disliked as obviously communistic.

After six years in office, on the occasion of being asked to speak on the subject of "America's Answer to Youth's Appeal," before the National Education Association in Portland, Oregon, June 30, 1936, President Sproul said in part:

> I cannot be sure that youth is making an appeal to America, even though I hear the clamor of a multitude of voices claiming to speak in youth's name. Every one with a panacea calls on youth to build a better world, according to *his* specifications. Should youth object to the plans or the materials he is straightway labeled as right or left, super-patriotic or un-American; brutal vigilante or dangerous radical. The cold fact is that most of us put the "appeal" in the mouth of youth and lay claim to his enthusiastic support without consulting either his will or his conscience. Or we paraphrase "youth's appeal" in terms of what we think youth should want. And with respect to the exact nature of even those more or less specious, and often spurious, appeals, who can say what it is, in the midst of confusion almost infinitely confounded.
>
> "Youth's appeal" is one of those phrases which may mean much or nothing. If it implies that the youth of America is banded together to demand "a brave new world," it means little, in my opinion, because it is not true. But if it means that a very considerable number of young men and women are becoming increasingly conscious of the social upheaval of our times, and increasingly aware of their vital interests in the events that are determining their future, then it may

mean much. The real truth is that youth's attitude toward the world reflects many things—their personalities, their backgrounds, their environments, and their responses to stimuli which are offered, indeed pressed, by those who self-ishly want for their respective causes the vigor and vitality of young blood. And the problems of youth to-day are neither new nor unique. They are the age-old problems of learning to live and to find a place in a world which exists for no single individual and no single group—young, old, middle-aged, proletariat, bour-geois, or aristocracy—but for all its inhabitants. . . .

The very youngness and inexperience of youths make them easy victims of those who would use them for ulterior purposes; and the more high-sounding, the more flamboyant, the more emotional the appeal, the easier it is to capture the young of any age or any nation. With them idealism is at the peak; emotions are in full flood; energy runs high; hope has not yet felt the sharp pangs of defeat. They lack the practical experience which must ultimately temper their idealism, but need not destroy it. Amongst them there is ability, excellence, even genius; youth often thinks more clearly than age, and does not naturally "bear the ancient grudge." But youth also takes the color of its environment; trained to believe that life is an adventure and that civilization will be advanced through their courage and resourcefulness, young people have often become the creatures of a ruthless state or the subservient followers of a self-seeking group. In a recent letter from an American student, now resident in a German university, there is this passage: "The great majority of students are sincerely in favor of the main objectives of the Nazi program, as they see them. Their admiration for and belief in Adolf Hitler are as genuine as they are great; and this is not based upon fear, force, or coercion. The majority do not wish a democracy—they prefer a dictatorship or a monarchy as the best form of government for their people and for a nation in their particular world situation. They are keenly aware of the very uncertain inter-national conditions. Most of them do not want war, but at the same time many believe that it is inevitable and not far distant."

The black-shirted youth of Italy march with hearts attuned to the commands of Il Duce, and the young people of Russia sing the *Internationale* with all the fervor of conviction. How about American young people? With many of the channels of yesterday closed to them; with many in school only because they can find no work; with others on relief or loafing in the streets with no outlet for the energy and enthusiasm of their years, is it reasonable to believe that American youth is thinking any more clearly than these or that it is not being similarly led astray? As a matter of fact, they are; and they are being mercilessly exploited, too, by the social racketeers who tell them that America is not the fair land of hope and opportunity that, always and everywhere, it has been pictured to be. Our own words condemn us, for they imply our belief that the youth of other lands is not thinking along lines that we call good. And if asked the question, "When is thinking clear and by what token?" most of us, if we are entirely truthful, must answer, "When it suits our point of view. . . ."

Education will always be deeply concerned with the highest concepts that man has yet known, and will always acknowledge their vital, indispensable part in man's very power to be a man at all. But twentieth century education is also most anxiously concerned with man, the social being, and with his adaption, with all his personal foibles and frailties, to an evolving, complex society. The salvation of the human race is less likely to be won by excessive worship of past achievements than by perfecting our social and economic structure so that there will be opportunity for even greater cultural monuments in the future. Twentieth century education is, also, detecting the relationships that should exist between the school and the society for which it is a preparation; between, in other words, the training of youth and its functioning in maturity. So would education build for democracy a stable but not inflexible organization of men, women and children, willing and able to accommodate itself and its individual members to the dynamic character of the world in which we live. . . .

I hear no mass appeal from youth today for "isms" or panaceas, even though their idealism, as always, renders them sensitive to the reforms which are so often in the vanguard of the thing called progress. In them "hope does not seem slain." The baneful brand of disillusionment has not yet been applied. If American education fulfils its destiny it will create a vast and ever-increasing army of informed, restrained, courageous, independent youth. Of such is the stuff from which new worlds are made.

Although President Sproul was speaking to a particular audience at a particular time when he made the above comments, the attitude he reflected for delegates to the National Education Association meeting was consistent with his official attitude maintained over twenty-eight years. Although students might act like a flock of sheep at times, and a herd of young mules at others, they were highly individualistic in their reasons for acting that way, and the President was opposed to every effort to paint them all with the same brush, whether gilding them as angels or turning them all into "reds." They irritated him on many occasions, as they may have exasperated their own parents, but time after time he would patiently explain to them the rules of the University of California and give repeated assurance that he had neither the intention nor the desire to restrict the responsibilities of self-government. However, he did warn them that he intended to hold every student leader personally accountable for trying to exercise what he regarded as "student rights" in an irresponsible way. One learns such tolerance and caution, perhaps, from being himself a parent of college students. As "Bob" Sproul facetiously remarked on one occasion, "When a good Republican finds that his own children are voting for Democratic candidates in spite of the best of home influence and every educational advantage, he learns to be humble in passing judgment on other people's children."

Each new generation of students in the 1930's seemed to feel honor bound to protect "freedom" for future generations of students by opposing all interference from vested authority. In 1932, for example, there was an effort started to revise the Constitution of the Associated Students at Berkeley for the purpose of extending the powers of the Student Affairs Committee to include jurisdiction not only over student disciplinary problems referred to it by the University, but also over the constitutionality of actions of the Associated Students, and over alleged infringements of "student rights" by the administration of the University. The editor of the *Daily Californian* asked for the blessing of the President of the University in the following carefully worded statement: "While it is entirely possible that you would not want to interfere unnecessarily in student government, nevertheless, it appears desirable to ascertain that you would have no objections to the changes."

President Sproul replied: "As you suspected, I do not wish to interfere in student affairs. I am honest in my statement that student government here at Berkeley is self-government and not government by the President through dummy student committees. Nevertheless, I cannot but be interested . . . and therefore comment in general on the situation. In the first place it should be remembered that student self-government exists by grant of the President of the University. In other words, it is not an inherent right of the student body. I remind you of this to establish a foundation for my next point which is that the President may not continue to give his hearty support to student self-government if the fundamental tenets on which it was established are changed too much."

In 1936 the students raised the issue that although the University had an acknowledged right to establish rules concerning use of campus facilities, the buildings occupied by the Associated Students should not be considered as campus facilities and the rules concerning their use should be established by the students rather than by the University. The reply to this effort on the part of the students was as follows:

"The President has delegated to the Associated Students the management and administration of the Stephens Union which is, nevertheless, a University building and subject to the general regulations governing the use of such buildings, as well as having special regulations of its own. The general regulations provide that: 'only those student organizations which are under the jurisdiction of the Associated Students may, in normal circumstances, receive permits. Other student organizations that desire this privilege may obtain it, if at all, only by express permission of the President of the University or his direct representative.'"

The ambivalent attitude of student leaders concerning University authority was clearly demonstrated on the Los Angeles campus following the move from the old Vermont Avenue campus to the new campus in Westwood. The cost of the removal and "settling in" was greater than expected and the income from football less than estimated. As a result the Association found itself owing money for taxes, rental of the Coliseum, team travel, and its opponents' share of gate receipts in the amount of more than $75,000, with no cash on hand. Under these circumstances the students were willing to agree that the University had to accept responsibility and that it was justified in taking a more active part in the financial administration of the Association. President Sproul reported to the Regents that it seemed essential to bail the Association out, and he recommended that a loan of $50,000 be made without security other than his personal assurance that a mature and experienced Board of Control would be established to keep an eye on expenditures. Subsequently it was proposed by the ASUCLA that to assure the solvency of the Association, payment of membership fees in the Association be made mandatory. The

Regents of the University agreed to institute a compulsory membership plan but only if the students themselves wanted such a plan and
would so indicate by a referendum vote. This vote was taken and
compulsory membership in the ASUCLA was approved by better
than a two-thirds majority. However, when the loan from the Regents
was repaid, and the Association finances were in satisfactory condition, the students raised a question as to why they should not have a
greater degree of local control. Provost Clarence A. Dykstra, with the
record of past financial difficulties before him, wrote to ask President
Sproul what his attitude should be. President Sproul replied: "Firmly
believing in the values of student self-government, I have always been
anxious to allow the maximum autonomy consistent with responsible
action and sound management."

Later he obtained the approval of the Regents to the granting of a
greater degree of local control over ASUCLA budgets and expenditures, despite the fact that the President of the Associated Students
wanted it understood that he was not surrendering any "right" to
come to the Regents for help, but just trying to eliminate unnecessary
interference. Some years later, when students protested that their local
Board of Control was not giving adequate consideration to student
points of view, the President upheld the veto power of the Board, but
made clear that students should have the same power. He said: "As
one who believes that student government should be fully responsible
for conducting its affairs, I should like to see its elected representatives ratify all actions of the Board of Control"

Students at Berkeley also ran into difficulty through trying to enjoy
the privileges without the restrictions of membership in a university
community. In the spring of 1940 the editors of the *Daily Californian* and
certain members of the Student Executive Committee began a campaign to deprive the alumni representative and the faculty representative on the Executive Committee of their voting privilege. The
Assistant Editor of the *Daily Californian* requested that the President
of the University reply to a long series of questions which he had
drafted. One of the questions was: "Can the decisions of the ASUC
Executive Committee be, logically and without qualification, called

completely student decisions if voting alumni and faculty representatives have seats on the committee?"

President Sproul did not object to being thus cross-examined. He answered: "Of course they cannot. But I see no reason for pushing logic to such a dead end. Practically, the decisions of a committee consisting of two non-students and thirteen students are student decisions."

He went on to say: "A completely student-controlled government is possible, of course. From an educational point of view there are many arguments in favor of such a government. I am not, myself, opposed to it. I have tried to say on innumerable occasions, and I repeat here, that the students can have any kind of government on this campus that they want for their own exclusive business. The only question is as to the extent to which business in which other members of the University family are vitally concerned shall be placed under the control and direction of a purely student government. . . . If two-thirds of the students voting on Friday approve a reorganization plan which removes the votes of the faculty and alumni representatives, I shall interpret their action in the light of the statement of my position published in the *Daily Californian*, as evidence of their desire for a student government, jurisdiction of which is confined to student business exclusively, and I shall act accordingly."

This effort to limit University interference with "student rights" was unsuccessful, and soon after the Associated Students found itself faced with a decision of the Internal Revenue Service that it did not appear to be an integral part of the University subject to the same control as other activities and was therefore not entitled to tax exemption. Consequently, another group of students, on the advice of the attorney for the ASUC, requested the support of the President of the University for a revision of the constitution and clarification of the status of the Association with regard to the Regents of the University. President Sproul agreed to support the movement if that was what the students wanted, and he was thereupon promptly accused by dissident students of being involved in a clever effort to gain control over the funds of the ASUC. When President Sproul asked the

President of the Associated Students why he permitted such a distortion of the facts to go unanswered, the latter explained that he didn't dare answer, because, if he did so, he would be attacked in the *Daily Californian* as a stooge of the President of the University.

Incidents such as these constantly aroused a suspicion, difficult to confirm, that opposition was being organized and directed, and students manipulated, by outside interests. As President Sproul said in the already cited letter to the Assistant Editor of the *Daily Californian*, at the outset of the difficulty: "I believe that the chief factor leading to a breach in student-administration relations is the domination of the student body by a group constitutionally opposed to all authority. . . . A representative of that group on this campus, who sits on the Executive Committee, has said 'We have nothing against Sproul, but we are against the system he represents. We are going to fight that system whoever is president.' "

Such incidents also help to explain why equanimity is such an important asset for a university president, and why a twenty-eight year tour of duty as President of the University of California is a truly remarkable achievement. As already indicated, in the final analysis President Sproul managed to avoid being backed into blind alleys because he never lost sight of the fact that the belligerents in the student body at no time represented more than a small though often well-organized group. In open discussions, even with the amateur or professional skeptics present, he could count on the majority of student leaders, as on the majority of all students, to listen to reason. During this same period of controversy, he requested the *Daily Californian* to publish a lengthy statement addressed to students in general. After briefly tracing the history of student self-government, as he had for generation after generation of students, he went on to say:

The present complex and in most respects highly effective student governments on the various campuses have developed from this small beginning without change in University policy. No change is contemplated now. The President will normally observe the autonomy of the student government in the conduct of student affairs, but reserves the right to intervene in matters affecting the welfare of the University or the responsibilities of its teaching or administrative officers. A student does not add to any rights he may hold as a citizen by registering at the University. Rather he accepts a new responsibility to live up to the spirit and letter of the regulations under which the campus community operates.

The concept of "Academic Freedom" does not confer any privilege upon students, nor does it confer a privilege upon any other member of the community outside of the classroom. This is clearly explained in University Regulation #5, issued February 15, 1935. . . .

Students are expected to live within the limits set by these principles. No individual student or student organization can be granted the use of University facilities to carry on propaganda for or against a cause or movement having no direct concern with student affairs on campus. Student organizations with outside affiliations requiring promotion of specific causes or movements, therefore, should not be given official recognition by the student government. Students who participate in such causes or movements off campus, should do so as private citizens and must not cloak their activities under the name of the University, or give any direct or implied impression that they represent the University or any agency of the student association.

In the application of these principles to specific cases, the President or his representatives will always seek to arrive at a just decision through friendly consultation with student representatives; but where consultation does not lead to mutual agreement the President or his representatives must assume responsibility for the decision. It is believed that a sincere effort on the part of the students to understand and abide by the principles under which the University operates will leave few problems which cannot be settled amicably.

It is clear from the record that even in the midst of heated controversies over "student rights" President Sproul held the respect and friendship of the great majority of students. When it was necessary to call in a group of them for a heart-to-heart talk, it was not unusual for the leader of the opposition to write a letter of thanks for the friendly way in which the President had met them, and for the frankness with which he handled the matter under discussion. This was not a calculated procedure but a reflection of an ingrained way of doing business. In any family discussion—with faculty, students, or other educators—he was not only a good listener but a cooperator. If there was opposition to his own point of view and the proponents of the opposing position forgot one of their own telling arguments he would bring it up himself. He called it "being the Devil's advocate" and explained that a conference was wasted unless all of the arguments were brought up and discussed. One important point of difference, if not remembered until after the close of the conference, might vitiate any agreement reached.

Shortly after he became President, Sproul took up the problem of settling long-standing differences of viewpoint with the junior college administrators of the state. He felt that neither the University nor the junior college would make its best contribution to education unless there was full and voluntary cooperation; so he asked for a conference, which he opened as follows: "It may be necessary for me to say frankly a few things that are distasteful to one or another of this company, who represents fervently, perhaps fanatically, a point of view rather different from my own. If so, I hope you will remember that different views may be honestly reached and sincerely held, and that no offense is intended." With this introduction he proceeded to lay before the group the points of disagreement that he discerned, and to propose a program that would recognize the unique responsibilities of the junior colleges and of the University, as well as the areas in which they should work cooperatively. He then suggested that a set procedure be established for periodic joint discussion of all matters of mutual concern. This was an unprecedented step in educational relations, but it was in line with the Sproul philosophy. He ended his presentation in the following manner: "With all this machinery, lubricated with the oil of good-will, which alone can make machinery operate smoothly and efficiently, I see no reason to believe that we cannot work out together the problems which are our mutual concern."

Subsequent history seems to demonstrate that Sproul was right, for the joint committee idea has continued to minimize differences and has steadily built up mutual confidence and effective cooperation.

This same approach characterized Sproul's consideration of problems with students. When the Internal Revenue Service informed the Associated Students that it could not simultaneously insist on its independence of action and enjoy the privilege of sharing in the tax exempt status of the Regents of the University, Sproul pointed out to the students that the authority of the Regents or of the President could not be changed by student vote, but that if they wanted to continue a constitution that ignored the authority of the Regents and the President and that was unacceptable to the Internal Revenue Service, he would not raise any objections, even though it meant paying taxes regularly. He asked only that they consider the problem on rational rather than emotional grounds. The editors of the *Daily Bruin* felt that they should put an oar into the water; so they suggested that it was all a plot to get control of ASUC finances, and that the Regents should be asked what they intended to do with the money after they got it.

Another area of frequent difficulty into which Sproul introduced his philosophy of free and open discussion around a conference table was that concerned with intercampus student relations, the maintenance of the single university concept in the face of local campus loyalties, and the rivalry engendered by intercollegiate sports competition. In 1934 a student named Hardy Smith, Class of 1936, who had attended UCLA and Berkeley, came to President Sproul with the suggestion that a positive program be adopted to make clear the statewide kinship of the various campuses and to temper the provincial emotionalism of the various student bodies on those occasions when they met for athletic or other competitions. Hardy pointed out that he had personally gone through an attitudinal metamorphosis as a result of registering at both major campuses, and that out of it he felt he had arrived at a loyalty to the University of California that was a step above his ties to either campus. In analyzing his own experience he said simply that the key was getting to know students on both campuses and discovering that friendship demanded an emphasis on what the participants shared in common, rather than on what their differences might be.

To President Sproul this was not just sentimentality, but the kind of spirit, or emotionally-based glue, that was needed to hold the University of California together; he promptly made young Hardy an undergraduate minister plenipotentiary to see what could be done. He wrote a letter to one of the chief administrative officers at Los Angeles to announce the nature of Hardy's diplomatic mission, in which he said: "I want you to give him all the aid that you can in making proper contacts with student leaders. I want you also to make it clear to anyone in the faculty or the administration of UCLA, who may be disposed to stand in the way of the plan, that it has my full approval."

It is interesting to note that Hardy Smith, now a business executive, on a visit to the Davis campus for the thirtieth anniversary of the California Club explained that the incentive behind his effort to do something for the University of California was an urgent need to get himself out of a predicament created by his scholarship average at the moment, and to prove that he did have ability.

Out of this effort came the establishing of the *California Club,* first with chapters at Berkeley and at Los Angeles, but subsequently on other campuses, to which student leaders were appointed by personal letter from the President of the University, and later also addressed by him on the importance of the responsibility involved, and the nature of the mission the club was expected to perform. To each chapter the President also appointed a faculty or administrative advisor, to give students promptly whatever assistance they needed. The general purposes of the Club were to assist the President of the University in perpetuating the unity of the institution, by promoting friendly relations and understanding between undergraduates on the various campuses, and by carrying this understanding to the communities around the campuses. Stress was laid on intercampus hospitality and courtesy for student transfers from one campus to another and for students in general before, during, and after intercampus competitions. In the last-named events, which stimulated migrations of hundreds or sometimes thousands of students from one campus to another, the courtesy involved assistance in finding overnight housing at fraternities, sororities, boarding houses, and private homes; joint breakfasts and lunches for student leaders; mixer dances scheduled after the games; all-University editions of the various student newspapers; special card stunts for the rooting sections, etc. Statewide-University floats for the Tournament of Roses Parade were one method used to reach the community. To give impetus to this program, conferences of California Club members were scheduled during the year at which speakers reviewed the history and status of the University and discussion took place on existing or potential problems relating to intercampus student relations.

The effectiveness of the California Club idea was apparent from the start. During the first year the Vice-President of the ASUCLA, a member of the Los Angeles Chapter of the California Club, announced her engagement to the Chairman of the Berkeley Chapter of the California Club. Both campuses agreed that this was evidence that students on the other campus were all right after one got to know them. One of the remarkable aspects of the program, resulting from the fact that the President of the University had very little money available for expenses, and did not feel that he should seek more until the idea had shown its effectiveness, was the method of support. The students financed their own operations through hiring name orchestras for intercampus dances after football games and selling tickets to these affairs. The California Club of 1938 proudly reported to the President that it had carried on a very extensive program on an outlay on only $1,000, which it had earned itself, and that it still had $700 in the bank as a reserve for the year ahead. The students at Davis petitioned the President for a chapter of the California Club in 1936, and the San Francisco Medical Center did the same shortly thereafter. To symbolize the statewide nature of the Club, money was raised to establish a Deming G. Maclise Scholarship, honoring the name of an alumnus of the Berkeley campus who had served as the assistant comptroller of the University both at Davis and Los Angeles, and who was well known and highly respected by all students through officiating at athletic events and serving as counsellor and advisor to students in need of personal help or the intervention of an *amicus curiae*.

For President Sproul the California Club was an evidence, as the Student Affairs Committee had been for President Wheeler, that the great majority of students do not have a constitutional penchant for creating problems, but drift into them for want of something else sufficiently challenging and exciting to do. They want to be participants in rather than bystanders at events, which is why they are so often willing to listen to any invitation to action on behalf of an appealing cause, without much concern for the past records or current reputations of those who issue invitations. If the Devil himself were to organize a campaign against racial discrimination in Heaven and charge that a disgraceful situation was being ignored just because the chief critic had horns and a tail, students would be inclined to give the Devil a hearing even though they wound up pelting him with ripe tomatoes. What students resented was being told they couldn't listen to the Devil at all.

In the dark days of the Depression it seemed to many students that although everyone agreed there was something wrong with the world, anybody who advocated a change was suspect. In the fall of 1933 a few students joined in a strike of cotton pickers in the San Joaquin Valley, and questions were loudly asked as to whether the University was an educational institution or a training ground for "reds" and "radicals." As a result President Sproul came to the defense of radicalism in youth before a Rotary Club Convention in Los Angeles. In 1934, as the political battle for the governorship of California began between Frank C. Merriam and Upton Sinclair, and "Running out the Reds" became a campaign issue, the debating teams on the Berkeley and Los Angeles campuses conceived the brilliant idea that it would be a very appropriate time and a good assurance of public interest to debate the question: "Resolved: That Communism is Fit for Americans." They were shocked to discover that there was objection to student discussion on this subject, inasmuch as politicians were shouting about it all over the state. Provost E. C. Moore at Los Angeles promptly found himself in the middle of an attack, on the one hand for suggesting a change in topic, and on the other hand for not having done something about it earlier. A bitter waterfront strike was in progress in San Francisco, and the Bureau of Occupations at Berkeley was accused by the undergraduate Student Problems Club of having sent students needing work to San Francisco for jobs that were alleged to be strikebreaking. Shortly thereafter the labor difficulties spread into a general strike; this required calling out the National Guard and led General Johnson of NRA to characterize the trouble as an attempt at civil war fulminated by subversives. A number of "Donnybrook Fairs" followed, resulting from efforts by propagandists for both sides to cater to the student desire to know what was going on and to decide for themselves who was right. In the fall of 1934 there was a near riot at Sather Gate with about 1,000 students gathered to hear the radical viewpoint, and others gathered to see that the speakers were barraged with eggs, fruit, and vegetables.

Meanwhile President Sproul had let loose with both barrels of a verbal shotgun aimed at extremists, right and left. In his statement to newly entering students he said: "I am no flag-waving jingo. But I have grown infinitely weary with the deprecation of America and American institutions by pseudointellectuals hanging on the fringes of a student body or a faculty."

At about the same time the Alameda County Joint Americanism Committee of the American Legion announced that it was taking matters into its own hands and organizing undercover activities to rid the University of California of radicals; and the Provost at Los Angeles found it necessary to suspend five students for using their positions, wittingly or unwittingly, but not unbelligerently, to promote the activities of the Communistic National Student League.

President Sproul's personal attitude was clearly set forth in the *California Legionnaire* of August 19, 1934: "The University must back its students to reappraise old values and must generate in them a more social-minded attitude toward the welfare of humanity and the solidarity of the social order. . . . This does not mean that the University, in the slightest degree, teaches or espouses radical doctrines be they one or many. Ideally it should stand apart from common controversies. It should have no opinions, no beliefs, no prejudices. It should propagate no doctrine or dogma . . .[It] has no right to espouse or oppose as such the orderly advocacy of proposals for peaceful modification of our political or economic system. It may not properly and legally suppress either reactionaries, unyielding in conservatism, or radicals, unreasonable in proposals for reform."

The American Legion accepted this as a frank statement of position, but strangely enough a professional liberal, Anna Wallace, writing in the *New Republic* for January 9, 1935, attacked President Sproul and accused him of supporting the rise of fascism; of opposing the Communistic National Student League just because it was against compulsory ROTC; of being in favor of spy systems, vigilantes, and student suspensions; and generally catering to "Big Business" on the Board of Regents. It is difficult to understand how this was brought into harmony with President Sproul's plea, in the *Oakland Tribune* of the previous August 31, for support of the Constitution of the United States and for loyalty with intelligence; or his plea, in the *Hollywood Citizen* of September 17, for public realization of the fact that our country is not perfect and that those who suggest change are not to be condemned for it as radicals.

At no time did the number of students involved in activities that aroused administrative or general public ire amount to more than a few per cent of the student body, but they were often successful in creating difficulties, perhaps because a large public university is, metaphorically speaking, as sensitive as a cross between Caesar's wife and an African elephant; that is, it is a paragon made conspicuous by size, attempting always to move with dignity, but constantly irritated by a string of baby firecrackers tied to its tail. The embarrassment of the situation is heightened by the fact that one is never sure whether the firecrackers symbolize the spontaneous ingenuity of healthy young Americans or a cold war planned and directed from off-campus.

In the midst of such anxieties some student problems are a relief. The managerial staffs of student papers have striven periodically to increase advertising income by selling space to questionably appropriate businesses such as local bars, burlesque houses, or enterprising graduate students guaranteeing to get anyone through college, for a price, by editing or ghost-writing all necessary theme papers and holding cram sessions before midterms or finals. Along with these, of course, the Communists periodically sought to get on campus by buying space to publicize lectures or meetings with free refreshments, etc., as inducements to student attendance. When questions concerning such advertisements were raised by worried parents and others who received the *Daily Californian* at home, the students defended their right to sell space by pointing out that similar ads could be carried by major metropolitan dailies. The editor further expressed the opinion that students should learn the meaning of the term *caveat emptor* while still in college.

Periodically, also, one or the other of the student newspapers would come up with the happy thought that anything that the University Administration sent in with a "must print" note on it, i.e., changes in courses or room assignments, changes in academic rules, or announcements of lectures, concerts or dramatic events, should be paid for just as other governmental agencies paid commercial newspapers for legally required public notices. They did not appreciate the canny Scot in the presidency. He said he would be glad to pay for such notices when the student newspapers agreed to pay rent for the University-owned land and facilities they were using. He also added, confidently, that such an arrangement would be quite profitable to the University.

However, even while fencing with one or another student over "rights" of some description, President Sproul encouraged the entry of more bright students who could be leaders and might in their turn challenge established authority. Less than four years after assuming the presidency he persuaded the California Alumni Association and the Regents to embark jointly on a scholarship program for outstanding high school graduates. More will be said of this in the next chapter.

In the year 1941, opinion polling of students became a popular pastime for various individuals seeking to prove the rightness or wrongness of this or that foreign or domestic policy. In too many cases it appeared that loaded questions were being asked of an inadequate number of individuals and that the results were being proclaimed as student opinion at the University of California. The students themselves tried to stop the practice by demonstrating that hundreds of signatures could be obtained on documents suggesting that all of the signers be hanged by the neck until dead, or drawn and quartered. The Executive Committee of the ASUC finally voted to set up a committee for the purpose of assuring that questionnaires were clear as to the issue involved, that they provided voting spaces for those against and for those without an opinion as well as those in favor of a given point of view; and that the results could not be announced until the number of people polled constituted an adequate sample. Inasmuch as President Sproul was asked to name the review committee, there were rumors started to the effect that this was just an effort to draw the University into its Ivory Tower while the world crumbled about its ivory ears.

President Sproul made clear to his administrative aides that he had no intention of issuing any orders involving matters of vital concern to students without conferring with them first, and in a memo regarding questionnaires he said: "The obtaining of a free and accurate expression of the opinion of students on matters of particular concern to them would seem to be in no way inappropriate." He further reiterated that not only students but even the President of the University had a right to a personal opinion on world events, and he utilized this right. He spoke over the Columbia Broadcasting System under the auspices of the "Fight for Freedom, Inc." in August, 1941, in the following forthright words:

> Until Hitler is defeated nothing else matters, for if he is not defeated, nothing that matters will remain—not safety, nor peace, nor property, nor the rights of labor, nor the freedom of men, nor anything else that we treasure. How then can some among us advocate that we stand idle while the catastrophe we can prevent occurs before our eyes? How can they ignore the lesson that neutrality is no defense against the New Order of Hitler, a lesson written in the epitaphs of twelve nations? That New Order is now a tragic fact, from the Arctic Sea to the Mediterranean, from the Dardanelles to the English Channel. If the Russians and the British are conquered, Hitler and his satellites will rule over an empire such as man has never before beheld. It is incredible that anyone should say that this is a matter of indifference to the United States. On the contrary, we have never faced a crisis of such moment to our future. We call upon every liberty-loving citizen to enlist under our banner to fight, not for Britain, nor Greece, nor China, nor Russia, but for America, and for the right, as God gives us to see it; to recognize that this peril is upon us too, and openly to strike our blow for freedom.

He further warned the college students of America, speaking from New York, a week before the Japanese attack on Pearl Harbor: "For the decade of the thirties and perhaps longer, the popular pose in

American universities, among students and teachers alike, was one of sophisticated dissatisfaction. The failures of the American way of life were magnified and the successes minimized to such an extreme that it came to be regarded as a mark of abysmal ignorance or incredible naïveté for any young man or woman to refer to American democracy publicly other than scornfully or critically. . . . Dissatisfaction, even sophisticated dissatisfaction, may lead to desirable reforms in a world at peace, but in a world of nations caught in a desperate struggle for victory or slavery, it is a greased skin hastening a people to national suicide."

Shortly after Pearl Harbor, speaking at the inauguration of President LeRoy E. Cowles, at the University of Utah, he added: "Human nature is not simple nor in all respects lovely. The virtues on which democracy is premised make high demands upon human behavior. That men will exercise good judgment and manifest good will in their political relations, that they will accept responsibility for what they do and freely make decisions under which they can live justly and well together, is an assumption not always and everywhere true. It represents a possibility in men, but has become a reality more or less only under the most favorable conditions. We have been able to enjoy a good measure of democracy in this country, for example, but not enough as yet to give us cause to be self-righteous about it or complacently at ease in Zion."

With the involvement of the United States in World War II the campuses of the University became abnormally peaceful and quiet. The 33,493 students who were registered in the year 1940–41 melted away to 20,482 two years later. The male population, particularly, declined rapidly, from 19,015 in 1940–41 to 7,528 in regular sessions in 1944–45. In this last-mentioned year male students represented only 35.3 per cent of the total registration, the lowest percentage in the history of the University. Those were serious times and the students remaining on campus were more impressed with the privilege of getting an education than with the earlier controversy over "student rights." The student activities program was greatly curtailed and finances were at a low ebb; these conditions might have been partly responsible for the change. But, also, it appeared that off-campus Communists were no longer trying to tear down democracy, but rather were urging it on to help defeat Hitler and the Japanese, and some of them appeared to be too busy trying to collect military information to send over to Russia to bother with a handful of students on campus.

This situation continued to prevail for awhile after the veterans started back to college under the provision of the G.I. Bill. The enrollment of men jumped from 7,528 to 31,687 in two years and continued rising to a peak of 34,409 in regular sessions in 1949–50. But the earlier arrivals, relieved to be home in one piece, appeared to be concerned, primarily, with completion of their college work. Their greater maturity, and seriousness of purpose were indicated by the fact that grade point averages for those who had been registered before entering the service and who returned after discharge went up 25 per cent. By 1947, however, the situation on campus was returning to the prewar normal, with one movement after another being organized to assert the independence of student government, to eliminate alumni and faculty voting from student legislative bodies, and to gain greater control over Associated Students' expenditures.

One of the first indications that student life on campus had returned to "business as usual" was the inauguration of a program of protest against a provision of University Regulation #17 to the effect that literature could not be distributed free or sold on campus in connection with meetings or events without permission obtained in advance. Regulation #17 was issued as a codification of various practices and rules respecting extracurricular use of campus grounds and facilities that had accumulated over the years. The restriction on passing out literature on campus without permission was part of a general regulatory action taken by the Regents of the University in the spring of 1935 to control parades, demonstrations, or meetings that might interfere with classroom activities, and to avoid continuous littering of walks, lawns, and shrubbery with advertising matter or propaganda sheets. One purpose of the action was to make sure that nonacademic organizations using campus facilities understood they would have to be prepared to reimburse the University for any extraordinary clean-up costs. Another was to make more specific the restriction on use of University grounds and facilities to authorized activities at authorized hours.

University Regulation #17 had been further revised in 1949 to make clear that the granting of permission to a student group to hold a meeting on campus did not automatically include permission to deluge the audience, and ultimately the campus landscape, with handbills, particularly by those having no connection with the meeting but merely attracted by the crowd. Handbills passed out at the door of a meeting hall on campus seemed more effective because they were more likely to be accepted and read than if they were offered on a street corner. On the other hand, citizens who did not like such handbills were inclined to interpret their distribution on campus as an evidence that the University favored or condoned some very strange causes.

Rumors were immediately started on campus, or off-campus, that the real purpose of the 1949 clarification was to deprive students of the right to circulate petitions on campus, a clear contravention of the Bill of Rights. It was learned that purveyors of handbills were sharpening the issue by labeling handbills with the word *petition*. As a consequence, the President of the University had to counter this plan with an announcement "in order that the right of students, employees, and faculty to circulate petitions under this Standing Order may be clarified." He pointed out that the only restrictions on the circulating of petitions were those required to prevent interference with instructional activities and to insure that the University of California was not directly or implicitly involved as an endorser. But the President was advised that efforts would be continued to distribute propaganda on campus by labeling each sheet *Petition*, and that some kind of definition of a petition would have to be established. So President Sproul added to his announcement concerning petitions: "Petition is defined here as a written document, couched in publicly acceptable language, for the bona fide purpose of obtaining valid signatures to a request for legal and proper support of, or opposition to, a stated position or action."

It was probably not completely a coincidence that the increase in student problems, and the recalcitrance of a few of the student news-paper editors, beginning in the 1950's, also marked a resurgence of communist propaganda activities. The conviction of eleven members of the Communist Party on the charge of advocating the overthrow of the Government of the United States by force, came in October, 1949. In the next few months Klaus J. E. Fuchs pleaded guilty to having systematically transmitted classified scientific information to Russia, Judith Coplon was convicted of espionage on behalf of the Russians, and Julius and Ethel Rosenberg, Morton Sobell, and David Greenglass were shortly on trial for conspiracy to commit wartime sabotage. In March of 1950, some 60,000 North Korean troops, spearheaded by 100 Russian-built tanks, invaded South Korea.

In the fall of 1951 the Communists held a youth festival in East Berlin. A few students from the University of California attended, and on their return submitted articles to the *Daily Californian* for publica-tion. One of the articles reported that the Korean people as a whole wanted to be left to settle their own affairs and were bitterly hostile to United Nations troops (mostly American), who were bringing so much destruction and grief on their country. Another reported that very few Americans attended the youth festival because Russia was advocating peace and America did not want its war psychology weakened. The publishing of this obviously communist propaganda aroused a storm of protest. Fighting was still going on in Korea, dur-ing which Communist bullets killed 33,629 young Americans. To make matters worse the editor of the *Daily Californian* defended his right to publish the articles.

Incidents of this kind were by no means confined to the University of California. They were occurring at major universities throughout the country and it was difficult to attribute them to coincidence. In the fall of 1952, *Editor & Publisher* ran several articles commenting on this situation, based upon information from thirty university presi-dents and deans. The President of Dartmouth said that he tried to accord to the student newspaper roughly the freedom that it would have as an outside paper, and then he added "There is no need to tell anyone who is at all broadly acquainted with American life that we pay a price for this freedom. That price is paid in the irresponsibility and malice which certain types of individuals practice under the guise of journalism." The President of the University of Illinois said: "Were the University of Illinois to assume any measure of responsibility for student opinion, two results would follow. First, such a policy would drive student opinion underground. Second, it would force the University to assume responsibility for every student utterance, since it assumes responsibility for some. Both of these results would be unfortunate."

President Sproul was in agreement with college presidents throughout the country that it would be unfortunate to deprive students in general of the privilege of a free paper because of the actions and policies of a few students representing one generation of editors. But he also recognized the justice of the complaint from students, faculty, alumni, and the general public that under a policy of allowing editors to choose their own successors, without regard to the opinion of the Associated Students as publisher, each generation of editors tended to perpetuate its own philosophy, whatever that might be. In response to a resolution of the Executive Committee of the Associated Students, he agreed to appoint a committee of alumni, faculty, and administrative officers as advisors to the editors of the *Daily Californian*. This committee was specifically informed that it was advisory only, but its existence was attacked immediately by student editors as a move toward censorship. Even while President Sproul explained to alumni that "We cannot have a free paper without mistakes being made, and I do not believe that freedom from mistakes is as important as freedom to make mistakes," the Editor of the *Daily Californian* protested against being obliged to listen to comments from an advisory board and charged that "The existence of such a board would mean a complete victory for those who wish to regulate University thinking." No mention was made of the fact that many students and others feared that the thinking of editors was already being regulated, and not by the University. About this same time such publications as *The Anvil*, *New Foundations*, and *The News* appeared on the magazine racks in the

Student Unions at Los Angeles and Berkeley. *The Anvil* stated its purpose to be the promotion of better relations between the Soviet Union and the Anglo-Saxon World. *The News*, a subsidiary of the newspaper *True*, published at 186 Gorky Street, Moscow, stated that it was "For Peace and Friendship Among Nations." Both were largely concerned with correcting alleged lies being foisted upon the American people by United States public officials and American newspapers. When questions were raised about these publications it was necessary to point out that the University of California did not sanction sale of publications on its premises if they were unacceptable for mailing under U. S. Postal Laws, if the publisher was not clearly stated and accountable for libel, if they were published by the Communist Party or editorially controlled by it, or if they advocated overthrow of the government of the United States by force. As a consequence these publications were removed from the stands, first at Los Angeles, and later at Berkeley. Mimeographed protests were immediately distributed to students under the title "The Issues of Freedom." The gist of the protest was that the classifying of *Anvil* as an official or unofficial publication of a political party (The Communist Party), was just hiding the real reason for the action. The editorial columns of the *Daily Californian* asked the question, "How far are we going to run, how much are we going to prohibit, before we have the courage to stop this negativism?"

For the next two years the editors of student papers grew more and more belligerent. It was finally necessary for the Dean of Students at Los Angeles to ask the editors to confine articles by off-campus torch-carriers to the "Letters to the Editor," section, and to give equal space to both sides of controversial questions. The response was an unrestrained attack on the University of California and on the Associated Students, by the editors of the *Daily Bruin*. On December 10, 1954, an editorial stated: "Our fearless administrators know that their job security depends on a tranquil-appearing campus. They carry a big stick for students, but they are frightened to death of the L. A. *Times* and *Herald-Express* . . . The *Bruin* has sometimes fallen down in news coverage. But some students are so biased that they do not recognize fair coverage when they see it, which is often. The Administration and the Student Legislative Council are notable for approving of biased coverage as long as it is biased in their favor, but screaming when it is 'slanted' (i.e., gives both sides)." Shortly thereafter it was necessary to remove the editors from office and to call for volunteers from the student body to staff the paper. Peace was also won at Berkeley but with less drastic action.

Although all of these incidents may seem to be inconsequential details in the life of one of the worlds' major universities, they are worthy of note because such matters often take up a good part of the time of an educational administrator, and how well he handles them may determine whether he has an opportunity to get on with questions of academic importance. He must necessarily walk warily, seeking to preserve freedom of action on the part of students in order that extracurricular activities may continue to have some educational value, and at the same time he must protect the institution from organized efforts to use students for ulterior purposes. There is always a healthy rivalry between youth and authority, and one expression of it on a public university campus is student probing for fallacies and weaknesses in the rules that authority lays down. An administrator who promulgates rules that are unnecessary or unenforceable merely establishes what could be called "an attractive nuisance." On the other hand, if he authorizes the disciplining of a student for action that is not clearly and specifically prohibited by rule he may also be in trouble. It is possible that one could demonstrate a rather close inverse relationship between the length of a university president's term of office and the number of rules and amendments of rules that come out too late. Conversely there is often a direct relationship between precipitate disciplinary action and the sudden ending of presidential appointments. Shortly before the writing of this chapter the president of the University of Colorado resigned as a result of a navigational error while making one of these constantly recurring runs between Scylla and Charybdis.

Needless to say, President Sproul's twenty-eight years in the presidency prove that he was able to navigate between these metamorphical rocks time after time with nothing worse than a few scratches in his paint or a dent well above the waterline, even though he did it on occasion with a very high wind blowing. There are always a few people, of course, whether students, alumni, or leading citizens, who think that it is better to hold a certain course and wreck the ship than to tack and live to sail another day. The problem is akin to that of deciding whether it is better to win a given battle or to try to win the war.

Throughout his career President Sproul managed to hold the allegiance of the majority of the people who counted, within and without the University. He was always a very human person who never retreated behind the dignity of his position. The crowd was never sitting back waiting for him to make a mistake, but rather always waiting expectantly for him to work his way out of an awkward situation. The enthusiasm with which students responded to a yell-leader's call, "Let's give twelve big ones for President Sproul," fluctuated from time to time, but it was always there. On two occasions when offers of important positions at considerably greater salaries came from elsewhere, the students organized impromptu serenades around the President's House, armed with drums, trombones, and placards, all exhorting "Good Old Bob—Stick to the Job." On his twenty-fifth anniversary as president, the Executive Committee of the Associated Students at Berkeley voted to buy him a new automobile and had no trouble getting its proposal approved by the Finance Committee. Watching him start the car with wheels spinning and gravel flying, shortly thereafter, one admiring onlooker remarked: "He sure would make a good drag racer."

V

Alumni and Intercollegiate Athletics

One cannot expect to cover the life of a major university over a period of more than a quarter of a century in one book without omitting much that is important. But neither can one expect to compress the life of an institution over twenty-eight years into such small compass that alumni affairs and intercollegiate athletics become unimportant. These are areas in which a president is always expected to demonstrate tactical omniscience or a reasonable facsimile thereof, recognizing that there are involved two separate fields of activity occupying, like stellar bodies in binary relationship, overlapping orbits.

Quite recently, Harold W. Dodds, President Emeritus of Princeton, in a humorous vein, summed up the changing role of the alumnus very well: "The old tradition was that the alumni are a hair shirt for the president. Some still are. But the early nineteenth-century admonition of an Episcopalian Bishop to the girls in his church boarding school to behave kindly to Presbyterians but not to 'listen to their sinful talk' no longer applies to alumni. They are the solid rock upon which many a privately sustained college or university has built its position, and

133

the tax-supported schools are increasingly enlisting their financial and moral support. If the institution pays them the compliment of assuming that they are interested in its high purposes, a gratifying and influential number will respond accordingly."*

President Robert G. Sproul would unquestionably agree with this as a general statement, though he would find it difficult to avoid commenting that the University of California, as the first major, multiple-campus institution of higher education in the country, has problems of which the President Emeritus of Princeton could have known only through hearsay. There is long tradition behind the metaphorical concept of a college or university as Alma Mater, and of alumni as sons and daughters bound by affection and respect. As Benjamin Ide Wheeler put it to the students of his day: "You cannot make a university out of minds and brains. In a university, as elsewhere in the world, heart is more than head, love is more than reason."

But Wheeler also recognized that hearts without heads to guide them were not of much service to a university community. On a number of occasions he expressed his opinion of those who wore their hearts on their sleeves and approached a problem with their "minds unbuttoned." What he would think of the University that developed within a quarter century after his death we don't know. But inasmuch as it had two campuses when he took over, a third at Davis some years later, and a fourth at Los Angeles before he retired, it is reasonable to suppose that he would have taken in stride the idea that an Alma Mater could serve as Queen Mother for a host of campuses.

However, there were many others for whom this change was disconcerting. They could not easily adjust themselves to the idea that Alma Mater was capable of playing a larger role than that of housemother for a single campus or a few geographically close campuses. This proved to be one of President Sproul's most persistent problems. It was a problem intensified by the involvement of two areas of the state that had been economic and social-status rivals for many generations, and by the eventual rivalry of the two major campuses in "big time" intercollegiate athletic competition for regional and national

* Harold W. Dodds, *The American President—Educator or Caretaker* (New York: McGraw-Hill Book Co., 1962), p. 205.

championships. The problem was further tinged, at times, by suspicion and bitterness, tracing back to the reluctance with which the Los Angeles campus had been accepted by the "northerners" and the condescension with which its ambitious plans seemed often to be greeted. There was both resistance to the idea of sharing Alma Mater with an adopted family in the south and skepticism on the part of the adopted family as to the bigness of Alma Mater's "yankee" heart. There were moments when the President was unsure whether to use his handkerchief to mop his brow or to wave it as a personal flag of truce. In one of those moments he offered to resign his position as President if his leadership seemed irreparably tainted by the degree he had earned at Berkeley. The fact that he didn't and that he continued doggedly to hold the institution together while time worked to heal the wounds was another of his greatest contributions to the University of California. Time did heal the wounds, and this can be looked upon as a triumph in drugless, Sproul therapy. The associated problems of intercollegiate athletics were equally frustrating, and, although not so much a threat to the structure of the University, they often periled its function and spirit.

In regard to both types of problems, Bob Sproul was undoubtedly aided by the fact that he himself was an alumnus of the University of California, and an alumnus who had taken an active part in association affairs from his election as permanent treasurer of his Class in 1913, and his election as Councilor and Treasurer of the California Alumni Association in 1917, until the time he was appointed President. During this period he came to know thousands of alumni from earlier and later classes, and they to know him as a friend. When his responsibilities for the welfare of the University suddenly expanded, he turned automatically to alumni as citizens who would understand his deep feeling and in some degree share that feeling. His long experience in Sacramento had also impressed upon him the fact that every alumnus was an important member of the family. Even the alumnus who took no pride in his affiliation with the University could not be ignored as an asset of little value, but had to be regarded as a potential liability unless he could be brought to understand the decree of *fiat lux*.

He was well aware that many alumni were more familiar with the roster of the varsity football squad than with the catalogue of the Academic Senate. But it was better, as he saw it, that an alumnus should know the football players than not know anyone at the University, and alternating praise or criticism following victory or defeat in athletics seemed preferable to chronic apathy. As a matter of fact, Bob Sproul did not need to look farther than his own reactions to know how alumni felt about intercollegiate sports. His own barometer rose and fell just as sensitively as any with each change in the athletic climate and he therefore knew when to expect emotional storms. No alumnus was more interested in attending intercollegiate competitions than the President himself, and none could wave his arms more wildly or cheer more loudly. But it was not the game alone that attracted him. It was also good to see old friends and make new acquaintances, and more than this, to participate in a gathering that brought alumni back to the campus voluntarily and eagerly, rather than with reluctant determination to discharge some obligation.

The more complex that civilization becomes, and the more diverse the responsibilities of a major university grow, the more difficult it is to preserve that common core of knowledge and community of intellectual interests that traditionally have been accepted as distinguishing the liberally educated from the technically proficient. The classical heritage that provided the common ground of knowledge and interest on which the minds of college men and women might meet and converse was steadily eroded away by progress and change. The serried ranks of black gowns and tasseled mortarboards at commencement grew longer as the ties that bound alumni to the university and to each other grew thinner, less personal, less intimate. Under such conditions an emotional interest in athletics is not necessarily a competitor with other ties between a university and its graduates. In a real sense it may fill a void.

Reflections like these seemed to influence President Sproul in his attitude toward intercollegiate athletics. From personal experience as an undergraduate in the days when able-bodied students turned out for one sport or another, not because they knew they were athletes, but to find out if they might be, he appreciated what it meant to make a team and, through disciplined effort in a common cause, win honors for the campus community and perhaps some little personal glory. He did not look on the contests of the few who made varsity teams as ends in themselves, but as part of the foundation for intramural programs on campus, and as a spark for the interest of thousands of youngsters engaged in sports at the high school level. Moreover, the strength of any group enterprise is related to individual pride in membership, and it is difficult to build such pride at the undergraduate level on statistical measures of academic virtue alone. The average freshman and sophomore may revere his Alma Mater in all sincerity but still vaguely wish she would do something to make singing, cheering, and marching in the streets appropriate—like roundly trouncing somebody's else revered Alma Mater on the gridiron or track oval.

In 1864, the year of California's first graduates, Benjamin Disraeli, Earl of Beaconsfield, summed up the then current controversy over evolution as simply a question of whether Man was descended from apes or angels, and he made clear to Oxford University that he stood on the side of the angels. In the long-continuing controversy over whether intercollegiate athletics were a liability or an asset to higher education, Robert Sproul stood for athletics as an asset regardless of how tainted they occasionally might become with commercialism and the insatiable quest for victory. However, he was also keenly aware that long before he became president many colleges and universities on the East Coast had found intercollegiate athletics a source of unbearable embarrassment. They had taken a diverting cub by the tail and suddenly discovered that the cub had turned into a full-sized bear. The problem for some of them proved to be a choice between evils, whether to hang on and tame the bear or let go and run for cover.

In the 1920's the Carnegie Foundation for the Advancement of Teaching published several reports on the threatening role of athletics in higher education. The third report, published in 1929, states: "The paid coach, the gate receipts, the special training tables, the costly sweaters and journeys in special Pullman cars, the recruiting from the high school, the demoralizing publicity showered on the players, the devotion of an undue proportion of time to training, the devices for putting a desirable athlete, but a weak scholar, across the hurdles of the examinations—these ought to stop and the intercollege and intramural sports be brought back to a stage in which they can be enjoyed by large numbers of students and where they do not involve an expenditure of time and money wholly at variance with any ideal of honest study."

However, the report further states: "The competitions and contests, the delight in bodily activity, the loyalties, and the honor that form a part of that vast organism called college athletics are the reflections in our college life of characteristics that are common to the youth of the world. In the pages that follow, these and other less pleasing phenomena of college athletics will be examined in the hope that those aspects which are good may in course of time achieve an unassailable predominance over those which are less worthy to survive. There can be no question of abolishing college athletics, nor should there be. What can be looked for is a gradual establishment through concrete action of a few general principles, to which all men would agree in the abstract. Even this slow change will be impossible without the sanction of an enlightened college and public opinion."

With all of the above, President Sproul, as his years of active service to the University of California drew to a close, would probably have agreed. Charges of professionalism were not entirely new. They had been bandied about soon after intercollegiate athletic contests began, in connection with rowing competition between Harvard and Yale in the 1850's. Over the years, various efforts were made to control the urge "to win at any cost" that seemed to precede other considerations just as surely as fingers came before forks. As early as 1879 the National Association of Amateur Athletes of America sought to define an amateur as one who had never competed in an open contest, or for a stake; for public money or gate money; or under a false name, or against a professional for a prize; or taught or pursued athletic exercises as a means of livelihood.

Colleges and universities, of course, were further concerned over the effect of amateur sports on the scholastic standing and health of students. In 1906 Benjamin Ide Wheeler and David Starr Jordan agreed that American football, as then played, caused too many injuries; so they switched California and Stanford to rugby. They expected that other Pacific Coast institutions would follow suit but only a few did, such as University of Nevada, Santa Clara, and Pomona. As a result, when California and Stanford found themselves unable to agree on eligibility of freshmen, and Benjamin Ide Wheeler severed athletic relations, there was no institution playing rugby which measured up to Big Game calibre. In the meantime, American football rules had been changed to make the game less dangerous; so in June of 1915 President Wheeler agreed to switch back to the American game. However, in the light of the Stanford experience, and prevailing practices at other institutions, he felt it was time to establish a basic code of conduct for intercollegiate athletics. In December, 1915, the Pacific Coast Conference was formed, and subsequently, Stanford readopted the American game and joined the Conference.

California's first games after the return to American football were rather discouraging. The coach had to take a trip to the East Coast to refresh his memory on rules and game strategy. Then came Andy Smith and the wonder teams, which apparently stirred all other teams in the Conference into an intensified player recruiting program. As a result California went into a slump, and in its turn decided that player recruiting needed intensification. The first organized effort under the Big "C" Society came in 1928, in part because of a protest by a member of the Class of 1928 that he had spent four years on the campus without ever seeing a football team or a track team win a single contest from either the University of Southern California or Stanford. He assured the Big "C" Society that this wasn't from lack of effort on the part of students or coaches. Alumni of the University of California at Los Angeles were equally sensitive on the subject, having been fielding teams for less than ten years, and having started so humbly that they were beaten 72–0 by Manual Arts High School and 103–0 by Whittier College in their first two football seasons.

Robert Gordon Sproul was not convinced that the University of California, with its relatively large enrollment, needed to scrabble with opponents for high school athletes in order to turn out effective teams. Unfortunately, in the year that he took over the presidency, the University of Southern California again drubbed Berkeley 74–0 and Los Angeles 52–0, and Stanford racked up scores of 41–0 and 20–0. Alumni leaders were convinced that the University of California could not compete against either of these rivals on the gridiron unless it also competed with them for high school stars. About this time the third report of the Carnegie Foundation for the Advancement of Teaching came out, and it seemed to confirm what the alumni claimed. The University of California was praised for having advocated a conference rule to prohibit athletic scholarships even though it had been offered a gift that would have made athletic awards possible. On the other hand, the report said: "The charge has been made, and evidence adduced to support it, that at a few institutions in the Mid-West and on the Pacific Coast, coaches, managers, athletes, and even university officers combine in a broad but intensive and systematic approach to prominent schoolboy athletes." The University of Southern California was named as the Pacific Coast member of this group. Stanford was named with the University of Southern California as being among the universities that maintained funds to provide "scholarships" for students selected as most worthy and needy, not by the faculty, but by the football coach. The magnitude of the two programs was made explicit by the mention of fifty-two scholarships at Stanford, and an annual fund of $40,000 at the University of Southern California.

In the face of all this President Sproul finally gave reluctant consent to a recruiting program provided that it did nothing more than sell the University of California as a first-class educational institution, and help students to find bona fide jobs off campus if they needed them. In explanation of this action he stated: "I should prefer that athletes come to the University without any solicitation whatever, even on the basis of the superior educational advantages we have to offer. The fact is, however, that high school stars are seldom, if ever, permitted to select a college or university on any such basis." He felt certain that any effort by the University of California to match other institutions in material benefits for athletes, even if it could be justified, would not accomplish the purpose that alumni believed it would. It would merely incite others to increase the intensity of competition.

Members of the faculty were concerned also by the pressure on coaches to turn out winning teams and by the intensified drill and training that took more and more of the student-athlete's time. During the season, they played on Saturdays and practiced every afternoon. Then they attended training tables, listened to chalk-talks, reviewed motion pictures of past games, and heard reports on opposing teams from scouts. They also traveled farther to play games. In 1935, President Sproul persuaded President Rufus B. von Kleinsmid of U.S.C. and President Ray Lyman Wilbur of Stanford to join him in a public plea for reason and sanity. Whatever effect this may have had on some individuals, it did not result in any general improvement in the situation.

The problem was not simply one of persuading a few intransigent individuals to obey generally accepted rules. Those who were interested in the athletic fortunes of a given institution of higher education seemed to feel that if their particular Alma Mater could not win under the rules then there was something wrong with the rules, and loyalty required that the rules be bent if necessary in the interests of practical justice. Such actions were further rationalized as a humanitarian attempt to prevent injustice to those young fellows who had to work their way through college and who could not afford to go out for sports unless they received help. The fact that pecuniary awards also went to prospective athletic stars who had no real financial need was dismissed as irrelevant or as a necessary concomitant of help to those who needed it. If all athletes were treated alike, solely on the basis of athletic ability, it was less embarrassing for those who really needed help to accept it, or so the rationalization went.

This effort to rationalize departures from tradition was just one aspect of an American cultural revolution. On the one hand, conservative leaders conscientiously proclaimed that: "An amateur sportsman is one who engages in sports for the physical, mental, or social benefits he derives therefrom, and to whom the sport is an avocation. Any college athlete who takes or is promised pay in any form for participation in athletics does not meet this definition of an amateur." On the other hand, there were thousands who felt that the traditional concept of an "amateur" athlete was just an antiquarian's delight, tracing back to good old England in the days when nobody went to college except the sons of the "upper crust." In their opinion this concept had no place in a country where all strata of society could aspire to college, and the majority of young people had to earn their own way, at least in part. Should the privilege of participating in sports be denied to the economically handicapped, or should they receive help? Athletic coaches, painfully aware of the fact that their jobs and means of livelihood depended on scoreboard statistics, usually found it easier to excuse illegal procedures that brought victory than to excuse defeats resulting from procedural virtue.

Universities thoughout the country were plagued by the fact that intercollegiate athletics had become such a popular form of public recreation, that academic conscience had to be compromised step by step to make sports "bigger and better" and thereby more truly American. Harvard and her closely related, so-called "stuffed shirt" Alma Maters, met this threat by restricting competition to members of the Ivy League, dedicated to holding athletics to their traditional peripheral position in academe. John R. Tunis, writing in the *Atlantic Monthly*, 1939, intimated that this was done as a means of assuring occasional victories for Harvard, and meeting the complaint that $4.00 was too much to pay for watching a football team play the way Harvard's did. The University of Chicago, after the humiliation of a 32–0 trouncing by almost-unheard-of College of the Pacific, in 1938, decided that the last straw had been loaded on the camel's back, and dropped intercollegiate football. President Robert M. Hutchins, writing in *The Saturday Evening Post*, made clear that "athleticism" was a kind of contagious disease that in his opinion could be cured only by taking money out of the games. This he felt was impossible because it would be resisted by students, alumni, the general public, and even the chief administrators of some colleges. He suggested that all of the problems might be settled overnight, if agreement could be reached to reduce the price of admission to about 10 cents.

The editors of the student newspapers at both Berkeley and Los Angeles commented on what President Hutchins had to say, and agreed with him in general that mounting commercial considerations in football should be restrained. The editor at Berkeley went further and suggested that if football could be saved for students of the future only over the dead bodies of some of the more rabid alumni, it might be worth trying.

President Sproul did not always see eye-to-eye with Robert Maynard Hutchins, and he also had the temerity to differ from the opinions of student newspaper editors on occasion. He expressed his deep concern time and time again over the dangers of competitive bidding for athletic talent, but he clearly considered abandonment of competitive athletics as a cure that was worse than the sickness. The record indicates that he consistently sought to establish something on the West Coast akin to the Ivy League on the East Coast. He was wise enough not to call it an Ivy League, or even to speak in praise of the Ivy League idea. Neither did he go around waving the banners of the Amateur Athletic Union or the National Collegiate Athletic Association. In the eyes of the Monday morning coaches, and the prophets of the fourth estate, this would have branded him as an effete at best and a traitor to "red-blooded" Americanism at worst. All his effort went into a fight for recognition of the fundamental point that a college athlete should first of all be a bona fide college student, and that as long as he continued to represent an institution of higher education he should maintain a satisfactory scholastic standing while making normal progress toward a degree.

Although it was true that several universities in the Pacific Coast Conference in the thirties did not have the same standards of admission or retention for students, athletic or nonathletic, as did the University of California, President Sproul was of the opinion that any institution calling itself a university should maintain such standards. He recognized the need for universities, state colleges, and junior colleges, each with a different educational responsibility, and each dedicated to discharging that responsibility in the best possible manner. It was his contention that no institution could offer all services to all kinds of talent and do a good job of it. In his opinion the rise of the University of California to greatness among universities of the world depended as much on the students it undertook to educate as on the faculty it gathered, each a stimulant for and dependent upon the other for the quality of result achieved. This may help to explain the persistence with which he worked to establish higher minimum scholastic standards for participation in intercollegiate sports. He felt that such standards would lay a good foundation on which to rebuild inter-institutional trust and respect.

The need for some kind of new foundation became apparent when the representatives making up the Board of the Pacific Coast Conference agreed to sponsor a survey of the degree to which the athletic enterprises of its member institutions were being conducted in compliance with the Conference code. The results of that survey, known as the Edwin C. Atherton report of 1939, so astonished the Conference Board that it promptly employed Mr. Atherton as Conference Commissioner for the purpose of investigating and, hopefully, minimizing the incidence of code infractions.

But the Conference Board was in a difficult position. Many coaches, athletic directors, and distinguished alumni took the position that the code was unrealistic, and that, like the Prohibition Amendment, it was unenforceable. Private, high-tuition universities maintained that they could not compete on a fair basis with public universities that had no tuition fees or only nominal ones. So in 1940 the Conference voted to permit any university in the Conference to make a grant-in-aid to an athlete in an amount equal to the difference between its own fee charge and the lowest fee schedule of any other university in the Conference. The argument was that this would eliminate the incentive to make illegal offers to high school stars.

President Sproul did not agree with those who believed that recruiters of athletic talent wanted merely an even break with other institutions. He was inclined to believe that the legalization of tuition scholarships for athletes would merely establish a new floor on bidding to get this or that high school star. The object of the game still remained the same—to persuade a particularly desirable prospect to choose one college rather than another, and if other sales arguments failed to work there would still be the temptation to make some additional, clandestine offer. Although the University of California did not charge tuition to legal residents of the state, it did require the payment of an incidental fee to cover some part of the cost of supplementary services by the libraries, gymnasiums, and student health services. Its fee structure, while low, was higher than that at some other public universities in the Conference, and under the new rules it would have been possible to offer prospective athletes a small amount of help, and the easiest course would have been to permit such offers to be made. But President Sproul, although never insistent on doing things to which the majority were opposed, was adamant against doing things which the crowd wanted done when he was convinced those things were wrong. He decreed that the University of California would not make any offers to athletes that were unavailable to other students. The staff at Los Angeles eventually was able to persuade him that the special circumstance created by the University of Southern California in the same city, made it essential that both operate under the same rules, as permitted by the Conference; but at Berkeley he held his ground for ten eventful years.

Long before this decade ended, it was obvious that the strategy of the Pacific Coast Conference was not working. The tuition-equalizing rule was supposed to make the code more realistic and to minimize rule infractions, but it fell far short of accomplishing this end. And this was not the only difficulty. The representatives of universities serving on the Conference Board found themselves in an impossible situation. There was no discernible single code of right conduct by which they could guide themselves. The largest and loudest chorus of voices sought constantly to impress upon them that the troubles they met were caused by their own rules rather than by the actions of coaches, athletic directors, and alumni. They were under constant pressure by their institutional groups to stop other universities from breaking the rules and to penalize them for every infraction. At the same time they were expected to function as defense attorneys when the institution they represented was under fire for similar rule infractions. But they were also expected to function as impartial judges in determining guilt and assessing penalties.

Some of the representatives had been on the Conference Board so long that they had become accustomed to a world of athletics that seemed to require its own codes of morals and ethics and needed protection from the naive and unrealistic thinking of inexperienced university teachers and university presidents. In this world the legalizing of tuition scholarships for athletes had seemed an essential bit of common sense. But time after time the Conference felt called upon to reject President Sproul's recommendation that the basic criterion of eligibility to participate in intercollegiate athletics should be demonstrated ability to perform satisfactorily as a college student. Whereas the University of California required a "C" average for continuation in college and for graduation, the PCC accepted a "D" grade as a minimum criterion of eligibility to play football.

The Academic Senate, the President's Administrative Advisory Council, and President Sproul could see no logic in permitting a student on the ragged edge of dismissal for low scholarship to give time to any extracurricular activity. Yet under the Pacific Coast Conference rules such a student was to be permitted to represent his institution in intercollegiate competition. Under this double code of behavior it was possible for a head yell-leader to be barred from his post for unsatisfactory scholarship whereas football players with approximately the same low standing continued to play, and at one point this happened. Needless to say, the pressure was great for the University of California to abandon its own standards and to allow the Pacific Coast Conference to establish a more realistic level of achievement. The fact they neglected, as President Sproul pointed out, was that some students would just fail to meet the requirement, however low it might be set, and that the vast majority of students looked to the standards as a gauge of the effort they should make. He felt that young people want only to know what is expected of them, and he had faith in their ability to meet that expectation.

Alumni and Intercollegiate Athletics

The fact that Pacific Coast Conference standards for athletes were making mediocrity respectable and putting pressure on all universities to conform if they wished to compete, was recognized by most of the presidents of the universities involved. One or two of them admitted that they were in a vulnerable position because any rise in the scholastic requirements for intercollegiate competition would make it more difficult to be an athlete than to matriculate or graduate at their particular institutions. President Sproul corresponded with all of them as to what might be done. There was general concern over the practice that coaches and athletic directors had adopted of holding meetings at the same time and place as the meetings of the Pacific Coast Conference Board. As a result it seemed that the Conference Board members were kept more aware of the problems of athletic departments than they were of general university problems. To meet this situation several presidents agreed that they should follow the same practice of meeting together when the Board of the Conference met, provided that President Sproul would assume leadership in persuading all presidents to participate. It was pointed out that he had been the principal advocate of radical changes, he was senior president, and for the moment California teams were doing well and were not under indictment for any illegalities. He could, therefore, take the initiative without being accused of acting through pique. Bob Sproul accepted the challenge, and all the other presidents accepted his invitation. The Council of Presidents met first on February 28, 1950, and continued to hold two or more meetings each year thereafter. It is possible that another president could have accomplished the same thing, but it is significant that all turned to him for leadership and accepted that leadership.

At the start it appeared that some of President Sproul's high hopes might be realized. Recommendations were made to the Pacific Coast Conference, then instructions were issued, and finally the matter of determining the tenure of the Conference Commissioner was taken over by the presidents. But it became more clear as time passed, that even the presidents could not fully control intercollegiate athletics. A horde of people, including athletic department staffs, some students, many alumni, sports writers, and a considerable segment of the general public, seemed to believe that intercollegiate athletics were too important in their own right to be hampered by purely academic considerations. Representatives on the Pacific Coast Conference felt that under the circumstances they had done as much as could be done to preserve respect for rules, and the decision to form a Presidents' Council seemed to imply that they had failed and that they could not be trusted to continue the job alone. They also felt that the ideas expressed by the presidents might be fine in theory but that they were very impractical.

While the presidents were organizing to put the brakes on further professionalization of undergraduate athletes, the Conference voted to permit tuition grants-in-aid at all institutions, and alumni were organizing to legalize grants-in-aid, not only for tuition, but for full subsistence. The Pacific Coast Conference again inclined to give up a restriction that they couldn't enforce and retreat to some better defensive position. The presidents, however, convinced that the atmosphere was already ominously unhealthy, voted to oppose further relaxation of rules even though they knew they would be heavily criticized for it. The presidents were convinced that the pressure for subsidization came not from the athletes themselves but from those engaged in recruiting, and that every rise in the ceiling on financial aid merely established a new floor from which competitive bidding started.

Three times in 1953 and 1954 the Council of Presidents rejected a recommendation from a special committee of the Pacific Coast Conference that the limit on subsidies be raised. Five times between 1953 and 1955 the Conference countered by rejecting a request from the Council of Presidents that a qualitative scholarship standard be established for eligibility to participate in intercollegiate competition. The Council of Presidents also tried to reduce the pressure on players and coaches by eliminating postseason, intersectional contests, but the storm stirred up by Rose Bowl supporters in Pasadena was more than they could withstand. President Sproul again experienced that "voice crying in the wilderness" feeling, but this time, at least, he had the presidents of other Pacific Coast universities standing with him.

Alumni and Intercollegiate Athletics

The tug-of-war went merrily on. The Council of Presidents agreed that it would be a step in the right direction to eliminate spring football practice. The Pacific Coast Conference twice voted against the presidents who had appointed them, reluctantly agreed with them the third time, and then under pressure from coaches reversed themselves a few months before the new rule was to go into effect in 1956. The presidents managed to bring an end to postseason basketball on their second attempt, but could not get support from their representatives for the shortening of both football and basketball seasons. The Conference representatives, however, did put a limit on the number of hours of practice per week—a more practical solution they felt. A request that they eliminate freshman competition was met by a compromise reducing the length of the playing schedule.

In a further effort to clean their own houses, the presidents insisted that the Pacific Coast Conference give more investigative authority to the Conference Commissioner, and each of them agreed to issue a warning to all coaches and athletic directors that would conclude with the following statement: "The purpose of this letter is to call the foregoing facts to your attention, to affirm in the most emphatic terms that it is the policy of this institution to conduct its intercollegiate athletic program in complete compliance with the rules, policies, and objectives of the Conference, and to advise you that I must hold you personally and individually responsible for your participation, directly or indirectly, in any activity involving the offer or grant of illegal subsidization to athletes."

One great blow to President Sproul was his inability to get Conference support for the C-average rule for participation in intercollegiate athletics. The University of California could not justify lower scholastic concessions for athletes unless it lowered its standards across the board for all students. To do this would have lowered the level of expected performance and started a whole chain of regressive concessions. But it was too much to expect coaches to compete against institutions offering greater leeway on scholastic effort, and also passing out tuition grants-in-aid. So in 1955 President Sproul reluctantly gave up his restriction on grants-in-aid to cover fees for athletes. But in doing so he sent the following instructions to all chief campus officers: "I am firmly opposed to the diversion of any regular scholarship or other University funds to this program. Moreover, since compulsory student association fees have now been approved by the Regents and are being collected by University officers for the account of the student associations, I would question the equity and advisability, if not indeed the actual legality, of making grants to one group of students from funds to which all others are compelled to contribute as a condition of University attendance. Furthermore, considering the rather erratic financial history of both student associations over the past seven or eight years, together with their desires to undertake additional financial commitments toward new unions, it would seem scarcely prudent that they assume this additional overhead expense . . . [therefore] all funds for the grant-in-aid program must be donated for the specific purpose."

Before making this decision he took the precaution of notifying other Pacific Coast Conference presidents that he was proposing only to permit help to athletes that all other institutions were already offering under Conference rules. He wanted assurance that his action would not be misused as a justification for another increase in the established level of aid to athletes. Each offer of illegal aid to a young high school graduate involved an assurance from some older man that it was all right to break the rules because everybody was doing it, and led the young men aided to perjure themselves by signing statements denying that they had received illegal aid. It tended to create a cynical attitude on the part of all students, indicated by passing remarks about the "campus Hessians" and "our paid gladiators." But no one realized how quickly the roof would blow off and demonstrate the fallacy of relaxing rules to save them from being broken.

In February, 1956, a national magazine revealed that an organized program of illegal payments to athletes was in existence at the University of Washington. Within a month, a former UCLA football player described an illegal athletic aid program at Los Angeles, and in May a secret fund for USC athletes was brought to light. President Sproul requested that all campuses of the University of California make an immediate investigation. This brought to light technical infractions at Berkeley also. Payments to cover fees were permissible under the rules of the Conference, but they had to be made with the knowledge of the administration, and the coaches at Berkeley had been maintaining an undeclared fund to meet registration fees of newly arriving athletes.

In life's most humiliating moments, President Sproul would probably have to accord high place to those in which these revelations were made. Not only was the University of California involved in activities that he had been fighting for years to eliminate, but coaches and others whose cooperation he had personally requested had connived in the violations and encouraged undergraduate students to join in the conniving. He was additionally mortified to find that what had occurred aroused little contrition. Instead there was violent anger on the part of some of those declared guilty because the Pacific Coast Conference penalized them for breaking rules that others, not yet exposed, had also broken. In the aftermath of this devastating discovery, it was extraordinarily difficult to keep alive the great tradition that competitive athletics were important in the development of good sportsmanship and high character. One coach made the public statement that they were in a mess and would continue to be as long as rules were imposed that had not been made by athletic people themselves. In other words, universities were a thorn in the flesh to leaders of athletics.

Despite the criticism leveled at him, President Sproul supported the Pacific Coast Conference in its contention that those discovered and found guilty of rule infractions should be penalized regardless of whether all of the guilty had been uncovered. He considered it most important that all universities take steps to prevent any recurrence in the future, and suggested to the Pacific Coast Conference that it review its penalties only to make certain that they had been assessed equitably. The presidents of the Conference universities, in a series of three meetings over a period of two months, agreed with President Sproul that if the Conference were to survive it would need to be greatly strengthened in the rules to which it subscribed. They agreed unanimously that financial assistance to athletes, including on-campus jobs and grants-in-aid, should be restricted to those in need as determined by university scholarship committees or boards, and should be administered by regular university agencies. They further agreed unanimously that qualitative academic standards of eligibility for intercollegiate athletics should be adopted forthwith, and that every athlete and every institution should make annual reports on financial assistance received and scholastic record achieved. It appeared to President Sproul that progress was finally about to be made. The Regents of the University of California had already endorsed such a program.

But the question of who was running intercollegiate athletics, and for whom, and why, had not yet been settled. The representatives of the presidents on the Board of the Conference at first accepted the agreement, and then point by point in three subsequent meetings either failed to take action or voted against the provisions of the agreement. They then went further, on the advice of coaches, athletic directors, and alumni, and approved a subsidy program including higher pay rates for athletes than nonathletes. However, by a 5–4 vote they did accept a qualitative scholarship standard for eligibility, even though they agreed to wait three years before putting it into effect.

Alumni who remembered the day when they managed to carry a full academic load, work in their spare time, and go out for intercollegiate athletics for the fun of it warned President Sproul that universities could not compete with professional teams, and that the real value of athletics in the educational situation lay in their nonprofessional, amateur character. They were of the opinion that the precarious financial position of the intercollegiate sports program was a result of declining public interest. This point appeared to be worth checking so President Sproul requested an informal analysis back over a twenty-year period. The figures compiled did not substantiate the view that there had been a decline in public interest, but did reveal something else. Both the ASUC at Berkeley, and the ASUCLA were having greater difficulty balancing their books in the period 1953–56 than had been true in 1936–39. But this was not caused by a decline in ticket sales.

In fact, income from intercollegiate athletics was up some 200 per cent at Los Angeles, and 79 per cent at Berkeley, the latter percentage being smaller because the base from which it was computed was larger. What caused the trouble was an even greater increase in the cost of fielding teams. At Los Angeles the cost went up 275 per cent, and at Berkeley it went up 175 per cent. General price increases played a part in this change, but the crucial factors seemed to be increases in the size of coaching staffs and a change in relative pay levels, mounting costs of training tables, and, most important of all, the inauguration of subsidized jobs on campus at artificially high rates of pay for subnormal productivity. As one alumnus commented when shown the Los Angeles figures, "If a $61,000 deficit is the price we paid for a Conference Championship and a game in the Rose Bowl, maybe we could save money by losing a few games."

All of this tended to confirm President Sproul's feeling that the people who were prescribing rules for intercollegiate athletics, conscientious as they might be, were not helping the situation. Consequently, he went back to the Council of Presidents with a list of five basic principles, approved by the Regents of the University, which he considered essential to the health of college sports.

(1) Eligibility for participation in intercollegiate athletics, freshman or varsity, shall be limited to students who have achieved a grade-point average of not less than 2.5 in high school or college preparatory courses, or 2.3 in junior college, or 2.0 (C) in senior college or university courses.

(2) Tuition grants-in-aid shall be awarded only to eligible athletes who have been selected by the university or college committee on undergraduate scholarships on the basis of need.

(3) Wage rates, both on-campus and off-campus, shall be no higher for athletes than for nonathletes, and no athlete shall be paid for time he has not spent or work he has not done. Campus representative jobs shall not be permitted. Eligible athletes may receive subsistence grants-in-aid, subject to need, in amount not exceeding the reduction in income due to loss of work opportunity during practice and playing seasons.

(4) Each institution shall be responsible for the enforcement of its published policies as to 1, 2, and 3, above, and shall agree to make available on request full information regarding the academic standing and financial aid of its athletes, both in the institution itself and in the schools from which they have come.

(5) Scheduling of games shall be subject only to the free choice of each institution, consistent with the principles stated in 1, 2, 3, and 4, above.

President Sproul was reasonably certain, before he presented these five points, that they would be accepted by his fellow presidents, and he was hopeful that the men they had chosen to represent them on the Board of the Pacific Coast Conference, whether they were in complete agreement or not, would consent to accept the advice of the administrators, which also reflected the attitude of the faculties. But to his consternation, after the Council of Presidents agreed to the principles, and the Board of the Conference voted to go along, there was again vacillation, a reconsideration, and finally flat rejection of the new policy. It appeared, again, that the opinions of coaches, athletic directors, and interested alumni were more determinative of policy than the decisions of the presidents.

When the Regents of the University were informed of what happened, they directed the President to issue a statement that read as follows:

"The University of California, having made every reasonable effort, without success, to secure acceptance by the Pacific Coast Conference of its principles of intercollegiate athletic competition as adopted on June 21, 1957, hereby reaffirms these principles and announces with regret its decision, to be made effective by giving immediate notice to the Conference, to withdraw from the Conference after fulfilling existing membership obligations extending through June 30, 1959.

"The University of California, Berkeley and Los Angeles, will: (1) Make every effort to schedule major sports with institutions having admissions and academic programs as nearly comparable to its own as is reasonably possible; and (2) Treat athletes on the same basis as all other students, taking into consideration such special circumstances affecting the student in athletics as would clearly warrant separate treatment consistent with the maintenance of high academic standards."

President Sproul sadly recapitulated the events leading up to this situation as follows:

> May I remind you that the requirements for granting aid to athletes, to which the Regents of my University are now committed, were endorsed by the Council of Presidents on last November 5, again on December 2, and still again on January 4. Yet, the Conference, after adopting this plan January 4 by a vote of 7–2, later rejected it, and instead, authorized a program which (1) continues to approve paying athletes at higher rates than nonathletes, and (2) allows athletes to receive pay for hours in which they have not worked, on the basis of "compensation for loss of opportunity to work" with no demonstration of need required to secure such payment. Thus the Conference violates the Constitution of the National Collegiate Athletic Association. The rules now approved by the Pacific Coast Conference also contravene those of the Amateur Athletic Union (and, it should be remembered, only those certified by the A.A.U. as "amateurs" may participate in the Olympic Games), which provide that "A person shall cease to be eligible to compete as an amateur . . . by accepting, directly or indirectly, any payment for loss of time or wages in attending or training for any athletic competition."

In a later, more personal statement to a president of a Conference university, President Sproul said:

> Believe me, the University of California's decision to withdraw from the P.C.C. after forty years of membership, was taken in no mood of exultation, but one of sadness and regret, and only after patient efforts to arrive at a basis for continuation had brought repeated disappointment and final failure.
>
> It has been at least a decade since we presidents, in our correspondence among one another, began to express concern over the deterioration of the Conference; and in an effort to save the situation, we started to meet seven years ago. Even then, we surmised that conditions had become ominously unhealthy—that a substantial proportion of football players and of star performers in other sports were being professionalized, and that the concomitant hypocrisy and bad faith were even more pernicious. Although the Conference had assumed responsibility for enforcing its code through a Commissioner, we then discovered that not one case of subsidization with evidence sufficient for taking disciplinary action had been developed during the preceding decade. Thereupon, we urged the Conference to provide the Commissioner with additional assistance and to take other more vigorous action to enforce its own rules.

Alumni and Intercollegiate Athletics

Two years ago, when a newspaper reporter disclosed code violations at Westwood, I immediately ordered rigorous investigations of their athletic programs by the campus administrations at Los Angeles and also at Berkeley, and those led to further evidence of infractions. With this self-examination, the University also undertook formulation of an athletic policy that would be in keeping with its traditions and objectives as an academic institution. The Academic Senate, North and South, not only participated but assumed leadership in the development of the five principles of a policy which received endorsement by the Associated Students of both campuses, and by the University administration—President and Chancellors. This was presented to The Regents last June and, adopting it by unanimous vote, they committed the University of California to its achievement, within or without the Pacific Coast Conference.

There was certainly no thought that this action would present the Conference with an "insurmountable hurdle." That athletes, like other students, should receive financial aid only when they demonstrate need has been accepted by both the Ivy League and the Big Ten Conference, and has been affirmed and reaffirmed repeatedly by our Council of Presidents—the last time a year ago. The principle that wage rates shall be no higher for athletes than for nonathletes, and athletes be paid only for work done has been approved by the N.C.A.A. Council. That institutions in athletic competition should exchange full information regarding the academic standing of and financial aid received by their student athletes was recommended by the Executive Committee of the American Council on Education in 1952, and approved unanimously by our Council of Presidents a year ago. That conferences can operate successfully upon the basis of assumption of full responsibility by member institutions for adherence to their own declared principles is demonstrated by the Ivy League. While concluding that opponents should be chosen from among institutions with entrance and other academic standards approximating its own, the University of California, in its announcement, specified requirements that still are substantially below its own.

As was indicated at our last meeting of presidents, the University of California did not expect, nor does it now expect, to achieve all these principles at once; but, to quote the Supreme Court decisions in the segregation cases, it is committed to their attainment "with all deliberate speed." Had the Conference, at its last meeting, demonstrated the aspiration to arrive at a basis for its preservation that prevailed during the preceding discussions among the presidents, its efforts could have resulted in success. The obvious absence of such a spirit, the flat rejection of all of the principles adopted by the governing body of this University, and the destruction of all hope for their achievement in the future left the University of California with no honorable alternative but withdrawal.

Alumni and Intercollegiate Athletics

Without question, the collapse of the Pacific Coast Conference was a great disappointment to Robert Sproul. He had hoped that it could be molded into the instrument it was originally designed to be, and that it would be a bulwark of defense for higher education in the face of emotionally charged public opinion. A less persistent fighter for what he felt to be right could have found ample reason for ignoring the trends and pouring oil on the troubled waters when storms threatened. President Sproul chose the less popular path, and his attitude was in part, at least, responsible for the equally strong stand taken by other presidents, some of whom were in a more difficult position than the head of the University of California. Even though the strength they evinced in union was not sufficient to overcome the opposition, it may prove, in the end, to have been more significant than a victory. No set of principles, dependent for their effectiveness upon the voluntary support of private citizens, could long survive in the atmosphere of opposition that prevailed in the late 1950's. The presidents made public their stand, and the collapse of the Conference clearly indicated that these were principles worth fighting for and deserving of more consideration than they had received. As Montaigne once said: "There are some defeats more triumphant than victories."

A good linesman in football seldom experiences the triumph of running half the length of the field and falling into the end zone with the ball in his arms amid deafening cheers from the rooting section, but his less spectacular efforts may often save the day. In the matter of intercollegiate athletics Bob Sproul's part shows up more clearly in the postgame motion picture review than it did at the time he played it. And the same can be said of his efforts to hold together the alumni of the world's first multicampus university. This is not meant to imply that he was just holding the line as far as alumni were concerned. Some of his most valiant opponents were also his greatest friends. They disagreed with him but even while doing so they defended his right to be stubborn, and they often made up for their opposition on one point by the enthusiastic support they rendered on other issues. When he suggested to alumni in 1934 that they ought to start a scholarship program for outstanding young people with economic handicaps, without regard to their athletic ability, they all pitched in to help. He suggested that alumni in various areas of the state raise an annual fund to help those top students who might have difficulty going to college at all without assistance.

With the approval of the Regents, President Sproul offered to match a specific amount of money for scholarships in each district. That is, he promised to augment funds which alumni might raise amongst themselves up to a definite maximum for each district, and to coordinate the work of undergraduate scholarship committees on the various campuses with alumni selection committees. The district organizations might refer prospective students to the University authorities, and the University would refer scholarship applicants to the district organizations of alumni. It was understood that a prospective student from any given district could select any campus of the University which he or she desired. In the first year there were just thirteen California Alumni Scholarship winners. By 1954–55 the number of scholarships awarded by Berkeley alumni alone increased to 219 a year, and a similar steady growth was achieved by the smaller and younger organization of Los Angeles alumni. Over a period of twenty-five years the Berkeley alumni committees participated in the award of more than 3,000 scholarships to young people from sixty different communities, involving cash awards of almost a million dollars. Scholarships were awarded to all winners in the annual competition but the cash award was varied with the degree of need in each individual case.

President Sproul early recognized that if the alumni scholarship program were to grow as he felt it should, he would have to find an additional source of matching funds. What he did is indicated by a letter written to Comptroller James H. Corley in 1946. "Beginning as early as 1936 and continuing down to 1941, I have been considering and proposing in various quarters the establishment of a system of state scholarships designed to equalize to a certain extent the educational opportunities of young men and women all over California, i.e., to put the high school graduate living in Alpine County or San Bernardino County on a basis comparable to the high school graduate living in Berkeley or Los Angeles. Most recently, you will remember, I proposed that a bill be introduced in the Legislature of 1941, but you thought that this would not be timely, and suggested postponement to 1943. Then the war intervened. Your recent letter renews my interest, and indicates that you believe that legislative approval of a well-planned program is now likely. Therefore, I am asking you to serve as chairman of a committee to work out a program and draft a bill for submission to the Legislature of 1947."

This plan did work out, and state support of university scholarships that had remained frozen at $3,500 a year from 1897 on, was brought up to date. Within three years the state was making $64,000 a year available for scholarships and thereby increasing the incentive for alumni to raise additional funds. Alumni had earlier taken the lead in raising funds for the California Memorial Stadium, for student union buildings at Berkeley, Davis, and San Francisco, and individuals or class organizations established a long list of special endowment funds for scholarships, loans, library development, art exhibitions, and expendable funds for benches, fountains, walks, etc. President Sproul's own class, the Class of 1913, which he modestly described as perhaps not the best class in the history of the University, but just a better class than any other, on its Fiftieth Anniversary, presented a gift of $50,000 to the Regents to establish a permanent endowment to be designated as the Robert G. and Ida A. Sproul, Class of 1913 Scholarship Fund. In the same appreciatory spirit, Camille J. Ehrenfels, Class of 1905, left a bequest for the sculpturing of a bust of Robert Sproul and the casting of two bronze replicas, one for the Berkeley campus and one for the Los Angeles campus.

It is doubtful whether any public university in the United States has enjoyed the sustained and effective support of a greater number of its alumni over a longer period of time than has the University of California. The growth of organized strength began in the early 1920's with the drafting of Robert Sibley, Class of 1903, as Executive Manager of the California Alumni Association. No one realized better than he that the day-to-day loyalty that promotes and maintains membership in an alumni association requires something more than fading memories of undergraduate days and football teams. He found what he needed in the personality and voice of Robert Gordon Sproul first as Comptroller, then as Vice-President, and finally as President, backed up by programmed service to the alumni themselves. To bring the University to life in distant parts of California he arranged alumni breakfasts, luncheons and dinners, and with the cooperation of President Sproul covered as many as possible of these on a circuit-riding basis. In the earliest of these programs it was considered essential to send with President Sproul an entourage made up largely of football coaches, yell-leaders, and glee club singers. But as time went on there came the surprising discovery that alumni, although enthusiastic about athletics, were just as much interested in hearing reports on the work of the University from President Sproul and a group of faculty members. As a result, the programs were gradually transformed from purely revival meetings for the old college spirit to cultural events for the communities in which they were held, and local alumni took increasing pride in the fact that their programs were not just private gatherings, but public events. To back this up there came, in addition to the traditional offer of preferential seating at intercollegiate athletic competitions, the idea of family summer camps, first near Shasta Lake, then at Pinecrest, and, finally, at Tahoe.

Reference has already been made to the problem that President Sproul faced in holding the University of California together after the establishing of a southern branch in Los Angeles. A long-standing rivalry between the two ends of the state, sometimes less than friendly, was accentuated by competition from the rapidly growing south in the field of higher education. Some were fearful that the birth of a University of California, Los Angeles, would be the end of their dreams for a truly great university on the Pacific Coast. It was difficult, in 1919, to conceive of a time when not only two, but as many as nine, public, first-class general campuses would be included in the master plan of university education in the state. Added to this general doubt concerning the wisdom of a multicampus university, and the skepticism in the south as to the future of a Los Angeles campus dominated by what was still regarded as a northern California rather than a statewide institution, there was a more personal and immediate problem. When the Los Angeles State Normal School became a part of the University of California there came with it a faculty that found itself, overnight, transmuted from leadership in the normal school field, to the bottom rung of the ladder in an established university system. They could not help but be aware that the qualifications they presented were in a number of cases not the same as those that the University of California required of members of its teaching staff. The note of insecurity that this injected into many lives was deepened by various intimations that the normal school tradition that they represented would be a drag on the institution until additions to the faculty created a university atmosphere. The fact that many of these teachers proved to be among the most valuable staff members of the new University, in administration as well as in teaching and research, did not mitigate the group feeling of resentment that arose when it was proposed that the University be moved to its new campus at Westwood, leaving the Normal School and most of its staff on Vermont Avenue.

As late as 1926, Director Ernest C. Moore felt it necessary to say:

"I am frequently asked how long it will be before the Southern Branch is an independent state university. Those who ask that question think of institutions only as they have known them; they have not asked themselves what they must become. If anyone will meditate on that aspect of the State University's existence he will see that it must always be one. It will not at all times be easy to keep it one. There are many factors of pride and locality that will seek to dismember it, but the conviction of every one of us should on all counts remain what it was at first—that the higher education of a state cannot flourish if its parts are set to contending against each other; and since that is so there is no degree of patience or self-denial too great to be summoned to the task of keeping it one."

The University of California had the rare distinction of possessing alumni before it officially opened its doors. This came about because it was preceded by the College of California, which began conferring degrees in 1864. The Trustees of the College of California, as mentioned previously, offered the assets of the institution—land, buildings, books, and other equipment—to the state on the condition that the state legislature would rescind its first decision to establish a college of agriculture and mechanic arts and plan for a real university instead, and that it would count as its own such degrees as had already been conferred. This offer was accepted, and, as a result, the University of California moved into an already established educational enterprise with a roster of nineteen rather extraordinary alumni, fourteen of whom went on to take higher degrees, and one of whom, John L. Beard, became the first alumnus on the Board of Regents.

This interest of alumni in the life of the University, starting with the appointment of an alumnus as Regent in 1876, continued and grew. By 1909 the alumni were sufficiently numerous and organized to secure the passage of an amendment to the political code of the state, naming the President of the California Alumni Association as an ex officio Regent. This was technically an unconstitutional action, but it met with such popular acceptance that no one challenged it, and in 1918 the people of the state removed the shadow of illegitimacy by approving a revision of the constitution.

The fact that there were already three campuses of the University of California in 1918 did not create any problem in selecting the alumnus who would serve as Regent because there was one commencement ceremony at Berkeley at which graduates from all three campuses received their degree certificates, and there was one California Alumni Association to which all belonged. But this pleasantly uncomplicated life did not last long after the decision was made to establish a fourth campus in Los Angeles. In the early years, while the southern branch was building up from a two-year institution to a four-year institution, the problem was not crucial, because those who matriculated in the south transferred to Berkeley or to one of the other two campuses to complete their work for degrees. But by the time Robert Gordon Sproul became president, the University of California at Los Angeles was a four-year institution and already had granted 3,791 bachelor degrees to young people who had done all of their undergraduate work in the south, and who had attended commencement services there because it was impractical to continue the tradition of one graduation ceremony for an institution with campuses more than 400 miles apart.

It was generally hoped, on the older campuses, that the graduates of the University of California at Los Angeles would join with graduates of Berkeley, Davis, and San Francisco as members of the California Alumni Association, and many did, for a number of years. But the schismatic factors already outlined contributed to a growing conviction on the part of the southern alumni that the Los Angeles campus would need to fight for its place in the sun, and if alumni were to play their part in that fight they should stay clear of any organization dominated by the larger, longer established, and financially stronger alumni group with headquarters at Berkeley. In 1934, the alumni of the Los Angeles campus voted to sever connection with the California Alumni Association and make their own way. President Sproul remained hopeful throughout most of his term in office that his personal interest in strengthening the University of California at Los Angeles would eventually eliminate the skepticism and suspicion of the staff, and that in reflection of this, southern alumni would recognize the value of one large association, both with regard to the services that such an association could render its own membership, and with regard to the services that such an association could render to the University. The President was correct in his opinion that time eventually would overcome much of the antagonism between the parts of the University, south and north, but he found that he was entirely too optimistic about the length of time it would take. Despite his personal efforts to meet the ambitions of the southern campus, the efforts of the California Club, and later the good results of the All-University Faculty Conference, there remained a hard core of graduates of the early, rather bitter years, whose loyalties, apparently, were unregenerate.

The California Alumni Association, urged on by President Sproul, and further stimulated by Executive Manager Robert Sibley, made various attempts to win Los Angeles alumni back to the Association under one or another plan that would protect their needs for a locally strong organization with sectional as well as statewide interests. But none of these plans worked out satisfactorily. The situation was in some ways reminiscent of that prevailing in the late 1890's when efforts began to bring about a closer affiliation between the alumni of the affiliated colleges in San Francisco and the alumni of Berkeley although in that case the San Francisco group wanted to be recognized and the Alumni Association at Berkeley long maintained that the continued existence of separate boards of trustees for the affiliated institutions, and the limited length of degree curricula, made their graduates ineligible. There was, moreover, a greater urgency about a working relationship between the alumni of the Los Angeles campus and the California Alumni Association, because completely separate alumni associations might eventually lead to demands for two alumni representatives on the Board of Regents, each of whom would feel obligated by the presence of the other to give primary attention to the sectional interests of his own constituency, and thereby change the traditional character of Board deliberations.

By 1936 it was clear that President Sproul was justified in his concern over the separation movement by Los Angeles alumni. In that year they indicated their urgent desire to be represented on the Board of Regents, either by participating in the selection of the alumnus who served, or, preferably, by amending the constitution to provide for a second alumnus to represent the University of California at Los Angeles, just as the existing one, they felt, represented the three older-established campuses. The California Alumni Association, in turn, offered to give up its privilege of being represented on the Board of Regents every year, and to support a request that the President of the Alumni Association of the University of California at Los Angeles be permitted to serve as Regent ex officio in alternate years. Unfortunately, this simple solution was found to be not legally possible under the wording of the state constitution.

Los Angeles alumni then proposed a plan whereby the two associations, in addition to their separate councils, would establish a third, joint council presided over by a president to be elected alternately from the north and from the south. President Sproul lent his support to the proposal although he was skeptical that Berkeley, Davis, and

San Francisco alumni would agree to one provision giving Los Angeles, with less than a fourth of the combined alumni group, equal representation on the joint council. There was no objection to the alternation of representation on the Board of Regents, but the provision for equal representation on the joint council was considered to be unrealistic. In notifying Los Angeles alumni of this reaction by Berkeley alumni, President Sproul took cognizance of the fact that some Los Angeles alumni were actively considering a constitutional amendment to have the president of their association named as an additional Regent ex officio, and he wrote: "If there were one representative from UCLA and one from Berkeley on the Board, they would tend to represent their own particular campuses and thus break down unity of spirit. A great factor in the strength of the University of California, in comparison with other state universities, has been that its Board of Regents has consisted, not of representatives of localities or parts of the institution, but of men whose devotion and service were given to the University as a whole."

The leaders of the California Alumni Association, in the months that followed, gave written assurance to the Alumni Association of UCLA, that although there might be difficulties involved in negotiating a workable merger plan, they were on record as supporting UCLA in its contention that graduates of that campus should share in representation on the Board of Regents. In the interim they offered to recommend to the Regents that the President of the UCLA alumni be invited to attend all meetings of the Board, and to participate in discussions. They further offered to have the President of the California Alumni Association confer with the President of the UCLA Association, prior to voting on any matter of particular concern to UCLA.

Two compromise plans for organizations of alumni were presented to the Regents of the University in 1939, but no action was taken on them at that time. In explanation of the compromise plans President Sproul said: "I should feel that I had done less than my duty if I did not inform the Board that these proposals represent an attempt on the part of two great groups of the University's alumni to correct a situation which is not 'for the good of the University.' The people of the state undoubtedly intended, when they amended the Constitution in 1918, that at least one Regent be chosen from the whole body of the University's alumni. Today that Regent is in fact chosen from a portion of the University's alumni, and another large group feels that it has been excluded from an opportunity which it should have. Every effort should be made, by all parties concerned, to correct this condition as soon as possible."

There was a general feeling among Berkeley alumni leaders that Los Angeles alumni had much to gain from a merger, and that eventually they might come to recognize this, or, at least, ameliorate their doubts about merging, in deference to the hopes of the President of the University and the Regents. Undoubtedly President Sproul shared this feeling along with being constitutionally optimistic about the willingness of human beings, once they came to know each other well, to sit down together and compromise their differences in the interests of unity and strength. Otherwise, he might have pressed for a decision by the Regents in 1939. He seemed to feel that it would be better to have the alumni work out a mutually acceptable plan, rather than have some decision made by the Regents that might be resented by one alumni group or the other.

By 1941 it seemed clear that a federation of two largely autonomous alumni groups was the best that could be expected, but even that solution was considered dangerous by the Los Angeles group unless the power of the federation council were to be limited by the requirement of a three-fourths majority vote for passage of any motion, and by granting one more than a fourth of the votes to the University of California at Los Angeles. The California Alumni Association was willing to concede one more than a fourth of the votes, and to stipulate that the federation could be dissolved by either group, if dissatisfied, at the end of six years; but it took the position that a deliberative body unable to move unless it could muster a three-fourths majority vote would be hopelessly ineffective.

President Sproul's patience still held out, though it may have been growing thin, and he asked his advisers to consider what might happen if the right of *any* alumnus to sit on the Board of Regents were challenged until some plan was agreed upon by which all alumni could participate in his election. There were still some UCLA alumni who thought that the best solution was to have a separate representative on the Board of Regents, and in 1943 a bill to bring this about was actually introduced in the state legislature. This bill did not pass because of a general reluctance to create a situation that might encourage sectional dissension within the Board of Regents. Twice more President Sproul persuaded representatives of the two alumni associations to enter into negotiations for a compromise solution. On the first occasion the representatives did come to a reluctant agreement, but at a meeting of the membership of the Los Angeles alumni group, this compromise was rejected. On the second occasion, the Los Angeles alumni abandoned all effort to reach a solution which they could support, and sent a telegram to President Sproul reading as follows: "It is our unanimous opinion that the Federation Plan can never achieve the ends desired by all concerned and therefore our original plan amending the state constitution permitting UCLA Alumni President to be ex-officio member of Board of Regents should be consummated by submitting an amendment to this session of the legislature."

From the depths of this discouragement President Sproul sent a wire to a leader in UCLA alumni affairs: "Since I am far more interested in the perpetuation of the University of California as one of the great universities of the world than I am in any job or any personal glory, I am quite willing to step out so that someone who is not a Berkeley man may be chosen if that will reduce or remove the suspicion and ill-will which now block the road to harmony and unity, and release the full power of the University for the tremendous job that lies ahead of it if it is not dismembered and destroyed. . . . I must admit that I am not hopeful of correcting in a few minutes the record I have evidently left upon the minds of UCLA alumni after twenty-five years of loyal, even if ineffectual, devotion to their longtime interests."

One year later, nothing more having happened, President Sproul decided to put the matter of getting final agreement in the hands of the Regents. He reviewed the long, disappointing history of the efforts that had been made, warned the Regents that unless some other solution were found quickly there would be another attempt to introduce a sectional representative into the Board's membership, and recommended that the Board appoint a committee to meet with alumni and decide on a plan that would be to the best interests of the University of California as a whole. One month later this committee, of which President Sproul was a member, rendered its report, and the Regents accepted the report. On May 29, 1947, they took action to establish policy: "Resolved that there should be created an 'Alumni Association of the University' composed of all members of the California Alumni Association and the UCLA Alumni Association, for the sole purpose of complying with said Constitutional Provision as to representation on the Board of Regents, whose President shall sit ex-officio as a member of the Board of Regents."

A first draft of a plan to effectuate this policy was also approved at the same meeting, but on June 27 the basic plan was amended to read: "That there shall be one representative of the alumni of the entire University of California serve on the Board of Regents, ex-officio;

"That in view of the fact that a large segment of the alumni of the University is not now represented, there should be created an alumni association composed of the alumni of all campuses for the sole purpose of complying with the Constitution provisions as to representation on the Board of Regents."

The two alumni associations were thereafter requested to draft an agreement to bring this about. The agreement provided that the President of the California Alumni Association and the President of the UCLA Alumni Association, elected for two-year terms, should serve alternately as President of the Alumni Association of the University of California for a one-year term, and during this term should serve as Regent of the University ex officio. When this agreement was ratified by the alumni of UCLA, after a year of discussion, the Regents, by resolution, invited the president of each alumni group to sit with them without vote during the year preceding his term as President of the Alumni Association of the University of California. Although this plan was less than President Sproul hoped the alumni themselves might achieve, the wisdom of his long struggle to avoid the precedent of separate campus representation has been confirmed as one general campus after another has been added to the University family. Patience and persistence were two virtues that President Sproul contributed in high degree at a time when they were sorely needed.

It should be reiterated here that this long struggle was not one that affected all alumni, either at Berkeley or Los Angeles, and neither was it the sole concern of the leaders who took part in it. They were also concerned with the welfare of their respective campuses, but regarded the concept of a large multicampus university with varying degrees of enthusiasm. Even among those who equated success in intercollegiate athletic competition with Nirvana, there was in the background, always, an interest in undergraduate activities generally, and in the undergraduate as a person and as a kind of younger clan brother or sister. One of the best examples of effective interest by alumni in this regard was that concerned with residence facilities for students, both fraternal and nonorganized. At Berkeley and at Los Angeles, alumni did what they could to develop house clubs, cooperatives, chapter houses, and University residence halls, but progress was slow.

For many years the Regents of the University took the position that housing and dining facilities for students were not among their primary responsibilities, at least as long as private enterprise was available to meet the need. They were particularly positive that tax funds should not be sought for these purposes, and they were not enthusiastic about the solicitation of gifts for housing, in view of the always long list of academic needs that remained unfilled. It is possible that earlier experiences of the Regents with residence halls at Berkeley helped to establish a tradition that involvement with them should be avoided. When the University of California was preparing to move from Oakland to Berkeley in the early 1870's it was confidently expected that a village would spring up around the new campus as academic buildings approached completion, and that places to live and to buy food, as well as other necessities, would be available. But in 1874, one year after classes got under way in old North Hall and South Hall, a committee of the Regents reported to the Board that:

"The lack of conveniences, and even of possibilities of residence at the University, on the part of students attending upon its instruction, is so absolute that we have to report that the institution is in peril from this cause."

In view of this emergency the Regents felt that they were justified in ignoring the implied prohibition on housing for students in the original Organic Act, which created the University, and they pledged their personal credit to obtain a loan of $18,000 at the then prevailing interest rate of 1 per cent per month, and made plans to construct a series of cottages, each designed to house twelve students, on the south side of Strawberry Creek. They had hoped to build perhaps ten to twelve cottages, but were astonished to learn that construction costs in backwoods Berkeley permitted the completion of only eight cottages at the outrageous price of about $187 per student housed. This meant that the room charge per student had to be boosted to the unheard of high rate of $2.50 a month in order to meet interest charges and retire the loan. A group of coeds, calling themselves The Young Ladies Club, leased an entire cottage at the special annual rate of $300 per year, payable in gold coin. But most male students apparently considered this charge preposterous, particularly in view of the equally high prices for food at the only restaurant available, and most of them preferred to walk from Temescal or ride the horse-car from Oakland. A meal, with nothing more than sour apples for dessert, cost 50 cents, according to one contemporary critic. The Regents found themselves with a number of empty cottages and a debt on their hands. They rented a few cottages to members of the faculty, including Professor Joseph LeConte, and even discussed renting them to people not connected with the University, but decided that it would not be appropriate to rent real estate commercially on the campus. They also considered selling them to any buyer who would agree to move the buildings off the campus. They finally lowered the rental rate to attract more occupants but ended up with little increase in income because The Young Ladies Club and other more or less permanent lessors demanded that they share in the new rate, thus reducing the rent per cottage to only $200 a year. Eventually one building was converted into an armory, and another into a headquarters for various semiacademic literary societies. Needless to say, residence halls for students became an unpopular subject and remained so for almost half a century.

In 1894 a new movement was started to build residence halls for students, but the Regents, after seeking advice from other public universities in the United States, decided to continue their policy against housing. The President of the University of Missouri pointed out that once an institution assumed responsibility for housing it could not avoid responsibility for epidemic health hazards, and for the good order and morals of students in extracurricular activities. It was not until 1923 that the Regents came around to recognizing that the importance of residence halls as a part of the academic environment might justify assuming the appendant obligations and responsibilities. Alumni interest played a strong part in this change of heart, but it was the personal guarantees made by Robert Gordon Sproul as Comptroller that reduced their worries about financial disaster. He reported to them, after a thorough study of the matter, that he was willing to offer assurance that loans of up to $1,480 per student housed could be repaid with interest in 25 years, and loans of up to $1,980 per student housed could be repaid over a longer period of time. The Regents did not follow the Comptroller's urging that they proceed immediately to build residence halls, but they did announce publicly that they would build at least one residence hall for men and one for women if alumni or others could provide gifts covering 40 per cent of the construction cost.

As a result of this announcement, which carried with it an offer of free land on which to build the residence halls, Mrs. P. E. Bowles, in 1927, generously offered to pay 100 per cent of the construction cost of the first residence hall for men at Berkeley, as a memorial to her late husband, Philip E. Bowles, Class of 1882. Shortly thereafter Mira Hershey made a comparably generous offer to construct the first residence hall for women on the Los Angeles campus. Within a decade, in 1937, Mrs. Sigmund Stern followed suit with a gift covering the cost of construction of a residence hall for women at Berkeley.

These gifts were most important in clearing the way for subsequent residence halls, in that they provided experience and assurance on what responsibility for housing might entail. But the Regents, as late as 1943, reiterated their conviction that housing for students was not a responsibility equal to that of providing higher education, and they could not justify adding provision for it to appropriations requested from the state. The State of California indicated that it was in complete agreement with this point of view. However, in 1938, on recommendation of the President, and with the urging of alumni, the Regents approved a program to erect one dormitory each at Berkeley, Los Angeles, and Davis, provided that the alumni associations raised one half of the cost by gift. Two years later they entered into a written agreement with the California Alumni Association to match a gift of $200,000 with a loan of $200,000 for a residence hall, but before this program could be organized the attack on Pearl Harbor ensued.

As World War II progressed, and prospects of victory grew brighter, it became clear that there would be an avalanche of veterans returning to college to complete their education, and that housing would be a serious problem, especially at Berkeley, where war workers from all parts of the United States had settled to work in shipyards and other industries. The Regents suggested that the Federal Government, in its program of housing for war workers, might give thought to a joint effort with the University of California to construct war housing that would also be permanent enough to meet postwar, veteran-student needs. This plan was not considered feasible, and by the winter of 1944–45, the situation became desperate. Some 200 women students planning to enter Berkeley in the spring of 1945 had to withdraw because they could not find a place to live. In order not to leave any stone unturned, President Sproul tried to build a Federal assistance program out of one provision in the Lanham Act passed by the 76th Congress that authorized housing for returning veterans in the District of Columbia. He also appointed a committee to investigate ways and means of meeting the housing crisis, and in his charge to the committee he advised them not to waste time gathering more statistics on the need for housing, or where it should be located, or how it should be planned, but rather to concentrate on the problem of finding funds.

By the summer of 1945 it seemed clear that the avalanche of students would start in the fall term, though even the most dire predictions did not do justice to what actually happened. Enrollment jumped from 11,000, the lowest in twenty years, to 18,000, the highest in history, in one sudden surge. But the advance warnings were sufficiently frightening to bring Vice-President Monroe E. Deutsch to the decision that he should ask the Regents, as an emergency matter, to lend unrestricted endowment funds enough to pay the entire construction cost of residence halls for women students at Berkeley, even though President Sproul was attending a conference in the East. There was no time for more than rough estimates of the cost of the project, to be carried out on gift land at the head of Dwight Way, but in view of the emergency, and with the strong support of an alumnus, Regent Jean C. Witter, Class of 1916, the program was approved. Although the cost proved greater than the first rough estimates, funds from two endowments were appropriated to provide low-cost housing for six units accommodating eighty girls each.

President Sproul was pleased to learn that the problem of student housing at Berkeley had convinced a majority of Regents that they should accept responsibility for building residence halls, even to the extent of lending 100 per cent of the construction cost; but he was concerned lest this establish a precedent for low quality, minimum cost construction, and also concerned over the fact that it was a piecemeal approach, dealing with student housing on one campus without simultaneous consideration of needs on other campuses. He was constantly insistent that one statewide university, if it were to last, required statewide planning. Consequently, he presented a general policy for consideration by the Board, covering these points: (1) that residence halls should be adequate; (2) that consideration should be given to at least one residence hall each at Berkeley, Davis, Los Angeles, and Santa Barbara; (3) that the State of California should be asked to participate in the program to the extent of at least $5,600,000 to be divided between the four campuses in proportion to enrollment;

(4) that loan money should be sought both by a proposal to the Federal Government, and by a request to the state legislature for authority to issue revenue bonds. This general policy was approved, the state legislature subsequently granted authority for revenue bonds, and in the sessions of 1946 and 1947, made $6,600,000 available for loan-matching funds. Federal aid was slower in coming, but the President continued to urge it.

In order to make these funds go as far as possible, and to bring the various campuses together on the matter, he then obtained permission from the Regents to have representatives from Berkeley, Los Angeles, and Davis participate in planning a basic type of residence hall to be a pilot project on the Davis campus. By 1949, working drawings were under way for a residence hall that could be constructed one wing at a time, to house 200 students per wing, up to four wings and 800 students, with a single kitchen and dining facility. Estimates then indicated that the construction of two wings as a unit would reduce the cost by about 12 per cent; so this amended plan was adopted. In the meantime, conference with the state Senate and state Assembly brought agreement that on a trial basis, two thirds of the construction cost might be met by state appropriations, if the remaining third were borrowed and the loan repaid from income. With this program started, and the need for a statewide policy clearly indicated, President Sproul reminded the Regents that they had discussed a goal of housing 25 per cent of students in residence halls at the major metropolitan campuses, and 50 per cent at the smaller campuses. This discussion had occurred six years previously. Then, just at this time, the housing supervisor at Berkeley, Mrs. Ruth Norton Donnelly, reported that as a result of the housing situation, students were complaining that they were being forced into unsanitary private boarding houses at what they felt were exorbitant rates. She reminded the President and the Regents that every survey of student needs for a period of fifty years had put housing at the top of the list. These facts, plus the apparent economic feasibility of financing a substantial part of the cost of residence halls through revenue bonds, particularly if housing aid from the Federal Government made it possible to sell bonds at a low interest rate, led the Regents, on September 24, 1954, to approve a program of investing reserves in student housing, up to a maximum of eight and a half million dollars. From that date on, the residence hall program went into high gear. The new policy was firmly established, thirty years after President Sproul had first proposed such a program, and had expressed his personal conviction that the Regents could safely borrow a substantial amount of the construction cost and repay the debt from revenue. During this long period it was the firm support of alumni that kept his hopes up, many of them the same alumni whose enthusiasm over intercollegiate athletics, and primary concern over this or that individual campus rather than the statewide system, saved the academic sky from becoming monotonously blue and cloudless. That Robert Gordon Sproul was able to deal with alumni on so many different fronts and, through patience and persistence, and firm retention of principle, prevent dissolution of the University explains his length of service and accounts for the fact that he was able to choose his own retirement date. Retired, he continues his distinguished career of disciplined service by religiously avoiding any involvement in University affairs unless he is requested by his successor to take part. When asked by an admiring student how he was able to maintain an office on campus and still avoid being pulled back into University affairs by friends and acquaintances, President Sproul laughed and remarked that a man over seventy is never sure he is bright enough to meddle unless he proves it by not meddling.

VI

Public Addresses

Public addresses play almost as important a part in the life of a college or university president as sermons do in the life of a pastor of a church, and to some extent the educational administrator and the minister of the gospel are faced with the same problems. They must conjure up inspiration for new approaches to traditional subjects and hold the interest (and hopefully touch the spirit) of audiences that retain basically the same membership year after year. This is a real test of creative communication. Had Abraham Lincoln been faced with the task of delivering a brief address at Gettysburg every Sunday morning for a year, or even every November 19 for twenty-eight years, we may be certain that few of his essays would have matched the deathless quality of the first. This would not mean that any of them failed to meet its purpose in a distinctively appropriate way.

There are at least two important criteria by which the merit of either a sermon or a secular public address must be judged: one the depth and quality of the thought that gives it *raison d'être*, and the other the personality and magnetic quality of its composer. Some oral communications are eminently worthy of nomination for immortality through preservation in printers' ink even though they leave their first audience cold and unimpressed. This was true of the Gettysburg

Address, which did not fully reveal its beauty of thought and expression until it was laid out in cold type on a printer's marble slab. It
loses nothing because its composer is absent, for he added nothing to
it in the delivery, as Lincoln himself said. On the other hand, there
are thousands of communications that achieve a transcendent level of
worth in their moment of baptism that paper and print can never
reveal, that memory alone may capture and hold. Regardless of the
message and the elegance of the wording, these addresses can never
offer to the reader what they brought to the listener on the occasion
for which they were created. This is true of practically every address
that President Sproul delivered. A Sproul address without Robert
Gordon is akin to the score of a symphony without an orchestra to
play it.

Another difficulty for an editor seeking to epitomize President
Sproul's public addresses is that there were so many of them! He faced
the usual round of annually recurring occasions from which a university president may be absent only if he is in the doctor's care, and
sometimes not then. New students must be welcomed to the campus,
and old and new addressed periodically at University Meetings. Dignified seniors and still more dignified higher degree recipients must be
given their "D Day" advice at commencement. The Academic Senate
must be addressed on occasion, and a host of other occasions demand
the presence of the President as master of ceremonies or introducer of
distinguished lecturers. Charter Day, the anniversary of the founding
of the institution, must be fittingly commemorated, and in addition
appropriate words must be said to alumni at the Charter Day banquet.

The presidency of Robert Gordon Sproul, because it involved the
development of a rapidly growing multicampus system, multiplied
the need for addresses to campus communities; in some years he had
to go through the major part of the round of events outlined above two
or more times with substantially different speeches. It is difficult
enough to prepare and deliver a Charter Day address once a year. Two,
three, or more, changed to fit the locality, can be a burden that tries
both spirit and mind. But if President Sproul ever felt himself withering under the demand he concealed it rather well. He liked to speak,

even though the program of preparation that he exacted from himself was an ordeal few could or would attempt. One thing did exasperate him continually. He would write a major address on an important subject about which he felt he had something significant to say, and by some process of conjuration that only he understood transfer the entire speech from paper to his mind in the course of writing, rewriting, and editing it. He would deliver it as if it were extemporaneous, and invigorated by the applause he invariably aroused, express the wistful hope that he could use it again to discharge some of the always long list of outside speaking commitments on his calendar. But with discouraging regularity the commitments would crystalize into requests for some omniscient analysis of another subject, perhaps: "Civilization's Debt to the Jersey Cow," or "The Relation of Higher Education to the Future of America's Territories and Possessions." At such times his entire secretarial staff walked on tiptoe.

It is appropriate to mention here, that the most adept tiptoer, on all occasions, was Miss Agnes Roddy Robb, known affectionately as "The Duchess," who served as secretary to President Sproul practically from her graduation in 1918 to his retirement in 1958, and then continued to run his office, part time, when he became President Emeritus. She was "the maid of all work" and the "Rock of Gibraltar" who marshalled work, pushed it along, stood guard at the President's door when necessary, and smiled and beguiled all visitors with never-ending patience.

Space does not permit of reproducing more than a small fraction of the thought that President Sproul put into public addresses during his 28 years of service as the chief administrator of the University of California. The best that can be done is to bring together a few complete addresses and such excerpts as seem best to elucidate the presidential policies and attitudes under which the institution operated for more than a quarter of a century. As he intimated on more than one occasion it is impossible to appreciate the warmth that lies behind the words of a university president unless one has sat in the chair from which they were written, and shared the blisters.

There is one outstanding attribute of Robert Gordon Sproul to which his public addresses amply testify. He did not arrive at stands on an issue suddenly, but once he had considered the question thoroughly and finally decided on his stand he seldom found it necessary to change it. He was just as deliberate about changing his mind as he was about making it up in the first place. In evidence of this, the pages to follow will present his first statement of personal attitude and convictions about higher education and the University of California, delivered before the Commonwealth Club of San Francisco during his first month in office and even before his inaugural address, and his first address to students at Berkeley shortly after the opening of the fall semester of 1930. These addresses reveal ideas and attitudes that the author had been developing and building through twenty years of intimate association with the University as student and staff member. They were not abstract generalities about higher education applied to a specific institution; they were rather the harvest of his own homestead, grown from seed he had helped to plant, watered with the perspiration of his own brow, and the brows of a faculty known to him personally for years before he thought of the presidency, and gathered as it ripened with his own hand scythe. He looked on the University of California as the promised land, and he felt a personal sense of dedication to it and to the ideas it produced. There was a substantial persistence about him. One usually knew where he would stand and one could count on him continuing to stand there, stubbornly if necessary, until he was sure there was a better ground. He could change tactics but did not lightly surrender strategies that he felt were right. The principles for which he stood at the end of his career as president in 1958, were substantially those with which he began it in 1930. They stood the test of time, and because they did, so did he.

FIRST STATEMENT OF PURPOSE AS PRESIDENT

The Commonwealth Club of California

July 25, 1930

Not long ago I was talking with Professor Jan Julius Lodewyk Duyvendak, of the University of Leyden, Holland, who taught Chinese literature and philosophy in the 1930 summer session, and the conversation turned to the University of California, its history, its accomplishments, its student body, its faculty. With many of these things Professor Duyvendak was familiar. But he had not known of the beginnings of the University, and expressed frank astonishment that it should have come into being in 1868, less than twenty years after the gold rush of '49, which opened California to the world. He was even more astonished when I told him that in the first constitutional convention, called to prepare this California of ours for statehood, long before that first Charter Day of 1868, the miners, merchants, farmers, mechanics, and other delegates from a more or less rough and turbulent pioneer community had discussed as one of the first requirements of the basic law, a proper provision for higher education, not only in agriculture and the mechanic arts, but in the seemingly less practical fields of liberal culture. "What a tribute," Professor Duyvendak said, "to the quality of your Argonauts! No wonder this state has become a new empire."

I mention these remarks because it seems to me that this quiet scholar, who, from the background of little Holland, has made himself known the world over in the field of Oriental culture, with characteristic Dutch sagacity hit the nail on the head as to one of the most powerful causes of the quality of our civilization. There was something to those men of '49, a breadth of outlook, a depth and buoyancy of spirit, an appreciation of the durable satisfactions of life, that gave impetus and direction to the State of California and to the University which it has cherished almost from the beginning. The founders of that University, too, were men of character and vision or they could not have builded so strongly for the future. Poor in the material things we enjoy today, they were rich in the fundamentals of university life and growth—the love of absolute truth, the appreciation of other than material things, the fearlessness of strong conviction. With them, high standards must have been usual, for they have bequeathed to us a University in which men must grow or grow ashamed. Modest as that University was when its founders launched it, it has come to be a mighty influence in the development not only of California but of the civilization of all the western states and of the lands across and around the Pacific. Wherever you go in this country, in Mexico, in South America, and in the Orient, you will find alumni of the University of California; alumni who graduated in years when educational opportunities were far smaller than they are now, yet who are today among the leaders in high, fine thinking. In government, in the pulpit, at the bar, upon the bench, in the medical profession, in commerce and industry, California alumni have played a conspicuous part. And while I would pray to be delivered from the smug practice, so human and so common among university administrators, of claiming full credit for the careers of distinguished alumni while washing the hands of all responsibility for the failures, nevertheless these fruits by which we are proud to be known, cannot all have been accidents.

But the pioneer civilization in which the University of California was born, and to which it ministered and contributed so largely, has developed into something almost infinitely different. Simplicity and order have given way to complexity and want of order. A flood of new machinery and new practices, and even a few new ideas have swept across the world and the university of 1930 has been washed out of the quiet groves of academe into the bewildering torrent of modern life. Even within the quiet groves themselves there is no longer unchanging quiet. The chemistry of my time was simple—even though I didn't think so—with fairly understandable symbols and formulae. In place of these elementary figures the chemistry of today has elaborate charts with atoms in chains and clusters, many-branched and in wide varieties of kaleidoscopic arrangements. The simple indivisible atom to which I was introduced has become a veritable solar system of orbits and revolutions, with goings-on within its complex interior beyond my powers either of description or understanding. We are told by Einstein that space is finite but without end and by Gilbert Lewis that time progresses both forward and backward. Natually these and essentially similar developments in nonscientific fields have had their effect on universities, which have found it none too easy to keep their traditional position of leadership in the procession traveling at airplane speed. Small numbers and limited curricula have given way to large enrollments, diversity of courses, and multiplication of departments. During the last decade or two the extraordinary expansion of subject matter in which the university is compelled by the logic of events to offer instruction, together with the rapid increase in students, has presented problems of the most baffling character, for which adequate solutions are only slowly being discovered.

As a consequence, universities have recently had the doubtful pleasure of hearing themselves discussed on every side, almost as much as subjects purely personal or prohibitory. To a few who have never emerged from "the golden haze of student days," the universities are absolutely right, to others they are at least equally wrong; while in the eyes of the larger class of more or less friendly critics, so conflicting is epidemic opinion as to the faults that mar, that the resultant of so many diverse forces must seem inevitably to be either stagnation or limitless power. One says too many students, another too few scholars; one says too much froth in the undergraduate mass, another too much dust in the faculty superstructure; one says what the university lacks is scholarly professors who are also great personalities, another that it needs two good half-backs and a fast rangy end.

Moreover, there is at least as much of this criticism within as without the campus walls, and from that I draw much comfort. For, it seems to me, if the universities and the public were both satisfied, there would be cause for alarm. Their common discontent is a happy augury of the ultimate correction of such weaknesses as actually exist. Now what are those weaknesses? What is wrong with the university? Of course, I can't begin to tell you the whole story in the time at my disposal, and one man's guess is as good as another's—at least he thinks it is—but I can outline three great problems as I see them. All three are general, but I shall discuss them largely from the point of view of the University with which I am familiar, the University of this state. The last indeed I shall discuss in terms of that University because it is the problem from which the University of California is commonly supposed to suffer most.

The first problem, of course, is as to what education should be, and what the university should have as its objective. There is no subject under the sun which admits of so much discussion and dispute. Perhaps it might be well to remind ourselves first of what the word education means, for there seems to be a very common, persistent, and official misunderstanding of that elementary matter. Education is conceived as entirely a process of imparting or pushing in knowledge to the human mind. Actually the word means the opposite. To educate is not to push in but to lead or draw out. It is true that these processes are inseparable, but the major process is not to load the young mind but to excite it. An educated man is not primarily one who can produce facts, but a man who can think and sort them out. He is not one who can solve crossword puzzles without reference to a dictionary, but one who by long training in learning, thinking, and doing realizes approximately the extent of his ignorance and incapacity. Education is shown far more by the ability to ask intelligent questions than to supply pat answers. True education first discovers, then leads natural ability. And as God fulfils Himself in many ways, so does the inspired teacher. The trouble in the modern world is that so many experts sit on the throttle of his inspiration.

It is one thing, however, to say what education should be and should aim at; it is another thing to say what instruments it should employ, or stake out the path by which it should approach its objective. It is here that educators dispute endlessly, rage, and utter vain phrases. If you asked the professors at the University of California what each one regarded as the proper means by which to achieve the purposes of that institution, you would have almost as many answers as there were professors, both as to purposes and means. With the varying philosophies of life that mankind has developed, it is not surprising that there should be no unanimity of opinion regarding a philosophy of education. But some things should be clearly defined and generally accepted, as to what we are seeking and the means by which we may attain it. Time and money, strength and genius, are being wasted because of the absence of these. An educational survey of the United States would disclose vast sums wasted on duplicated courses and huge plants and equipment that need never have been. So would such a survey of California. There is no reason why every junior college, college, and university should cultivate all fields of knowledge, or the same fields of knowledge. More to be commended is a careful restriction of instruction and research, so that, within its estimated income and its community requirements, each institution may support comfortably the departments of known value and established need.

Furthermore, largely because objectives are not clear and methods are uncertain, all institutions of higher education that I know have student bodies so lacking in homogeneity, so varying in mental power, as to be almost unteachable, as a whole. And size of student body affects this problem but slightly in degree and not at all in kind. In the universities of today we are attempting to be all things to all men, and are about as comfortable as a chameleon on a Scotch plaid. Some of our students are as brilliant and ambitious for learning as any scholar of medieval times. Some have the mind but little desire to use it. Some are beautiful but dumb, and some are not even beautiful. But we try to educate them all by similar means—an unattainable purpose. And yet, if we sorted them, and grouped them into homogeneous units, most of them might be educated profitably.

I have read somewhere that the present generation of university men and women may be divided into four homogeneous groups. First come those who are not bent on learning as such, but who want vocational training without much regard to cultural values, for the sake of making more money and rising to a higher place in society. Often these come from families that have known toil and meagre resources and which believe that their children may escape through education the narrow lives that the parents have lived. These young people usually make our most earnest students. They may not have the highest qualities of mind or of educational ideals, but they have a purpose in coming to us, they work everlastingly, and they are generally a source of satisfaction.

In the second group are those who come to a university to satisfy the wishes, even the demands of their parents. They have no desire for further schooling, but would prefer to go to work or to be married. It would be a great thing, too, if they could be put to work, so that those really fitted for it might learn the worth of the education into which they are being forced, and the others might find sooner their various proper careers along other lines. For these second-class students have no interest in scholarship, study only enough to get by, and clutter up the educational machinery no end.

In the third group come those who enter college for social reasons, because it is the thing to do in their set, because they want to make a fraternity, because it is a good way to meet the socially elect and the matrimonially eligible. These think almost wholly of the externals, the glamour and the tinsel of college life, and not at all of its true purpose. The term *student* is for them a courtesy title, for they simply cannot conceive of a burning desire for learning.

In the last group are those who come to a university with a fair idea of what it is all about, and with a certain singleness of purpose for scholarship. With these a vocation, and they usually have one in prospect, is of secondary importance for the time being. They have in mind that culture which gives breadth and depth to life and they realize that many things which are unseen are eternal. Contrary to general belief, there are a good many of these in universities, genuinely bent on education, and willing to pay any reasonable price for it.

None of these four groups is by any means hopeless from an educational point of view. The problem is to separate them and give to each the kind and amount of higher education suited to its needs. What we are doing now is to maintain a conglomerate condition which overtaxes the ability of some and never uses others up to their capacity, which is harmful to the more brilliant minds because it sends them into the world cocksure and soft, and harmful to the weaker students because it eliminates them with the impress of a permanent inferiority complex. What we need is not lower standards of admission to the universities, but higher and better ones, so that this condition may be improved. What we need is not more standard universities and colleges of lower quality, for those disappointed even by our present generous system, but other, altogether different institutions which will train these students better and get them to their lifework sooner. What we need is not more four-year colleges that will admit anybody without examination or question, but another type of institution, extending not more than two years beyond the high school, which will provide curricula designed for those whose talents do not lie along the line of a university career, but who are interested in further education. That, in my opinion, is the great field of the junior college, and I pray that its leaders may have the wisdom to see their opportunity and to make the most of it.

The second problem of every university to which I would call attention is the faculty. In earlier days when the map of the world's knowledge was a simpler affair, with fewer frontier lines than now separate our growing number of studies, a "faculty" was a fairly coherent guild of scholars held together by a common intellectual interest. A high degree of group consciousness, *esprit de corps*, and the intimate interchange of opinion on common problems was then possible. But that has all changed. Small numbers and limited curricula have given way to faculties running into the hundreds in number, to expanded curricula, and multiplied departments. The old unities of scholars and scholarship have disintegrated, and specialization has grown by leaps and bounds. This process of progressive division and subdivision of fields of inquiry and instruction has not only destroyed the earlier character of a "faculty" as a community of scholars, but has increased immeasurably the demand upon the limited supply of brains which are capable of meeting the requirements of the academic life. One of the great present problems of the universities, under the discouraging conditions of the modern world, is certainly the maintenance of the faculty on the high plane which it has always occupied.

The glory of a university is obviously the men who constitute its faculty. It cannot be too often repeated that it is men and nothing but men who make education. The reason why the University of California occupies the high position it does throughout the academic world is that there has never been a time when its faculty could not boast men who were finding their way along rough trails, illuminated only by the spark of genius, to the heights of scholarship. Within a few years after the receipt of its charter from the state there were to be found in the University a goodly number of men whose reputation is even yet undimmed, such men as Daniel Coit Gilman, later president of Johns Hopkins University, Hilgard in Agriculture, LeConte in Geology, and many others. Nor is the present faculty devoid of men who in their respective fields hold high the lamp of learning—Campbell in Astronomy, Kofoid in Zoology, and G. N. Lewis in Chemistry, to pick out a few of the most obvious. In a very real sense, such men are the University of California, and similarly elsewhere, for material development is futile without brains to use and direct it, and personality to irradiate it. Students are getting a gold brick if they go for education to a school where there are no great teachers.

Nobody, I am sure, will question that those are the facts. Yet too often they are ignored in the development of an institution. It is only human for a president to place the emphasis on buildings which will be a continuing monument to his administration, instead of seeing to it that available funds are used, and new funds sought, to secure the best scholars and teachers to be had, and to keep them happy after they have come, so that they may be as productive as possible. As a result the maximum salary for a professor has increased very little for many years, and the average at California, $5,200, is far below that of the institutions with which we must compete for the very limited supply of first-class men. Limited, because few of the best college graduates can be persuaded to undertake a scholarly career, when they feel, quite properly, that a man is foolish to enter even a pleasant field where the laborer is held to be not worthy of his hire. Those who might be the commanding educational statesmen of the day, who might foresee and prepare for the social structure of the future, who might without pressure or compulsion undertake important innovations in educational practices are enticed into commerce, or industry, or other professions than education that offer those adequate inducements which are necessary to secure the services of the brightest minds. If the stream of our civilization is not to be dried up at the source, we must pay salaries in education that will attract first-class men in competition with business and other professions. If the university is to command confidence, if it is to treasure and convey the wisdom of the ages to coming generations, which may thereby have a more orderly understanding of modern life as an environment in which to find happiness as well as material success, it must hold within its ranks those minds that are capable of discovering, recognizing, and assaying the valuable trends and aims in nature and in society. If it continues engaging the present proportion of second-rate minds which make knowledge an end in itself, which stifle the desire of youth for learning, which do not relate education to the living of a good life, which stuff book knowledge into heads without teaching them to think—we must expect it to fail in its highest purpose. The reason that we do not have higher quality in higher education everywhere today is that the great genius of our country is not to be found in university faculties. Individual universities have individual brilliant men, though many universities and colleges in America do not have a single one. But the statement is generally true, and so long as it is true, there will be dissatisfaction with and criticism of higher education, no matter what the size of student body or the methods of instruction. The only way to meet that problem is to make scholarship respectable, to enable the universities to meet the financial competition of the business world for the brightest minds rather than to accept perforce those who seek in some quiet faculty a refuge for mediocrity.

And that brings me to my third problem, the problem of numbers. The last ten years have seen an influx of students that has almost overwhelmed the undergraduate departments of American universities. The ambition of parents, increased wealth, the attractiveness of college life, assumed vocational advantages, and, above all, social prestige have transformed and reinforced the motives which formerly led students to college, and have resulted in the present vogue for the "collegiate" among great groups of young men and young women who really have little idea as to what it is all about. The cultural influence of Alma Mater seems to many to have been swamped by the ever-increasing waves of young people demanding the delights and advantages of a university education without the labor and the application necessary to attain in reality that desirable distinction.

From these conditions have arisen criticisms of colleges and universities of every kind and size and quality, but particularly of the state universities, and in this locality most particularly of the University of California, widely advertised when state appropriations were needed as the largest university in the world. The question as to whether these criticisms are well-founded, and if so, what to do about it, is one of the major problems of the president of the University of California, and to it I have been giving a great deal of attention. . . . The University of California today is no great congeries of wandering students and harassed professors, drawing from each other neither knowledge nor inspiration. It is quite the equal of any but the very small college, in the personal quality of its teaching and the spirit of its student body. For once you exceed an enrollment of a few hundred students, the widely claimed advantages of the small institution vanish completely, and the university with 3,500 and the university with 10,000 are on a par so far as personal contacts which make for better education are concerned. For instance, the ratio of faculty to students, which is what counts, is at Michigan 1 to 13, at California 1 to 12, at Yale 1 to 11, at Stanford 1 to 10—all practically the same.

So I am not as worried as I might be over the fact that California is a large University. Indeed, I am disposed to approve mass education—so long as it does not become herd education. The important point is that the qualifications of entrants to do university work be maintained, and that the standards of the University be not impaired, either from within or without, with a view to making it possible for larger numbers to meet the requirements. Subject to those limitations, I believe that the University should welcome all who desire to come to it. The state cannot but profit by serving the splendid group of young men and women who seek an education on the various campuses of the University. An increase in that number, if quality be maintained, cannot but be desirable.

The success of a large university in providing sound education is primarily a matter of organization. The quality of the faculty, the wide range of opportunities in the way of departments and courses, the splendid facilities in libraries and laboratories, all make the University of California a most attractive place for students. If such a university is able to furnish enough instructors of proper qualifications and sufficient facilities, as we now are, I know of no reason why a very large number of students should not receive an excellent education on its campus. As long as we maintain high standards of admission and graduation there is no need to limit enrollment. As to eliminating the first two years, I should prefer that others make that experiment. We shall observe the results with interest and be guided as to our future policy by them.

These, then, are three problems of the American university. In discussing them I have tried to let you see something of what my attitude will be toward the administration of the University of California. Now to make it more definite, let me close with just a brief statement of policy. I believe that the chief purpose of the modern university and particularly the state university is the cultivation of intelligent leadership in the body politic. Certainly it will be a grave indictment of these centers of learning if they fail to breed men who can solve the problems and meet the crises of the world in which they live. I pray for the University of California an influence in quickening the intelligence of the youth of its succeeding generations; in deepening their seriousness; in assisting them to define their problems and to aid in defining the problem of their communities. The troubles of this world will never find a better remedy than trained intelligence. The solutions must be worked out in toil and patience day by day and bit by bit. Man's chief problem is man himself, and never did his situation call so loudly for leaders of broad vision and deep understanding. If these leaders come not from the universities, what are the universities for?

FIRST UNIVERSITY MEETING

August 22, 1930

Frankly this is the moment that I have for months awaited. Neither my election to the presidency nor my assumption of that high office touched my heart and exalted my spirit as does this moment when I stand before you, the student body of the University, and address you as your President. Whatever of woe the coming years may hold—and those more experienced in presidencies than I am assure me that there will be plenty—it matters not; for once in my life the cup of my joy has been filled to overflowing. Already I can say, "It has been good to be here."

A few days ago I welcomed the Class of 1934 to the University and told them that they were unique in at least one way because they were starting out with me, the Class in the University and I in the presidency, and that no other class would ever duplicate that peculiarity. Today I cannot say the same thing because many of you started under my distinguished predecessor, Dr. William Wallace Campbell, but I can hope in all sincerity that just as you started before me you may also finish before me, and that each of us may come in proper time to his commencement.

I told the Freshmen also that this is a wonderful University of which we are all a part. I see no reason to change that statement today, even though some of you have been here longer and may have affected the University more than those newcomers who had then not even registered. The men who founded the University of California back in 1868 must have been men of character and vision, or they could not have builded so truly for the future. . . .

Because the University of California has been such a splendidly successful institution, under conditions quite different from those which exist on the campus today, there is a disposition on the part of some, including not a few of our alumni, to believe that it cannot now be a very good institution at all. Mass education is a most frequent phrase in the mouths of these folk and their favorite argument is that methods which are effective and economical in the manufacture of automobiles, cork screws, clothespins, and bricks are fatal to the production of educated men. Perhaps that is true; but we have of such methods on this campus no more than other American universities. We are subject to the criticism that mechanization and academic bookkeeping dominate our life; but certainly no more and perhaps somewhat less than is true of the overwhelming majority of our contemporaries, including every other university of which I know in the West. This University is hard to enter (you will vouch for that and many a star athlete who is elsewhere today will confirm your statements). It will be sufficiently difficult to graduate from (that part I leave to the faculty). You will be well educated along the way if you will lend yourselves to the experience and cooperate in it, and in no other way could you be well educated at any institution anywhere.

As a matter of fact, despite my natural inclination to look back upon the golden days I spent under the Berkeley oaks as an ideal which could hardly be improved upon, when I leave sentiment for the more solid foundation of reason, I envy you your stake in the University of California of today, with its splendid facilities in libraries and laboratories, with its wide variety of opportunities by way of courses and departments, with its large and distinguished faculty of teachers and investigators in almost every field of knowledge. Perhaps it has lacked recently a little of the spiritual quality which drew older classes together in the disorders of hygiene sections and class meetings, in the disciplines of military drill and campus politics, and which sent them off the Greek Theatre stage on Commencement Day not so much doctors, lawyers, business men, engineers, and bond salesmen, as they were sharers in the spirit of a great and dear mother. But that is something you and I can correct if we but will, and I invite you here and now to join me in the great adventure. Let us make this University once again a hearth about which a great family gathers, a place where many of unlike minds may break the bread of learning and quaff the joys of fellowship, a place where the potential usefulness and value of the personal equation of each individual student is not lost but refined and sublimated in a melting pot of a ten thousand student power furnace.

I envy you young people not only your place in this great modern University of 1930; I envy you even more your stake in the world of today where intellectual curiosity, scientifically directed and intelligently applied, is ferreting out solutions to the problems of nature and of man, of the universe and of life. This is the age of science and democracy. The work of the laboratory capitalized in the factory and by industry has built up a great civilization. Alongside of these great developments we have carried forward the idea of majority decision as the basis of our government. The combination is irresistible so long as we do not delude ourselves into thinking that a majority vote can change the facts; and the danger that we may believe that we are determining truth by a count of noses grows less and less as science takes a stronger hold upon democracy in the extraordinarily interesting world in whose latest phase you have the good fortune to find yourselves. . . .

It is these things that cause me to envy you the world in which you are to play your parts. How many of you will take advantage of them? More, I hope, than have ever taken advantage of intellectual opportunities in the past. And how shall you prepare to take advantage of this your world while you are in the University? Certainly you cannot be a real part of it by laboriously taking notes from professors and regurgitating them in examinations. You cannot be a real part of it by giving to the most exacting adventure of life—the discovery of the new, the conquest of the unknown—such moments as you can spare from the round of social duties, of carousal, and from extracurricular activities. You can seize this most precious chalice of opportunity only as you seek not to learn but to think, not to accept but to question and to solve, not to take the word of a book or a professor for anything except as a basis for your own investigations. Whenever you read or are told anything by anybody, from the President of the University up, put to yourself two questions: Is it so? and, What of it? By these tests you will eliminate much misdirected action, many harmful conclusions based on wrong premises, and much useless speculation composed of elements which even if true are of no importance.

I wish there were more of that sort of questioning in this University despite the problems that it might bring me as President. It shocks me deeply to hear young minds quote prejudices with complacency and acceptance, as they often do. We hear a good deal these days of the revolt of youth but I have seen few important evidences of it. There has been recently a demand for freedom but of a rather small and very cheap variety. Girls will be boys in demanding minor and somewhat unworthy privileges: boys will be defiant in defense of petty rights; but there is altogether too little demand for freedom in the things that really count. Youth must be served; but not with manufactured enthusiasm, ready-made slogans, and fat-mindedness. The revolt of youth, to be worth anything, must be against all that is built upon sham and hypocrisy, against all that impedes progress toward the truth. To be young and an intellectual vegetable should be a contradiction of terms.

The average faculty man, I admit, does not encourage such an attitude. He seems to proceed on the theory that the student is in the University to resist education and that he must circumvent it. Now I don't believe this is so and I don't believe the professors have proved the case by scientific methods. I have a little black dog called Ginger —and by the way I regret to inform the older classes that he is on the campus and perhaps making a nuisance of himself. At any rate recently he was ill and needed a dose of castor oil. Remembering my own youth and my continued aversion to that healing substance, I gathered my family together when the time came to administer it and they held the dog so that he could not move and so that when the spoon was introduced into his mouth he could do nothing but swallow. As they let him go after a truly terrific struggle, and as I stood exhausted with the spoon hanging from my hand, the dog came up, licked it off carefully and proceeded to search about the floor for drops which had fallen. Perhaps there is a moral to that tale.

At any rate, too often the supposition is that everything must be done for the student. I believe it is Bernard Shaw who says in his preface to *Back to Methuselah,* that if you wash a cat in its early infancy it will never learn to wash itself, and that the right method is to besplatter it with mud so that in its frantic efforts to clean itself there may be fixed forever in its makeup the technique of cleanliness. Well, I do not advocate seriously your rolling in the mud of the gutter so that you may gain experience in keeping clean, but I do advocate a similar procedure in less earthy realms. Specifically, nobody can teach you anything; it is up to you to learn. The professor can put before you the truth as he sees it, but it becomes yours when you see it, and not one minute before. It never becomes yours when you only memorize what he has seen. It becomes still more yours when, because you have seen one truth, other questions arise out of it in your mind and demand a solution. And it becomes most of all yours when you consult your instructor on the doubts which have arisen in your mind and he says, in answer to your questions, "I don't know, but let's see if we can find out together." I am afraid you won't find any too many of your professors with the humility to make such a confession, but when you do find one cling to him, for he will interpret to you the spirit of this University as expressed in its motto, "Fiat lux," "Let there be light."

You will never become educated merely by passing regularly, even though it be with A's, fifteen units of work per semester exclusive of physical education and military science. That will give you a degree, but it will give you little of an education. For the educated man is not an encyclopedia but a human being capable of arguing from cause to effect, of positing an intelligent question and thinking it through to a logical answer, of applying the tools of learning to the business of living and so helping to solve the problems and meet the crises of the world in which he lives. Education must be active and those who serve it truly must be ever at work widening its frontiers and seeking, perhaps finding, new knowledge. There is no real education that is not self-education. You will grow only as your emotions are brought into play and you engage actively in enlarging your world. Information, unless you do relate it to thinking and living, is useless, for the mind is not a pail to be filled but a dynamo to be set working.

And the fault is by no means all on the student side. Much of what we label education from up here on the platform is ineffective because it does not get down into your real world and help it to expand, but instead parcels out learning in formal abstract divisions that mean little or nothing to one who comes for the first time to a new subject. Education to be worth much must be humanized and related to the student's life and world. Knowledge must be made real. Scholarship must be shown to be the real adventure that it is. If these things came to be, the curricular activities of a university would be so attractive and stimulating that you would put into them a large part of the energy that now goes into extracurricular activities, into sports, publications, drama, and all the rest of the hodgepodge that fills the gravy train and gilds the vest with brazen symbols.

Not that I believe these extracurricular activities are harmful or even useless. I most certainly do not. As I have experienced and watched them they have seemed to me one of the most live and helpful factors in university life. Certainly university life without the romance of camaraderie and the joy of physical and emotional as well as intellectual stimulation would be a sorry place indeed. I would never consider the possibility of eliminating all the color and enthusiasm of present-day life at the University of California, no matter how effectual an educational method might thereby be evolved. I would not be attracted by such a method, and I would be doubtful of a university which did not evolve extracurricular activities. Such activity is not only an outlet for undergraduate energy; it is something more. It is romantic life, especially the athletic side of it, which binds the university into a social and spiritual unit. What I should like to see, and believe altogether possible, is a student body active in enlarging the boundaries of its knowledge and understanding of the world, and at the same time supporting a healthy extracurricular life secondary and supplementary to its main business.

That kind of student body would become an alumni group capable of transforming the world. It would have the technical knowledge of subjects necessary to get on in business or in professions. It would have the advantage that comes with studious and orderly habits acquired early in life. It would have the capacity for intense, sustained, independent thought that marks the intelligent leader, and it would have added to all these keen-edged tools the haft to drive them home in the knowledge of human nature acquired through competition and other contacts with fellow students. He who knows not that last will be at a hopeless disadvantage in the hurly-burly of living. This is an age of strain and steel, electricity, chemistry, and science, but as always the main element is man. Accordingly, as extracurricular activities give you any just estimate of human relations, they give you a start in the most intricate, complicated, and useful science of them all.

You are, largely, an undergraduate student body. Overflowing with life and energy and still unshackled by responsibility you seek adventure and the joy of living more abundantly. Your great need, whether you know it or not, is outlets for your energy and emotional drive, outlets adequate and worthy of the power that is in you. Extracurricular activities furnish perhaps one of the best of these outlets that we know. When the faculty devises a better "'ole," I am sure you will go to it! In the meantime don't forget the other outlets. A little study will convince you that they are not without great attractions also. If you use them they will bring you assets that you cannot get otherwise. They will give a wider picture of your possibilities than you can get in any other way. You will learn in an atmosphere of great things. Instinctively you will absorb an ambition for real success and real service, not the spurious success and service at which the Menckenites rail. The University will become a part of you and give you vision to play the full role in life which your talents qualify you to play. There are thousands of men scattered throughout the United States whose value to the country is largely lost because in their youth they had no opportunity to see beyond their immediate surroundings, no chance to study the permanent satisfactions and durable values of life, and no inspiration to set as high a standard for themselves as they could attain to. A university such as this one can enlarge your knowledge, vision, and ambition so that what ability you have may be turned into fields a hundred times greater than it might otherwise enter.

Despite the scoffers, the cynics, the wisecrackers and the minority of desiccated academicians, a university can do all these things better in an atmosphere from which sentiment has not been extracted and in which emotion is an element; for who shall reach his goal without a burning heart. The truly great university is not a thing of books and papers, test tubes and reports, grades and mechanisms. It is a creature of the spirit built out of the lives of men—faculty men, student men. It is founded on great loyalties as well as on great intellects. And so I choose to close with the stirring words of a great university president, Benjamin Ide Wheeler, spoken in his first speech on this campus, characteristically a speech to students, words which I have often quoted and which I shall often quote again, for they epitomize my own attitude toward this University, which I hope may come to be yours also:

"This University shall be a family's glorious old mother, by whose hearth you shall love to sit down. Love her. It does a man good to love noble things, to attach his life to noble allegiances. It is a good thing to love the church, it is a good thing to love the state, it is a good thing to love one's home, it is a good thing to be loyal to one's father and mother, and after the same sort it is good to be loyal to the University, which stands in life for the purest things and the cleanest, loftiest ideals. Cheer for her; it will do your lungs good. Love her; it will do your heart and life good."

AN EARLY STATEMENT TO ALUMNI

From an Address at the Annual Charter Day Dinner

March 23, 1932

Last year, on the evening of Charter Day, I took occasion to speak of the dangers facing higher education in the State of California and to urge that the alumni of this University familiarize themselves with the high standing of its faculty, the variety and quality of its offerings, the efficiency of its equipment in libraries and laboratories, that they organize themselves to fight for its principles and its continued exist-ence against the inroads of those representing other points of view, sometimes hostile and often unfriendly to the University of California. I urged that you join me in building once again a state spirit for a state university.

Since that time there have been both confirmation of the fears ex-pressed and progress in the direction of that calm study which alone is likely to lead to sound and purposeful planning. The legislative attack was beaten off, chiefly by the reflective judgment of those repre-senting districts with no self-interest in the contest. The Carnegie Foundation has been called on to make an impartial survey and has been about its task for some six months. A commission of distin-guished educators has been recruited by President Suzzallo of the Foundation to digest and draft conclusions from the mass of fact and opinion which has been unearthed. A conference of the parties inter-ested is to be held in Sacramento on March 28, 29, and 30, at which data will be presented, ideas sifted, issues resolved, and the trend of conclusions indicated. It seems only fitting that at this moment, here in the bosom of our great family, I should speak to you of the spirit in which the representatives of the University enter upon these most important conferences, and the policy that will guide them.

In the first place, we do not go before the Commission with selfish motives, with an eye single to the interests of the University, or with malice toward any other institution or type of institution. We are seeking honestly to interpret and intelligently to serve the highest interests of education in the State of California. To that end a strong group drawn from our faculties, both in Berkeley and in Los Angeles, has for some months been making a critical study of the University's scope, function, and educational policy. We believe that we have attained a clear and forward-looking view of the University's proper role in the higher educational activities of the state, a role which might well be expressed in this credo:

(1) We believe that the University should be the repository of the highest learning and best traditions of our democracy. This implies libraries and similar collections which represent the accumulated knowledge of the human race. It implies, also, the maintenance of the highest ideal of human behavior and human action to which the civilized world has attained, and a never ending effort to realize these or better ideals which the wisdom of man may from time to time dictate.

(2) We believe that the University should be the training ground for the scholars needed in every generation to carry the light of learning forward into the darkness of the unknown, of the teachers in high schools and colleges and universities whose devoted lives must form the basis for the intellectual advancement of our country, of professional men in medicine, law, dentistry, pharmacy, engineering, agriculture, business, and public life upon whose integrity and proficiency depend much of the mental, physical, and material well-being of our people, and finally, of that large proportion of the state's population which is capable of studying and profiting by the various branches of knowledge beyond the realm of the secondary schools.

Viewed in the light of this statement of scope and function, certain University policies denounced as undemocratic and certain University aims criticized as extravagant are given clarity and reason. The selective admission requirements established by the University, in conference with the representatives of the high schools of the state, the standards of substantial attainment demanded for the various degrees and professional certificates, the constant emphasis on excellent library and laboratory facilities, on research institutes and variety of curricula, come to be, obviously, the only means to the desired ends. Such analysis also accounts for the friendly and sympathetic attitude of the University towards the other educational institutions of the state and implies with clearness and logic the points of articulation between secondary and higher education, between the University and the high schools, the junior colleges, the teachers' colleges, and vocational institutions. . . .

EN FAMILLE

University Meeting

September 2, 1935

In accordance with time-honored custom, this University Meeting, the first of the college year, is dedicated to the welcoming by the President of both new and returning students. Included in the group who have come to us as freshmen and transfers from other institutions are 3,561 men and women, and by adding themselves to our number they have made it the largest we have ever known. The greeting of the President comes a little late this year because of the change in our academic calendar but it is none the less sincere and hearty. Even your numbers we shall not hold against you if, while you are here, you will demonstrate that you stand for quality as well as quantity.

To be the president of a university with a student body so numerous, so intelligent, so handsome as you from a distance would appear to be, seems to me about the most satisfactory post a man could hold, and so at the beginning of each year I tend to swell with pride. And then I read a little later in the newspapers of one of you who has strayed from the path of rectitude, or at least staggered upon it, or of my own latest pusillanimous failure to defend the ideals of eighteenth-century America or to stake my all upon a doctrinaire, new social order in which I have no confidence, and I humbly come back to normal dimensions. But, thank goodness, it is not true that all I know about you or about myself is what I read in the newspapers, and so, though my pride is chastened, it is never destroyed nor even seriously diminished. I realize that there are students here, as in every university, who should not be here; just as there are here faculty members, as in every university, who should give thanks each night for the tradition of professorial tenure; but just as I know and shall prove that we have one of the best faculties in America, so I feel certain that we have the best student body. On this point, at least, I am sure that you and I are in perfect agreement.

Because I think so well of you I hope you will give me the pleasure of knowing better each one of you. En masse, you may see me monthly at these University Meetings, which are deservedly well attended (for other reasons) and which you should resolve right now never to miss. Here you may get a sense of belonging, here you can partake of the spiritual force, the quality of soul which is one of the hallmarks of a true university. But that is not enough for me. I want to know you as individuals—apart from the mass—as many of you as I possibly can. And so I wish you would greet me on the campus and visit with me in my office, either at the student hour from 10:30 to 11:30 each Wednesday morning, or by appointment at any time. Come as you are and for no better reason than just to see whether I am really human. I shall face you bravely, for I believe that I am, and I shall keep up at least my share of the conversation. Come up and see me sometime. . . .

The faculty of the University will spread before you the fare of plain living and high thinking on which greatness is built. The world will offer more tempting and more spicy dishes. The choice will be yours for, though you can lead a student to college, you cannot make him think. Your ears will hear Tennyson singing, "To seek, to strive, to find, and not to yield," or Robert Louis Stevenson crying, "My purpose holds to sail beyond the sunset," but something within you must awake to a new world unseen before, or the table will be spread in vain. Only you can choose between these things and the cheap magazine with the gaudy and impossible girl on the cover. You will learn of "the glory that was Greece and the grandeur that was Rome," of the grouping of figures in the Sistine Madonna, of the marvel of Corot's light streaming through the gnarled trees of the forest; but will you still prefer the "funnies" and the colored Sunday Supplement? You will be introduced to the great men of all time, to the leaders of spiritual and moral progress, the Lincolns, Spinozas, Aristotles, Merciers, and all their kinds; but will you still prefer the Longs, the

Coughlins, the Townsends, and the Darceys? Fortunate you will be if you come to possess life's intangibles, for there is no poverty like aesthetic poverty.

Every one of you should do more in this University than accumulate credits by passing course after course, forgetting each as you go on to the next, and finally amassing the minimum number with the minimum average. We are proud of these men on the platform today who this summer represented the University in one of the most public of its fields of endeavor, who have met the challenge of stern competition, and who have proved what may be accomplished by hard work, dogged determination, high courage, and team spirit. Why shouldn't we have a *whole* student body that accepts as seriously the challenge of this institution of *learning* and sets out to contribute its best to scholarship, perhaps even to win a championship or two in the field of creative thinking. You have an even greater stake in high academic standards than has the faculty. At a college or university where these do not exist, the student is getting a shoddy substitute for higher education no matter how good the football or track team may be, no matter how much talk there is about intimate contacts between teacher and taught, about student-centered rather than subject-centered instruction, about good teaching as distinguished from scholarly research. The proper division of responsibility charges the faculty with maintaining the highest standards of teaching and you with maintaining the highest standards of study. Loyalty to the University, in its finest form, is a clear recognition by each student of what the institution should be and a determination to do his share toward its attainment.

If history repeats itself, you will hear much while you are here about freedom of speech, freedom of thought, and freedom of assembly. The University of California never has, and, I trust, never will stifle freedom of discussion. We do, however, draw the inevitable line between liberty and license—liberty that protects the rights of every individual and license to organize disorder. The disciples of discontent here and elsewhere developing a doctrine of despair, proclaim a program that, if it were realized in action, would deny to all but a particular group the liberties that they mouth, and prate, and demonstrate so much about. And yet there are in every student body sincere, young idealists, urgently anxious to right the wrongs of a mad world, who are peculiarly susceptible to this kind of propaganda. Let me urge you to think straight and hard on these matters. Don't be fooled or deceived by sophistry, by casuistry, or by the constant seizing of issues that are not in question. Watch out especially for quack remedies peddled by egocentric psychopaths, be they conservative or radical, right or left. Progress has never come from the heedless acceptance of easy panaceas. The chief contribution that you can make to the welfare of humanity while you are a student in this University is to prepare yourself for effective, productive living. Your task is not to master government and society for untried and doubtful ends, but to master yourselves and the tools with which you must work if you are to accomplish anything.

The overwhelming need of today is the need of knowledge of contemporary problems. I urge you: With all your getting here, get, if you possibly can, an understanding of the fundamental principles of government, economics, and social relations, together with the historical data illustrative of these. It is in order that you may have a fair chance to get this understanding that we fight for the theory and the practice of academic freedom. In no other way can study be education and not propaganda. I realize that the democratic republic, to which this University is altogether loyal, is today attacked on many sides by those who have no concern for the principles on which it rests and to whom the long decades of human struggle and accomplishment in furtherance of American ideals mean nothing. We are compelled in the University, as elsewhere, to listen day by day and almost hour by hour to the enemies of ordered progress under the law. On mimeographed sheets and in fevered conversation you will hear violent abuse of all who are in authority, rabid appeals to selfishness and hatred, and tireless attempts to stir your worst emotions. Only clear thinking can meet such provocation. Neither in exterminating the enemy, nor in ignoring the fact that he exists, nor in suppression of knowledge about that for which he contends, lies the vindication of our convictions and the safety of our country. Rather it lies in proud recognition of how great America, with all her shortcomings, has been, and grim determination through self-discipline, fortitude, and moral stamina to make it what it might be. . . .

ADVICE TO YOUTH ON COMMENCEMENT DAY

DEPRESSION YEARS

The Sixty-ninth Commencement, May 14, 1932

Today, in my opinion, is not a repetition of 1893 or 1907, or whatever may be your favorite panic of the past. In origin and character it is quite different from anything that I have studied or known, and I am convinced that the old formulas will not apply. It is up to you to find new formulas, and the courage to apply them despite resistance and discouragement. That is the great challenge which faces you as you go out from this campus to play your parts in the drama in which your predecessors have proved themselves so tragically inept. That challenge is peremptory, ominous. It is not mere commencement rhetoric. Discontent is moving toward disorder and the time has come for thought and action by all those who have faith in our underlying social, political, and economic principles, and in the institutions that have been founded on them.

Thought, and action, were the words I used. The world that confronts you is full of facts—realities—which must be squarely recognized in a spirit of realism; and dealt with in human understanding and human sympathy. The world that confronts you is full of questions which cannot be met by stubborn resistance to change but must be answered; and answered with open minds and enlightened liberalism. Are our historic ideals false and useless? Are social compulsions preferable to uncontrolled freedom? Is progress to be made by turning our backs on the past and beginning civilization all over again on a different plane by diametrically opposite methods? Why is it that with all the progress the social order has made, there should be so much of unemployment, poverty, disorder, and human misery? Why is it that with overproduction everywhere there should be so much of under-nourishment? Why is our civilization so unequal in its distribution of happiness? Is democracy a failure, and must we turn to tyranny of an individual or of a group? These are not questions which to ask is to answer. These are questions which university graduates should be prepared to answer, for a people cannot move faster than its leaders. I hope that we have taught you better than the universities of yesterday taught us about some of the things you will need to know, for example, economics and international relations.

The stupendous challenge of today's world's problems is peculiarly a challenge to the university graduate. It is he presumably who has been prepared to meet it. So I say to you: Face the world with courage. The adventures, the conflicts, the opportunities for devotion and sacrifice in pursuit of high ambition: all these are spread out before you. Your lives will have in them enough of chance and danger to satisfy the most daring spirits among you. Seek for stability, for poise, for restraint and repose in your life and that of your country. Above all things seek for wisdom and understanding. So may your study and endurance and struggle be to better purpose and effect. Turn back as you need them to your University for renewal and enlargement of your knowledge to fit the changing needs of changing times. May you help your University and may your University help you through all the unknown years ahead. As Disraeli said fifty years ago, "The claims of the Future are represented by suffering millions; and the Youth of a Nation are the trustees of Posterity." Set straight your course under the guiding stars of courage, sympathy, and intelligence, and I have faith that you will discover in your generation, if not an Isle of Atlantis, at least a more sanely prosperous country and a better world.

The Seventieth Commencement, 1933

The greatest danger you face in the world you are about to enter is the fallacy that things are more important than men. Your greatest peril is that the idealism of youth may be dwarfed and twisted, and the mysticism of the spirit cramped into a materialistic mold. If tragedy awaits you in whatever career may lie before you, it will probably come, not through failure to achieve material success, but through failure to realize that the supreme goal of any life consists of three things: first, a trained and useful mind; second, a cultured and serene spirit; and third, an empowered personality. That is the end of true education—personal completeness. The end of university training is not to bake a cake, or build a bridge, or plow a furrow, or kick a field goal, or polish a quatrain, or dig out a Greek root, but the development of a whole life for the whole of living.

Intelligent choice of values is the sole foundation of a successful career. What are, after all, the highest values of living, the values we cannot afford in any circumstances to sacrifice, the values which reveal to us sources of supreme satisfaction independent of the senses, of the things we possess, of the external world in which we live and move and have our being? Not all of us will answer that question in the same way. Not all of us will, or should, make the same choice of values. But the wise among us will make the momentous decision mindful that it is only through idealism we can penetrate to the core of reality. Ideals are "the things that men live by." Without them we skim over the surface of existence and never sound its depths. . . .

The world that we have created is today too much for us. The machinery we have invented manufactures products which we did not foresee, which we do not want, and yet which we seem helpless to avoid. The industrial organization that has grown up around us is carrying us along, we know not whither; we know not why. We have more gold, more food, more things, and more power than at any other period in history. Yet we are poorer, hungrier, more helpless, more confused than mankind has ever been. The intelligence of the race has thus far failed before the problems that the race has raised. But with the lamp of knowledge in the hands of educated men and women, we can and we will light our way out of the dark labyrinth in which we wander. Insight, understanding, intelligence, discriminating appreciation of values, are now as always the hope of mankind—provided they are translated from matured thought into forceful action.

As Walter Lippmann said at Berkeley on Charter Day, in an address that I hope I shall never forget: "Men have learned what their ancestors did not know, that an ordered society is not ordained for them but has laboriously to be constructed and managed. They have learned that the good life in an ordered society will not be provided for them by the unconscious working of destiny, but that they themselves have to make themselves the agents of destiny to achieve the good life." Not to be ministered to, but to minister, is the true goal and chief justification of culture and power. Character and wisdom become stale and profitless unless they are made vital in conduct and action. Sir Philip Sidney, who has been called the "choice darling of England," while at school wrote to his brother, "If there are any good wars, I shall go to them." Living, he swayed the course of empire, and wrote *The Defense of Poesie*. Dying, he pressed his canteen to the lips of his wounded friend in Flanders. May you also resolve, as did Sir Philip, "If there are any good wars, I shall go to them." Down through the ages, the great tragedy of human progress has been that the educated, the privileged, as a group, have refused to act in obedience to the truth their intellects clearly discerned—until finally the frustrated forces of change accumulating in uncontrollable and destructive revolution have wiped them out. Up to now every social order that through the centuries mankind has painfully evolved, mankind has inevitably cast into the discard because it would not admit the necessity of changing its form and adapting itself to new conditions.

The world today is in the midst of another and incalculable upheaval. Your generation cannot count upon a life of ease in a paradise its predecessors have prepared. A great adventure awaits you, graduates of the University in 1933. It challenges you to make something of it. Do not be dismayed by the fact that it involves an acceptance of new ideas and new ideals. Free your minds from illusion while holding fast in your hearts to faith. The only disaster that can truly overwhelm you is the loss of your inner integrity. Test the new and when you find it true, fight for change instead of fearing and defying it.

Out there the enemy is intrenched; social wrongs and economic injustice are still rampant; life is crowded and cramped and twisted;

happiness is frozen and blighted; moral purpose is sterilized and robbed of purity; might is braggart and shiftlessness is sullen; holy impulse is stifled and hope often gutters down like a candle in its socket; pagan practices are crushing Christian civilization. Knowledge has been prostituted to the murderous policies of war. Machines have been held of more value than the human beings who tend them. Wealth rather than personality has been made the yardstick of achievement. It is no wonder we are in misery and must fight to "let knowledge grow and life be enriched." It is a good war. Go to it and play an active part in the making of a brave new world.

The Seventy-first Commencement, 1934

This is an age of transition. Commencement addresses have always begun with this thought, whatever the words in which it may have been expressed. That the world of yesterday is passing into the world of tomorrow, that all is in flux—this has ever been the theme of the moralist. And it is true, for external change is the one unchanging law of nature. The only variation is in the tempo. Changes which used to require a hundred years may now be made in as many days. We are hardly accustomed to one machine or one process before another has displaced it. In the bewildering revolutions of the modern world we are continually having to face new fashions in dress, new forms in literature, new conventions in morals, new ideas of right and wrong. The obvious peril is the loss of standards, of criteria of judgment, and of the compass points of conscience.

If these forces of change affected individuals only we might perhaps ignore them, but they affect whole peoples and the social institutions under which they live. Today, even in America, the question is being asked why our vaunted progress is so ineffective in satisfying the hopes and meeting the needs of so many of our people. The material means with which to satisfy every human desire and to afford every human comfort are produced in ample quantity and at moderate cost, yet many who need such things desperately cannot possibly acquire them. Somewhere, somehow, there is a gap, a want of balance between our social, our economic, and our political systems which we have not found ways and means to fill or to supply. So much is familiar to all. There is no disagreement as to the outlines, and little as to the details of the problem.

The difficulty is to find an answer or answers to the questions that arise as we pass from an economics of want into an economics of abundance. Yet the answer must be found, for great masses of men will not indefinitely sit quietly by and see themselves and their families reduced to want in the midst of riches and power. It is not enough to see that there must be change; we must apply to the situation criteria of some kind as to what the change shall be. It may well be that in your choice of standards, there lies for you and for American democracy the possibility of greatest peril.

Noisiest among those who will claim your attention are the impetuous and headstrong adherents of revolutionary doctrines. Theirs is a quick answer to all the questions of the day: Let us dig humanity up by the roots, cut loose from encumbering traditions and ideals, and begin all over again on a different plane and by methods contrary to all those that have proved effective in the past.

These guides who will thrust themselves upon you feel no need of property, of family, of faith, or of religion. They stand flatly on the absolute negation of everything in which our people have believed, on which our institutions have been founded, and from which civil and political liberty and popular government have been developed in the long, slow, painful advance of civilization. Are they right? Are our historical ideals really futile and false? Are social compulsions truly preferable to freedom? These questions you will have to answer as you face the world outside these gates. On what you say and do will depend the future of multitudes, as well as the life that each of you will lead.

Before I finish I shall indicate which side I hope you will take, but my deeper hope is that you will think the problem through and come to a conclusion, not because of what I have said, or anyone else may say, but on the basis of your own reasoning. If we are to avoid disaster in the irrepressible conflict, the educated men and women of America will have to exercise their mental muscles and do some thinking. Empty phrases and sounding slogans have no valid substance. There is no salvation in blind following or blind hatred. That each of you should take an intelligent and valiant part in the battle between democracy and communism is an obligation you owe to your University and to the great body of men, including this faculty, who through the years have contributed to learning and to civilization. I do not, however, commend thinking to you so much on the ground of obligation, as for the satisfaction it will give you to exercise your minds and to take your stand on one side or the other because of convictions that are your own.

Constitutional democracy is neither dead nor futile. Whether it can be successfully administered in the future will depend upon the individuals that are its constituent parts, and particularly upon you, the oncoming generation. If you cannot become fully developed, well-rounded men and women instead of bumptious go-getters, if you cannot show character to match your opportunities, if you cannot stand firm when things go wrong and courageously assume your responsibilities as citizens, then our democracy will fail, as would any other system of government.

But if you will be broad-minded and open-minded to suggestions of change and improvement, if you will set yourselves like flint against those who, in their lust for power and greed for gain, would exploit, to the public disadvantage, the opportunity that is our heritage, then the days of real achievement for America are only now beginning. The physical frontier is gone, with its many chances for sudden wealth and material prosperity, but along the spiritual frontier the vision of a new and better world is opening before us—a world in which the resources we are to derive from science will be controlled for the benefit of all and not for the few, a world in which the socialization of national purpose will prevent a barren and unsatisfying individualism.

To the building of that new world I call you in the name of America. The obligation and the opportunity are enormous. The goal is not to be won without a burning heart, a heart which keeps alight not the sickly green flare of cynicism but the pure and steady flame of honest patriotism. The turbulent world you enter is no place for cowards. A courageous sinner is much more at home in it than a timid saint. The call of the hour is for leadership, sympathetic in its understanding, tolerant in its outlook, and dynamic in its courage. We are not suffering nearly so much from an overproduction of material goods as from and underproduction of honest thinking. Do not permit yourselves to be embittered by the disappointments of your elders. Do not permit your confidence to be impaired by their suspicions. Do not permit your judgments to be clouded by their inferiority complexes. They are paying the penalty of their mistakes; you should profit by them. Above all, don't be content with contemplative inaction. Don't be content to interpret the world. Go out to change it. But remember that change need not mean destruction. Any attempts to recreate the world in seven days will result in chaos, social disorder, and general ruin. Utopias never work out as planned. But if you can keep our American system of government successfully working, as it has worked since the days of its beginnings with Washington and Franklin, you will be keeping clear the way to the land of promise and you will help to lift from the hearts of men the awful load of sorrow and suffering which is now crushing them to earth.

Your reward will be a greater, finer, and richer America than we have yet known. For whether America shall be exalted or abased depends wholly upon America's citizens and the quality of their leadership. To those who can keep the faith, the way lies straight ahead.

The Seventy-second Commencement, 1935

The first and most urgent responsibility that your generation must meet is the re-establishment of public confidence—confidence in one another and confidence in the state. Men will not move forward unless they have confidence in the honesty and fairness of their social, economic, financial, and political order. There is only one straight and narrow way to this essential achievement, and it is quite likely to be at times a hard and lonely road. In order that there shall be confidence in the state and in one another, each individual citizen must establish high standards of rectitude in his personal and public life, and hold himself to them. *There* is a test to prove your mettle. Men must be able to trust their fellows; they must be given protection by society against exploitation, persecution, and theft. Only so will men act willingly in cooperation with their fellows under the aegis of a democratic government. If democracy prove unable or unwilling to achieve the self-mastery that this requires, men will be forced, indeed they will choose, to act at the dictation of despotic but efficient authority.

That democracy sorely needs citizens who can so maintain a balance wheel of sanity and clear thinking has been, and is increasingly, apparent. For democracy, with its recognition of *all* citizens, must needs reckon with its archenemy—demagogy, multiplied in power these days by the twentieth-century magnitude of its vociferosity. Consider the number of fundamental conditions generally agreed to be important causes of the present depression which are the result of surrender to popular whim and prejudice against the sober wisdom of men of knowledge and judgment: the exaction of impossible reparations payments, the enactment of too high tariff laws, the obstruction of partial disarmament, the emphasis on selfish nationalism. Every one of them has played a part in bringing the world to its present unhappy pass, and every one of them is the consequence of the free play of democratic forces. "Out of this morass," says Dr. Nicholas Murray Butler, "Out of this morass there is one sure way of escape, and that is by the aid of a really well-instructed, a really alert, a really courageous, and a really liberal public opinion."

The Seventy-third Commencement, 1936

Real progress comes neither from directionless effort nor Micawber-like waiting for something to turn up; neither from jumping up and down on a soap box nor from sitting idly in an ivory tower. Before we can make headway in the whirlpool of life, amidst the violent intensity of social and economic storms, we must get our bearings and know which way is forward. The University has tried to demonstrate to you that the only way to do that is to get the facts, to strive to understand them, and to act accordingly. Facts are often harsh, unpleasant, awkward things, but you can't avoid them and you can't ignore them. You must live with them, and in the end you'll find them far better companions than the most charming fallacies.

The University has tried, also, to let you see for yourselves that the present is the child of the past, and that only by studying the story of what man has done in earlier days can we achieve real knowledge of the times in which we live. History is to mankind what memory is to the individual. If men are to look ahead and discover anything worth seeing, they must learn first to look, with understanding, backward, that they may trace the way by which they have to come. To project the line of human progress into the future we must, any surveyor will tell you, have at least one point in addition to the one on which we are now standing. In spite of the tragic story of Lot's wife, I urge you to have the temerity to look back before you rush forward. History supplies the only data on which we can safely rely; the basis of sound thinking must be the world's past experiences. Patrick Henry, who was certainly not a conservative, spoke wisely when he said: "I have but one lamp by which my feet are guided, and that is the lamp of experience. I know of no way of judging the future but by the past." Others have voiced the same thought.

To some of you these words will smell of lavender and old lace. You have read or seen so much of difficulty and distress, of selfishness and stupidity, of corruption and crime, that it is your perfectly understandable disposition to cover the past with a blanket indictment and to proceed either with the desperation of the hopeless or the valor of the ignorant. Many of you are disillusioned, suspicious, and insecure, blaming everyone and anyone but yourselves for the discomforts of today and the miserable uncertainties of tomorrow. But this is only a passing phase at one time or another in all men's lives, and with glad relief you will realize again that pilgrimages of the spirit to the sources of a people's supreme traditions are essential to a healthy national life. There are full-statured men and women in all ages. Seek them out and learn from them, not from cripples. Your generation—any generation—is but a bridge from the past to the future, and if this bridge breaks its connection at either end, traffic stops and the continuity of development is broken.

Times like those through which we have been passing encourage feeling rather than thinking. Kind hearts are wrung by suffering; tortured minds are moved to approach reform through destructiveness. The thinking man can sympathize with but he does not follow the adventurers along this path. Revolution destroys more than it creates. The contribution of educated men should be to evolution—slow but sure. Daily your generation should experiment. Daily it should move upward. But each step should be built on one below. No man attempts to climb Mount Everest in one spectacular dash, but only by care in preparation, patience in progress, and restraint in adventure, as well as daring and determination in action. This is the way of wisdom, and of heroism and courage as well.

Right now there is grave danger in this country, as in this University, that restless radicals will attempt to go too far and too fast. Bryce says: "Revolutionists, intoxicated with their own aims, recoil from no means needed to secure their ascendancy, because they have not learnt, in Cromwell's famous phrase, to believe it possible that they may be mistaken." I do not fear that radicals will overthrow our government or our institutions, for the American people are too sensible to follow them. But I do fear that the overreaching enthusiasm of extremists will inevitably and properly invite reaction, and thus prevent the progress which might otherwise be made. If I know my country, the bombs of revolutionists are not dangerous because they may start a conflagration, but because they will call out the fire department of reaction. And with the smoke of propaganda, the water of suppression, and the axes of terrorism, the damage will be done, and the building of civilization set back another generation. . . .

THE ROAD TO WAR
The Seventy-fifth Commencement, 1938

The compelling task of your generation is to maintain and strengthen democracy upon which alone can ever be built a world at peace. How shall you go about it? How shall the many and deep-seated strains pervading the structure of man's organized society be eased and removed, their recurrence prevented? For the moment most of the world is turning to heroes and demigods, looking for miracles. In recent years some hundreds of millions of people in a folly of desperation have deserted democracy for dictatorship. But no such legerdemain will work. No short cut to wisdom, no panacea has been or will be discovered. What the world and you are facing is a long job, a hard job, a democratic job. It is a labor that calls upon each and all; a slow emerging and articulation, through democratic processes, of that ultimate folk justice of which Lincoln has said, "Is there any better or equal hope in the world?" Men of high purpose and creative imagination, and most of these should be university graduates if universities are worth their keep, must envision the larger possibilities, turn vague hopes into clear concepts, point out beyond the intervening ranges the distant, shining goal. And, thus, gradually there will develop a social organism which will fulfill the needs, the desires, and the aspirations of men and women made after the likeness of God. In the meantime, our surest reliance is human decency—good will, patience, honor, faithfulness, mutual forbearance, and hard work—elemental solvents for the ills of men.

Let me now make one or two practical, quite prosaic, diagrammatic applications of these principles in the brief time at my disposal this afternoon. One of the most significant phenomena of the day is the deep and eager interest of an active and intelligent minority of American students in the prevention of war. And one of the saddest commentaries upon human nature is the suspicious, contentious, intolerant way in which so many of these advocates of peace seek its realization. For beneath the peace of the world, and inherent and essential in its attainment, is the immutable law of ordered human society, the law of good will. Harmony among nations can never be secured by promoting hatred among men. No lasting progress toward peace will ever be made by bitter partisans who denounce and vilify those who press toward the goal by roads different from their own, nor by nations that mock at international treaties and international agreements and consider them mere scraps of paper. The one element indispensable to a world of just and enduring peace is a common spirit of good will, a common endeavor toward good will.

Such an approach is admittedly intangible and immeasurable in scope and duration. And so it is natural, perhaps, impatiently to ask, Would it not be better to concentrate on more immediate steps to save our hard-won progress toward world peace and order from imminent disaster? No! Unless the foundations are well laid, the superstructure will never survive the earthquake shock of war. At a thousand points the long-range policy must affect the short-range action. The only way to prevent war is to remove the causes of war, and to stimulate good will in the hearts of men, so that eventually shall be established the rule of law to displace the rule of force in the settlement of international differences and disputes.

One more example and I cease. There is a powerful doctrine abroad in the world today that modern democracy is merely the spawn of a decaying liberalism. There are violent movements, too, which would cure the ills of industrial capitalism with communistic sentiment and ideology, or with the irresponsible force of fascism, or with a misshapen combination of the two. These doctrines and movements thrive upon the destruction of trust and confidence, the promotion of intolerance and ill will. They have their roots in the want of social faith. America has been bound together by tolerance and patience and a sense of duty. The crystallizing principle of our national life has been the obligation of man to man, of class to class, of race to race, of faith to faith. Thus Americans have found and cherished liberty, thus they have builded a civilization which, with all its faults, is kindlier, more humane, more just than any man has known before.

Through one hundred and fifty years our people have established the idea and the practice of majority rule. They have maintained it not by force of arms but though the confidence of the minority that its rights would be upheld, and the confidence of the majority that its position would be assailed only through the mechanisms of free speech, a free press, and a free, secret, and convenient ballot box. Today these confidences are being undermined by those who hold that majorities sometimes have emergency mandates to ignore the rights of minorities, and also by those who hold that minorities have a duty to seize power by violence and to oppress or liquidate those who disagree with them. These claims are based always on greed for power. Don't let either of them fool you. Don't be misled by the argument, logical enough but based on the false premise of class self-interest which rejects the possibility of truth in the contentions of opponents. The peril of American democracy today is a developing arrogance which, for wealth, creates its own privileged class morals, and, for labor, justifies violence and condones cunning. This is an ominous state of affairs, indeed, for what little wisdom men have acquired in the course of their cruel history clearly demonstrates that no one knows enough to rule another violently, and that no end is good enough to justify the sacrifice of the methods of persuasion. By this wisdom are quarrels composed, violence averted, and the democracy maintained by which men live and let live.

The principle which is paramount for democracy is this: Political progress comes through the suppression of lawless and arbitrary violence in human affairs, and through the laborious development of habits of courtesy and good will in the relations of men. Never can a campus, a community, or a world be at peace if good faith is not practiced and believed in. The vice of imputing unworthy motives, of looking for a fight instead of conciliation, is a reversion to the primitive, a decivilization of mankind, a descent to barbarism. There is evil in the affairs of men, of course, but evil does not pull the great tides of history, and the man who looks upon anything he does not like as the product of malice, or deceit, or conspiracy, may properly be regarded as not quite sane. The difficulty is not that the modern tasks of democracy are insuperable, but that modern men seem to be becoming more and more irreconcilable. The United States has no social or political problem which cannot be worked out by counting heads rather than breaking them if our people will but play the game according to its simple, elementary rules.

The Seventy-sixth Commencement, 1939

There is a vast fund of leadership in our nation that suffers neither from the rigor mortis of reaction nor the delirium tremens of radicalism. It is for you to find and follow that kind of leadership, to help lift the standards around which stable intelligence, effective power, and sound social sense can rally. Thus will the fruits of this age of science be brought into the lives of the millions, and America be maintained as a self-governing democracy with politics the servant, not the sovereign, of our lives.

The future of free institutions is bound up with their efficiency. To survive, democracy, in competition with other forms of government, must prove itself a superior system, or it will be replaced. The decline in democracy abroad, its disappearance over large areas, the weakness, short-sightedness, and vacillation with which democratic nations have frittered away the moral as well as the physical profits of the World War, are too well established to be considered merely accidental. They put thoughtful men squarely on notice that democratic institutions need to be strengthened, and adapted to handle modern problems more effectively, especially those in the economic and social fields. Underlying the dictatorships was a prior failure of democratic regimes, especially on problems such as unemployment. The crisis now facing civilization results from the ineffectiveness of democratic governments, as now organized, to cope with present-day problems. The central problem facing your generation is the adapting of the American way to the society and the economics of 1939. To survive, democracy must work.

Before each one of you who aspires to live his life creatively, lie tasks that will tax every physical, mental, and spiritual strength and resource he possesses. New ways are slowly opening out before democratic America. If ever there was a time when we needed to pay a duty to intelligence, that time is now. Trained thinkers with disciplined emotions must be alert to changes and fearless in facing them. I hope and believe that this University has built in you the creative attitudes and the staying power you need for the vitally important work that is yours to do. The world's problems now crying out for solution are a challenge to the university graduate. It is he, presumably, who has been prepared for the coming hour. With your readiness to strike out on new courses after sounding the way, with your ability to scrutinize new proposals with a mind stored with the wisdom of the past and trained in the analytical methods of the present, there is hope for this and every other free nation. In the words which Thucydides puts in the mouth of Pericles, these, like Athens, will owe their greatness "to men with the fighter's daring, the wise man's understanding of his duty, and the good man's self-discipline in its performance."

Fortunes may accumulate and dissolve; depressions may follow periods of lush prosperity; political chicanery may win a brief power; commercial dishonesty may have its little day; but if you perform the functions for which you have been trained, if you stress effectually in your lives sound learning, intelligent loyalty, civic responsibility, and personal integrity, there need be no fear for the future of America.

The Seventy-seventh Commencement, 1940

Today the civilization of Europe which has meant so much to the preservation of the great and significant values of the world, is in disorder if not decay. It is a cursed fate for some, no doubt, that they should be born in this uneasy time when they might have decorated elegantly a quieter epoch. Yet, for the magnitude of its enterprises, the present century has no parallel. To be confronted by such problems and competent to play a part in their solution, is for courageous souls a challenging opportunity.

For those who love peace and believe that peace is the mother of democracy and progress, as power lust is the chief determinant of war, the only practical course would seem to be to raise defenses behind which, undisturbed by the ideologies of hate on principle, we can maintain ourselves in the development of the democratic tradition, while lending effective moral and material support to the rule of equity and law elsewhere, and to those peoples whose ideals we share. If we are then attacked by the dictators, by the priests of political witchcraft, we shall be able to strike back, and not strike softly!

That we may do so, if the dread time should come, certain things we must prepare beforehand to accept and act upon. The weakness of democratic nations before the dictators has been democracy's divided counsels before totalitarian unity. Therefore, we must put the commonwealth before private wealth, and the basic needs of the common man before the lesser needs of the possessing few. If not, faction will multiply on faction and there will be no disciplined liberty to confront successfully armed regimentation. There must be no tolerant, or belligerent, talk of "the working classes." We all belong to "the working classes," or those who do not had better make haste to qualify. If dictatorship can provide not only "bread and circuses" but also a minimum economy of health and decency for all its citizens, and if democracy cannot, it will be the worse for democracy. The test is a concrete one, and it will do no good to plead either the ideals or "the system." Democracy must concern itself with citizens as citizens in a community, differentiated in function but by intention classless—all recognized as being of the common clay. It must concern itself with the minds, the eyes, the teeth, the stomachs, the mental and physical health and fitness of this and future generations. How can we ask common men to fight, if we accept no common obligation?

A political liberty that is not implemented by a minimum of economic security is a reduction of democracy to absurdity, as Carlyle showed long ago. This does not mean no high incomes—the dead level of socialism—but the high income must carry social responsibility, even as it did under feudalism, and it must, moreover, be socially warranted. The tragedy of commercialism lies in the divorce of private wealth and public duty. The citizen in a democracy, even with the humblest occupation must be able to hold his head high as a member of a community earnestly concerned for him and for his self-respect. The core of democracy is the self-respect of the humble, and democracy can only succeed, broad-based, where this is true.

If we are "to continue to maintain inviolate upon this continent a civilization that will invite the souls of men," we must exalt the values of civilization and we must have faith. Somehow, we must find a religion of our own that will overcome the political religions of Marxism and Naziism, each with its Book and its Prophets. We must not become entangled in other men's errors; our fight is to build freedom in at least one area of the world. If we do not wish in these United States collectivism and totalitarianism advertised and lauded as more complete democracy, we must labor with sincerity of soul for a truly free American community. Unless our loyalty and devotion to this free community is more powerful than the fanaticism of the communist for the class war, or the bigotry of the Nazi for the Nordic race, then they and not we will shape the future of the world. And our loyalty and devotion must be guaranteed, as Pericles said, by the bravery with which we guard them.

Democracy is the resolution to remove those actual and unnecessary divergences of interest that are the springs of class war; to replace class consciousness by public sensitiveness; to stimulate the willingness of men to recognize, without envy, inequality of function and also of talent. All this is not an easy task. Democracy demands discipline, the discipline of educated men and women, but it is the only method by which Russian Sovietism and National Socialism can be defeated in equal combat while freedom is retained. To you, graduates of the Class of 1940, we look to see the American tradition take form in deeds, in classless living, and in putting first the common good. Especially we look for sincerity in the cause of humanity, for a vision of peoples transcending class, for a concept of eternal justice that does not fail, and of rational justice sufficient to the needs of the day. To ridicule the self-sacrifice of Soviet Russia or to hate the heroic courage of the "Battalions of Death" of Nazi Germany is to confess some inner weakness. It is for you to do as well, as firmly, as proudly, but more sanely, for democratic America. It can be done, I believe that you can do it.

The Seventy-eighth Commencement, 1941

The specter of war, which has haunted the Class of 1941 throughout its senior year, bids fair ere long to overtake all its members, either directly or indirectly. To many of you this experience has been a rude shock, not so much physically, for no generation of Americans has ever been fitter or braver, but intellectually, emotionally, and spiritually. For years you have been schooled by your elders, by me and others like me, to distrust force, to abjure violence, to abhor war. Now, "with stunning suddenness," as a student editor has said, "the signals have been switched," and you are called upon to employ force, to approve of violence, to prepare for war.

In the hour of freedom's peril and democracy's test, both must be backed by a fighting faith in the democratic idea and the democratic system, by a passionate love of country and of a way of life. Are we not seeing this magnificently demonstrated day after day and night after night across the sea? Planes and battleships and armored divisions will be as useless to us as the Maginot Line was to the French unless they are manned by men who know what they are fighting for and who are convinced of the rightness of their cause. No way of life can survive unless those to whom it is entrusted are infused and inspired by an aggressive belief in its value. Such belief men and women must achieve personally. They cannot be preached, or exhorted, or coerced into it. Obviously, also, they cannot enjoy the fruits of democracy if they do not believe in it and are not willing to work and fight for it. Democracy is a jewel of many facets, a word of many meanings. In one of its most glorious aspects it is an affirmation that men and women can find within themselves a common faith, an instinctive loyalty to ennobling concepts of the human spirit, a faith and loyalty utterly alien to the frenzy induced by lying propagandists, whose victims are spied upon and whipped by secret police. Democracy is the creation of free men. It can live, remember, only in the air of freedom. For democracy is simply a way of achieving ends, good, bad, or indifferent, that men have the ability and the will to achieve for themselves within the limitations of the hard world in which they live. It is not a gift—this democratic way, our American way. It is, on the contrary, born of travail and suffering. Nobody is going to give you faith in it, but if you get that faith for yourselves, nothing will ever destroy this country of ours. You will not only fight for it—as soldiers, if necessary—but also as engineers, lawyers, doctors, states-men, artists; and you will fight for it successfully—you will repel the attacks of barbarous retrogression for yourselves and assure a livable future for your children.

In that struggle your University will be fighting alongside of you, strengthening you in the heat of combat even as it has hitherto sought to prepare you for the more normal tests of life. For the University of California is dedicated to the service of the forces of freedom in the United States and in the world. It is not neutral, it is not even objec-tive in this vital business of mankind. Passionately loyal to truth, its position, as it always has been, is critical and independent. The Uni-versity will continue to seek the truth and to try to tell the truth, even amid the obscene agonies of war. It will give no comfort to the foes of democracy, be they Communist, or Fascist, or just plain, old-fashioned Tory. It will support and encourage every agency honestly enlisted for the defense of the United States and of democracy. It will continue to teach that our form of government is an infinitely precious heritage, to be preserved at all costs. Unceasingly the University will declare its faith that men and women can govern themselves and that they need not abdicate that prerogative even to the wisest and the best, let alone to a self-styled "super-race." It will continue to stress the great achievements of our country, but also to point out wherein it has thus far fallen short of its ideals. The University will deal with controversial issues courageously but objectively, so that the children of a free people may know and decide in the light of the facts. It will continue to summon the enthusiasm of youth to the unyielding defense of the sectors of democracy already won, and to encourage pioneering spirits to push out new salients into every field of human endeavor. This is the pledge of your University—to sharpen and temper its ancient weapons, the rational minds of selected men and women—so that in this hour of democracy's crisis it may help to win a victory in which all humanity shall share, the only sort of victory that free men can count as victory.

I cannot foresee what lies immediately ahead for you and for all of us, nor is it within my power to shape it. Only one thing is clear. In the world that you are entering, there will be short shrift for weaklings or for fools, whether individuals or nations. Would you, as individuals, hold fast the integrity of your being? Then you must, each of you, oppose to the challenge of totalitarianism an unconquerable will to live—or die—in freedom and with honor. Such a determination can come only from a united people. Only as youth and age alike are inspired with an understanding of the American tradition can we hope to safeguard the true spirit of liberty, to preserve that freedom under self-imposed law that is our heritage.

IN THE REALM OF POLITICAL PHILOSOPHY

Address at the Annual State Chamber of Commerce Breakfast

Sacramento, September 7, 1946

Day by day, at every meeting of the United Nations, of the foreign ministers, and of the Security Council, a persistent, frustrating conflict of political philosophies takes the center of the stage and usually obstructs the play. At stake in the conflict is the whole system of free government, private property, respect for human personality, consent of the governed, representative authority, and legal checks and balances for which the English speaking world has struggled during three hundred years. At least a hundred years after it was thought that liberty had been established in Western civilization, the very opposite philosophy of the meaning and objectives of government has arisen to deny every principle that Americans have been taught to regard as liberal and progressive.

Our country was founded and has grown great on the philosophy of liberalism. Challenging the substance and reality of the gains of liberalism is the philosophy of socialism; to be more precise, the philosophy of a totalitarian, regimented society. The liberal philosophy holds that government is an agent of its citizens, the socialist philosophy, that it is their master. The first philosophy would limit the exercise of political authority to the restrictions of constitutional law, and so preserve some humane consideration for individuals and minorities. The second mocks at this "legalistic" theory of the state, and holds that it is the function of government to remove all disabilities to anybody's enjoyment of a life of material abundance, to substitute for the consent of the governed the economic demands of pressure groups, supported by physical force. The liberal philosophy holds that there are certain necessary truths about the good life, to which individual and social behavior ought to conform. The socialist philosophy holds that such truths are mere "ideologies"—i.e., they are merely a way of making people believe whatever is deemed expedient that they should believe in the struggle for the material advantage of a class or political party.

At first the socialist philosophy seemed innocent enough, even if Utopian. It was only a humanitarian siding with the "under-privileged." It meant the brotherhood of man, it would substitute economic liberty for the masses in the place of mere political and civil liberty. It would substitute cooperation for "cutthroat competition," and would justly distribute the material wealth of society. But it has become clearly evident with the passing of the years and the accumulation of data that the radical movement—socialism in its original and broadest sense—is the wolf in sheep's clothing. Dictatorships, secret police, concentration camps, contempt for human personality, and military conquest are not the accidents of the movement, they are essential to its realization.

Call it what you will, every socialistic movement means (1) the destruction of a government of checks and balances, of principles, of rights, of parliamentary meeting of minds, and popular suffrage; (2) it means government by decree, bureaucratic planning, and concentrated, irresponsible authority; (3) it means the regimentation of the population by means of the expropriation of employing capital, and the taking over of the ownership of the wealth of the nation by a class of successful professional politicians; finally, (4) it means the end of the system of free enterprise.

Such in brief are the major conflicting philosophies of the modern world. In the dust of their conflict it is difficult to discern, much less understand what is happening in the world today, even in these United States of America. We Americans hear much about national preparedness for war, but what can arms and munitions—even atomic bombs—avail if our hearts and minds are open to the very subversive influences against which our ports and borders are closed. The best answer to the world challenge of communistic socialism is the recognition, for what they are, of all the steps that lead toward an imposed, planned economy and totalitarianism, and the regeneration of the society of opportunity for all, which is our heritage. Let Americans oppose dictatorship at home by taking the lead in a moral and political housecleaning. Thus we shall prove that we are still worthy of the liberties our fathers won for us, and need have no fear for the outcome of the conflict of philosophies in the world beyond our borders. If we are unwilling or incapable of realizing these truths and acting upon them, the coming decades may well visit upon us the sad fate of our European contemporaries.

IN QUEST OF PEACE
The Eighty-sixth Commencement, 1949

Whether I can provide you with directions or sustenance for the journey on which you now step forth, I am frankly doubtful. Once I had a childlike faith in the efficacy of the commencement address. But that faith was long ago mortally wounded, and by one who is now a Regent of the University, and on this platform today. For he delivered a commencement address in June, 1914, in which he conclusively demonstrated that the forces determining peace had made such progress in the world that there could never be another war. He had hardly stepped off the platform when all the nations of Europe were at each other's throats. While I have always consoled myself that it would have been different had the rulers of Europe been privileged to hear what he had to say, my trust in the commencement address has not since been fully restored.

Nevertheless, I can, perhaps, from a slightly longer perspective than yours, diagnose some of the ills of our times, and identify some of the contributing causes, the correction of which could not but have a beneficial effect. One of these ills, certainly, and one which must command our special attention, is the failure of educated men and women, not only in this country but throughout the world, to do any really independent thinking: their reliance upon the mechanics of an industrial society and the machinery of government to achieve results that can be accomplished only through the acts of individuals; their willingness to drift with the currents of contemporary life on the theory that what goes on is either beyond their comprehension, or beyond their ability to combat successfully.

We, who represent and are the products of the civilization of the twentieth century, may be justly proud of our advances in technology —our airplanes, our automobiles, our Frigidaires, and our washing machines—but can we be equally proud of our progress—or lack of it—in the many things which have a more direct bearing upon the human aspects of that civilization—religion, philosophy and the arts; literature, or the home life of the American family? Science has bestowed upon us bounteous gifts wherewith to make our tasks easier and to enrich our leisure; but we have become so deeply engrossed in the machinery of it all that we have lost sight of "the whirling stars." We have forgotten that no machine can be better than its inventor; that neither the mechanics of science nor the machinery of government can produce results inconsistent with the quality of the humans who devise or operate them.

It is almost certain that man will continue to gain more and more control over the physical world. From ancient times to this very day, every aspect of our culture has been affected by the advances of science and technology. The artifacts of man, the food he eats, the clothes he wears, the houses he builds, his means of travel and communication, his prevention and cure of disease, his conduct of war have been shaped by the findings of science. Moreover, these achievements of physical science have come about through the unfettered exploitation of the experimental method, operating at the impulse of free ideas, which is the glory of the university. They have given us a control over physical nature that has in a generation revolutionized our manner of life, and utterly outstripped our ability to match it with the necessary social, and ethical, and economic readjustments.

Much of this technical advance has been benign in the highest degree. Man has gained control over many diseases which formerly decimated populations and occasioned widespread suffering and sorrow. He has ameliorated innumerable conditions of living and has thus brought greater happiness to thousands. But in the process, there has been wrought much that is ill, temporarily if not permanently. Laborsaving devices have impoverished hundreds of thousands who have been thrown out of employment. The machinery of warfare has been made so awful that another war bids fair literally to destroy both man and his civilization. The methods that have been pursued in every war that you and I have known, whereby women and children and other innocent noncombatants are brutally slaughtered quite as a matter of course, represent a reversion to sheer barbarism. These malign acts, it cannot be gainsaid, are the applied products of scientific thought imposed upon a world that had not yet achieved the moral and spiritual controls to protect itself from the misery of their misuse.

We have had a lopsided development of creative thinking directed to physical problems, perhaps because these were the easiest to solve, but probably because they were the problems that interested the men of the industrial age. For always the achievements of men have been determined by their interests even more than by their talents. Aristotle would have been as capable of inventing the steam engine as he was of analyzing the processes by which the tragic drama purifies the soul. The age that produced a Shakespeare could just as well have produced an Edison. And our world—some are wryly saying—has not even noticed that it lacks a Raphael or a Beethoven: it is quite happy with "modern art" and "bebop."

Men began the conquest of nature and the harnessing of nature's forces, fully a thousand years after they could have done so, because it was only then that they became interested. Imagine a Hebrew prophet, a Greek philosopher, or a Roman senator caring what makes garbage rot. Pasteur did care, and the science of bacteriology became a major force in the modern world. More recently, men have cared to know how to make machinery and how to get rich, and so they have done both. When we care about something else, we shall do that successfully too.

Men have cared, and so mankind has progressed. But—and for too long—they have not taken thought for the social and ethical effects of

234

their caring. There were medieval devotees who cared so intensely for the rapt vision of the crucifixion that it left actual stigmata on their hands and feet. There were conquerors who cared so much to slaughter that they piled the bones of their victims higher than the pyramids. And there are fanatics ruling Russia today who care so much for a formula they read in a book, that they oppress a whole people with incredible privations, and with proselyting missionary zeal, in season and out, abuse and threaten all other types of government and especially democracy. From *your* generation the world needs desperately that earnestness of caring in the areas of spiritual and ethical insight.

For there is a great wind sweeping across the world, so great that no man knows whence it comes or whither it is going. Yet none but the deaf can fail to hear in the noise of its passing, the ominous words: "Get ready!" What does it mean? Get ready for what? Men differ in their answers. Some think it means get ready for World War III. It is a terrible and bloody wind if this be true. Some think the wind calls us to get ready for government-made security, with food and warmth and shelter within the regimented reach of every man. But those who thus read the wind never remind us that the cattle standing to their halters in their narrow stalls have all these things.

I venture to assert that neither of these interpretations is true, that when the present turmoil in men's minds has quieted down, the eternal verities will still hold sway. I venture to think that the wind, with all its violence and strength, is saying, especially to you, young men and women: Get ready to play your independent parts as free men should; get ready to use and not abuse the great gifts which science is pouring forth; get ready with character, wisdom, and valor to defend and enrich the inheritance of culture and liberty into which a benevolent Providence has permitted you to enter. Get ready, says the wind, get ready with better trained minds, more knowledge of the past and reverence for its lessons, higher courage for the future, and a deeper devotion to the cause of human freedom.

Get ready, too, says the wind, to adjust your economic, political, social, and spiritual views to new conditions, to changes in environment and altered material forces. But never forget that human nature remains basically the same, and it is human nature that the leaders of men must reach, and inspire, and guide. Remember that shifting conditions are normal on history's long trek, and that they will continue throughout your lifetime. Remember that the principles you have learned in the University are fundamental, and have eternal force and power. But remember, in addition and above all, that your real success in life will be measured in terms of your continuing growth in knowledge and character, by the stature you attain as intelligent, reflective human beings.

Therefore, question authority, respect tradition, love liberty. When authority tries to impose itself upon you without convincing you, ask what its origin is, what its sanctions are, and pay attention only when it gives you satisfactory replies. But respect tradition, because it comes carrying with it, in maxims and institutions, the wisdom of the past. Respect tradition, too, because it is being made new all the time—indeed, you have made, and are making, some of it yourselves. Respect tradition, because it is what you are passing on to the next generation.

Above all, love freedom and liberty, not merely in the vagueness of generalities but in the day to day actualities of political and economic living; and remember that a nation cannot through coercion, effectively control the agricultural, industrial, and commercial procedures of its people without control, also, of all the other aspects of their life. From a practical point of view, the absolutist states are quite right in suppressing intellectual liberty as they have done, for there must be no sabotage of the policies of the state if a totalitarian regime is to work at all, and free, moving thought is always a potential disturber of the peace. That is why communism, with its foundations laid in the complexities of the Marxian Bible, has reduced its universities to intitutions for the promotion of propaganda, and its professors, even of genetics, to the status of puppets of the ruling regime.

Not so long ago, that public official whose proud business it is to control and discipline the Soviet press, announced that no such thing as individual liberty exists. "There is no freedom of the individual," he said; "there is only freedom of peoples and nations, for these are the only material and historical realities through which the life of the individual exists." The astounding assumption of this speaker that individuals are not even realities, but merely facets of a community, was answered long ago by Goëthe, whose centennial we celebrate this year, in the dictum: "Mankind? It is an abstraction. There are, always have been, and always will be, men and only men."

And so long as there are men, subject to all the weaknesses and frailties of human nature, there will be points at which the rule of force may be necessary, just as in your community there is need of police in order that riots and personal assaults may be prevented and punished. Certainly, there must be force in reserve—moral force, political force, economic force, and, in last and unwelcome resort, even military force—as the nations slowly make progress toward greater liberty and larger opportunity for all men. The only practical choice is between force dedicated to dictatorial control and force devoted to the survival of democracy.

In taking leave of you, then, I urge and warn you to preserve the priceless American heritage—the heritage of a free, self-governing people, devoid of caste, loving peace, and resolved, at whatever cost, to attain in time the ideal of justice, equality of opportunity, and individual dignity for every citizen. American democracy, as is the experience of all human aspiration and endeavor, has made its errors, its failures, its blunders. But, with all its defects, contrast our republican form of government with that of its autocratic rival, and who can hesitate for an instant in making his choice, or who can doubt that, with patience and intelligence and good will, we shall find the way out of our troubles. Keep our American system of government working and improving, and you will not only be keeping clear the way to the land of promise for yourselves and your children, but you will also be helping to lift from the hearts of men and women elsewhere in the world the awful load of sorrow and suffering and fear which is now crushing them to earth. Whether America shall be exalted or debased depends wholly upon America's citizens and the quality of their leadership. To those who can keep the faith, the way lies straight ahead.

The Eighty-seventh Commencement, 1950

For the last time, one may speak to you as undergraduates. Tomorrow you will be alumni, "old grads" in the vernacular, eligible to prod the University into improving its football team, and to receive appeals for contributions from the Alumni Association. What can one say on such an occasion which will not drift lightly off the tops of your minds like mist before the dawn?

I can only pray that many of you will be challenged all your lives by the capacity that resides in each human being to grow in knowledge to the very end of his days. There are resources of the mind at the command of each one of us, little gifted though he may be, which can never be drained completely; there are horizons before us which can never be overstepped; Pierian springs for our refreshment which can never run dry. These resources and the satisfactions they bring are the true wealth of educated minds.

The value of your university education does not lie primarily in the skills it has given you, whereby you may draw larger salaries, or secure positions of more influence, or obtain more quickly and more certainly an adequate pension, or other hallmarks of success. It lies rather in the power it gives you to discriminate between the transient and the eternal; and in the measure of restraint that it enables you to impose upon yourselves when tempted to seek rewards that would turn to dust even as you laid hold on them.

If you will but heed as best you can this advice I offer you—even though I have heeded it none too well myself—your lives will never be drab or commonplace; never blighted by disbelief or despair; never frightened by the dark complexities of modern civilization, or even by the riddle of the universe. You will have confidence and strength; you will have joy and satisfaction; "you shall run and not be weary." Even though the sky is now darkened with clouds, and chilled by the atmostphere of a cold war, the future still beckons with its rainbow of promise. The troubled world awaits even now a new era, in which any one of you may record new progress, discover new truth, or otherwise serve well in whatever place may be your lot.

The American system of political democracy combined with capital-ist economy, and rooted in opportunity and justice for all, has been abundantly proved to be a sound and fruitful partnership. Through almost two centuries it has advanced human rights to a degree that no other political or economic system in all history has even approached. With its emphasis of the rights and duties, the free enterprise of the individual man, it will, if I know anything of the course of history, soon resume its forward march, shoulder to shoulder with other democracies, to a world of peace for our time and hope for the genera-tions yet to be born.

As Winston Churchill puts it in his book, *Europe Unite*, "If we all pull together and pool the luck and the comradeship . . . and firmly grasp the larger hopes of humanity, then it may be we shall move into a happier sunlit age, when all the little children who are now growing up in this tormented world may find themselves not the victors nor the vanquished in the fleeting triumphs of one country over another in the bloody turmoil of destructive war, but the heirs of all the treas-ures of the past and the masters of all the science, the abundance, and the glories of the future."

One final word: Remember as you go out from this place, that you are forever a part of the University of California. It is to you, its sons and daughters, that the University must look for justification of its works. For it is still true of all institutions that "By their fruits ye shall know them." It is upon you, primarily and increasingly, that the University must rely for intellectual, moral, and even financial sup-port. Upon you, as life brings you to positions of influence in your neighborhoods and communities, and, some of you, in much larger areas, will devolve a responsibility for the direction of this University in which you once were students. Hold her ever in reverence, hold her ever dear, help her whenever the chance comes to you. Only so can you be true to your trust; only so can she achieve the full measure of the destiny that is rightly hers.

The Eighty-eighth Commencement, 1951

More than five years have passed since the "Victory" days—V.E. and V.J.—yet the world has not gained stability, and peace is still a far-off dream. In reaction, seemingly inevitable, from the heroic struggles and sacrifices of total war, wearied peoples have turned to what they deemed to be their own affairs. Absorption in personal, too often selfish, interests has displaced the spirit of service. That the eager hopes of 1945 have not been realized is patent even to the most undiscerning. As we look about us in the world of today, we see not peace but a universal hatred that seems to smother every generous impulse. Suspicion is rife among men. Idealism in the relations among nations is seldom to be seen. Western civilization finds itself both baffled and depressed; and the way out has not yet been charted, or even clearly hinted.

Nor is the problem one to be solved by clever adjustments, or in a short period of time. No one can doubt that the free nations are today engaged in a fight for their lives, and that the United States, the most rich and powerful of them all, is inextricably involved. The whole world is being tried as by fire. Society everywhere is in revolution. Western civilization is not only being challenged by a hostile, militant, fanatic ideology; it is desperately defending its very existence against evil forces, manipulated and deployed by power-mad, ruthless men. Victory in such a struggle cannot be won by local domestic arrangements; acceptance of international responsibility is inescapable.

Above all, I believe, the hope of our nation, as of all free nations, lies in a generation of youth trained to see clearly, to view broadly, to judge fairly, and to act fearlessly. It is for the development of these qualities in our youth that the University was established, and never before in its history has its responsibility been so heavy as it is today. Confident in the vitality of the ideals of individual opportunity, individual enterprise, individual liberty, upon which America was founded and upon which it has prospered, the University has sought resolutely, in your lives and the lives of the generations who have preceded you, to sow the seeds of knowledge and of faith. These are the saving elements of any human society, and if men would but learn the lessons taught in universities, and remember them in their hours of decision, the future might be faced with far greater hope and far more certainty than is now possible.

The University has done what it could, then, to help you to get knowledge that is certain, and to form sound mental habits. For all your lives she will continue to follow your careers with keen solicitude. The University has tried, too, to give you some understanding of the principles that the people of the western world have come to venerate as the very foundation stones of civilized life. These principles—honor, ethics, morals—are plants of slow growth. They have been developed out of the trials and troubles, the defeats and despair of mankind, for thousands of years. They vary from continent to continent, and from nation to nation; but even though these differences of standards exist, certain broad principles, representing the best among all peoples, have emerged: principles of probity, of freedom, of justice, and of good will. It is disheartening as we look out over the world scene today, to note how these fundamental principles, which are not inherent characteristics of the human race, but which have been worked out through centuries of trial and error, pain and death, are being flouted and ignored. Herein lies the most serious threat of all.

Nor are we in these United States free from this critical danger. Who can look closely at our nation today and deny that we, as a people, in both high places and low, are exhibiting tendencies and traits not alone contrary to our national ideals, but also destructive of our way of life. The boldness of crime in our large cities, the feeble acceptance of responsibility in public office, the scarcity of common sense in the administration of political affairs, the disunity of our diplomacy, cannot but cause grave concern to every thinking American. It is these laxities, above all, that we have sought to prepare you to resist as citizens with backbones of integrity.

Most disturbing of the evidences of our national uncertainty and unrest are the outbreaks of intolerance which have seized a significant minority, perhaps even a majority, of our people. The right of the majority to rule is too often interpreted as a mandate to translate a personal opinion into a code of conduct to which all must conform. Schools and colleges are too frequently targets for grossly unfair attacks. Fanatical attempts are made to legislate group prejudices into laws. Misguided conservatism too often seeks the suppression of trends which the patient search for truth has demonstrated to be logically inevitable, just as insane radicalism agitates for the destruction of what has been proved by the same methods to be sound and beneficial. Thus impulses and tendencies are being given rein which are entirely incompatible with the freedom of individual thought and action upon which our system of government was founded.

Aware of these dangers that confront our country and the world, we of your University, who will remain on the campus when you have gone, ask not primarily that you succeed in a material way, although we shall not, of course, wish that you should not do this, too; but, rather, that you play a full and faithful and effective part in the democratic life of the communities in which you settle. We expect you to be loyal to the principles of our American system of government, that is, self-government of a kind similar to that which you have known in your own student organizations; and we expect you, furthermore, to help to advance and perfect the practices dictated by those principles. Only through the thought and toil of enlightened, dedicated men and women such as you can our form of government endure, our society prosper, and the perfection of the aspirations they represent be more fully attained. Your idealism, the courageous idealism of youth—too often the butt of ridicule and the whipping boy of resentment—in the final analysis is both the shining hope of the world, and its safeguard when tempered by the experience and wisdom of the ages.

The Eighty-ninth Commencement, 1952

The past half-century has been easily the most destructive in history. Two world wars, a series of revolutions, a worldwide depression, and the current cold war—all these in one generation—have profoundly disturbed the equilibrium of all of us. Technological developments have converted rural peoples very largely into city dwellers; independent, self-employed men and women into organized workers, and pioneer individualists into regimented societies, depending upon collective action rather than individual initiative to attain their objectives. And the everpresent menace of atomic war has loomed so large upon the horizon that, even in our University buildings, there are signs today pointing the way to bomb shelters.

Nor can we forget for a moment the threat which Stalinism presents to the western world, a threat which is not only, and not even primarily, one of lower standards of living, or the destruction of liberty. The Russian people had known poverty and lacked freedom for centuries before Stalin came to plague them. Yet Russia, in the years before communism imprisoned her, enjoyed a rich and spontaneous life of the spirit, which fertilized not only the writers, and artists, and musicians among her own people, but also, by a steady stream of exchange, the civilization of the West. Stalinism put an end to all this by pressing the minds of Russians into intellectual strait jackets, by prohibiting disinterested seeking and lonely daring, and by inhibiting, as far as possible, contemplation and meditation, let alone free expression. So a monotonous uniformity of thought has spread like a blight among a gifted people, and engendered a purely utilitarian technology, an appalling dearth of intellectual discussion and artistic imagination, conforming to principles and regulations handed down from the Kremlin and the Politburo.

Nevertheless, it is my conviction that the problems which confront us all, though frighteningly difficult, are not insoluble, if only you and others of your oncoming generation will grant them the high priority they deserve in your thinking and doing, whatever your job or your profession may be. In this era of high specialization and keen competition, it will be hard for you to find the opportunity for adequate attention to social, economic, and political questions, but find it you must if these questions are to be answered satisfactorily, and in time. The obligation of those who have had the superior advantages that you have had, is to keep alive the spirit of individual freedom, of venturesome enterprise, and especially of general participation of all citizens in the business of government, the one business of which each of us is a part.

The key to the continuing success and well-being of the American republic is not the imposition of duties in times of crises, but the voluntary assumption of individual responsibilities in normal times. When enough American citizens accept this key in principle and use it in practice, when enough of them realize the virtues and potentialities of our free systems of economics and government (even when these are balanced humbly in perspective alongside the past, present, and possible future values and contributions of other forms of human society), victory in the grim struggle between the free peoples and Stalinist imperialism will be assured. For communism is a doctrine of despair, and the sure answer to its evil exploitation of human needs and fears lies in that "hope that springs eternal in the human breast," and in clear proof of continuing progress toward eradication of the shames of greed and oppression without resorting to hate, violence, or dictatorship.

I am not unaware, of course, that much of what I have been saying falls under the head of platitudes, but perhaps they are platitudes because they are true. Thoughts that have survived cannot be dismissed because they lack novelty. What I have tried to make clear is that the human feeling of being trapped by circumstances is to be regarded as a challenge to each generation. If you can understand this, you can meet and overcome discouragement with a high heart. The burden which civilization imposes, is the consciousness that life at the human level is a process of finding answers to perplexing riddles. Animals are weighed down by no such worries, for nature provides them with all the answers they need: but for civilized man there can be no such state of nature.

And now you are about to leave behind you the University years, in which you have been sheltered more or less from the sordid and disfiguring forces of the world of which I have been speaking, and in which you have had a unique opportunity to develop the best that is in you. Being a realist, I do not expect, of course, that every one of you, even in the extraordinary Class of 1952, will attain to a post of high distinction, or even of great usefulness, and thus be able to affect the destiny of the human race. But I do like to think of you who are being graduated today as men and women who will contribute to the enlightenment of the groups of which you are a part, to the appreciation and improvement of our American heritage, and to peace among the nations of the world. And so I wish you Godspeed!

ALUMNI AND THE UNIVERSITY

The Ninety-first Commencement, 1954

It is the custom in America, at least, that commencement speakers shall dwell upon one or another, if not all, of the current, unsolved problems of the world, and offer advice to the graduates as to how they may find the answers, thus crowning their careers with distinction, and their university with honor. As I look back over my quarter century of such endeavor, I might well become depressed at the results of my oratory, but I assure you that I am not.

On the contrary, I am happily persuaded that the well-known tendency of young men and women to reject advice, and to seek their own experiences, is one of the most priceless gifts of youth. For I shudder to think of some of the errors into which your predecessors might have fallen, if my words of wisdom had not been phrased in such generalities that those who listened might ride off in any direction, or even in all directions, secure in the belief that they were following my guidance. And those who did not listen, of course, were not harmed at all.

Today I am going to depart somewhat from the traditional course which may well have brought commencement addresses to a point of no return—return, that is, in the sense of profit. I am not going to moralize or philosophize in terms of your personal affairs. Instead, I am going to propagandize for colleges and universities, and especially for this University, from which you are being graduated today, but of which you will, nevertheless, be for all your days a part. For graduation does not terminate membership in the University; it merely changes your status from student to alumnus, and, we hope, eventually from beneficiary to benefactor.

As each of you lays down the privileges and obligations of undergraduate life, he takes on almost immediately the responsibility of a university alumnus not only to be himself an enlightened member of his community, but also to share with his neighbors the light he has received from one of the greatest beacons of reason in all the world. If you become a good alumnus, you will, I naturally assume, contribute money to the University for buildings, and scholarships, and other purposes, although we are not yet listing these gifts as assets on the ledgers of the Regents.

Every one of you, however, can, and I hope will, make the basic principles and purposes of the University known to your fellow citizens, thus helping to generate a wider popular belief in its values, and defend its integrity against those who would either weaken its resources or encroach upon its freedom. The great evolutionary forces in history have stemmed always from the intellect, which you represent whether you possess it personally or not, and from the spirit. The man who knows and who thinks clearly and with conviction about what he knows, is an influence that no demagogue can ignore. Even dictators have no answer to him but death, and over the centuries they have never been able either to exterminate his kind, or to reverse the forces that they have set in motion.

I am confident that it is because the American people believe these things to be true, that they send so many of their children to colleges and universities, and that they have contributed so generously both privately and publicly to the support of these institutions. Nevertheless, at the recent session of the state legislature, a note of criticism most discordant to my perhaps ultra-sensitive ears, was sounded in about these words: The faculty of the University of California ranks among the foremost in public and private universities of the nation, and first among publicly supported institutions. It is a grave question, however, whether or not the State of California can afford this level of instruction, and this quality of research.

It is this question I wish to discuss briefly with you, your parents, relatives, and friends in this great audience. As you might expect, I think I know the answer. Certainly, I am fervent in my belief, not only that this state of ours can afford public education of the quality it now offers to its youth, from the elementary schools through the graduate divisions of the state university, but also that it cannot afford anything less than this and hope to measure up to the limitless possibilities of its natural resources: in the words inscribed on one of the state buildings in Sacramento, to provide men to match its mountains.

From the early beginnings of our freedom-loving republic, America's system of public education has been a principal road toward its goal of liberty and justice for all. America's colleges and universities have been a sturdy part of the backbone, not only of the progress of government of the people, for the people, by the people, but also of our way of life. Today these colleges and universities, both private and public, are imperative for America's survival. In this technologic, atomic society, with its insistent demand for new scientific principles, these institutions simply cannot be permitted to wither on the vine, and become incapable of producing the fruits essential to our national health.

In the fell clutch of the circumstances that confront us in the world of 1954, two conclusions seem to me axiomatic: (1) that the trustees of both public and private colleges and universities must be able continuously to demonstrate that the goods they offer are worth the money they cost, and (2) that the American people must realize that they cannot have the kind of higher education their children have enjoyed in the past unless they are willing to pay for it at present-day prices.

Further, it seems to me almost axiomatic that neither the trustees nor the people can justify any amount of money spent upon institutions without appropriately high standards of admission, instruction, and graduation. Certainly, the conferring of a degree does not make an educated man and woman, and the ultimate cost of proceeding as if it did would bankrupt our society much more quickly and surely than the cost of education *per se*, whatever this might prove to be.

AFTER TWENTY-FIVE YEARS
The Ninety-third Commencement, 1956

Perhaps you will be interested this afternoon, while the memory of your student days is still fresh and clear in your minds, and just before you set out on your respective careers—careers that I hope will offer some of you opportunities to improve the standards of higher education for a later generation—in certain conclusions that I have reached after twenty-five years in a university presidency that offers experience without limit. One conclusion of which I am certain, perhaps the only one, is that reform, if needed, is not to be achieved primarily by skillful administration. In fact, I am not disinclined to accept President Nicholas Murray Butler's famous dictum that "Administration is the art of doing very well that which had better not be done at all."

If administration offers no panacea, how then shall we proceed toward the end product desired? To answer this question, one must first attempt to define the essential purpose of an American university. From the reading of many university charters and similar documents, it appears to me that one purpose is generally accepted, although in such general terms, unfortunately, as to be recognizable only with difficulty. This is the preparation of young men and women for citizenship by equipping them in a measure to face the problems of the present and future, by bringing them into contact with knowledge of the present and past.

Certain obligations are implicit in the acceptance of this undertaking, the first of which is that the student shall be disciplined to think reasonably, that he shall learn to recognize and reject half-truths, that he shall proceed logically from facts that he can establish to conclusions that he can intelligently defend, that he shall come to know "academic freedom" for what it truly is—freedom of the mind from mental inertia and ingrained prejudice. In order that these wonders may come to pass, he must be provided with what one of my predecessors, who shall be nameless only because I have not been able to locate the reference, once called "the furniture of the mind."

For a mind without furniture, without equipment, cannot put its powers to use, its mental activity operating in a vacuum can produce no more than dialectics. This is why the university preaches, although it does not always practice, exposure of every student to the learning of the past as well as to the discoveries of the present: literary, scientific, and esthetic. Such exposure has practical values in that the student may secure through it the material and the inspiration to build a more abundant and even more successful life. An abundant life, I should add, is that which results from dwelling in a special, well-furnished mind.

To these obligations of a university labeled "discipline" and "furniture," I would add a third: the creation and maintenance of an atmosphere in which young men and women will acquire a sense of individual responsibility, that will determine and govern their lifelong attitudes toward the society of which they are a part. Out of this will come, inevitably, a realization that one cannot and should not expect to get something for nothing; that responsibilities are the price one pays for rights; and that society owes no man a living who has not diligently and earnestly sought to earn it.

None of these obligations of the true university, I am convinced by my years spent in this one, as a student and later as an administrator of one kind or another, can be met satisfactorily by any single educational formula. Consequently, I have with admirable restraint, consistently refrained throughout my presidency from offering presidential panaceas for the guidance of either my betters in the faculty or my fellow learners in the student body. Formulas and processes are useful only to the extent that they stir up controversy and rout complacency. But they are positively dangerous if they divert a university from its main purpose, which has to do with human beings—with young men and women—over into the subsidiary problems of methods and organization.

Methods and organizations are valuable only as they help to bring the student and the teacher together in a favorable atmosphere, where flint may strike steel and spark find tinder, or, at least, moss find new boulders on which to cling and lend beauty to an otherwise desolate landscape. The only thing that really counts, if my observation is worth anything, is the relation between a student with an observing eye and eager mind, on the one hand, and a teacher with an overflowing mind, library, and laboratory on the other.

WHEN A PRESIDENT GRADUATES
The Ninety-fifth Commencement, 1958

Regents, faculty, relatives and friends, we of the graduating class salute you on this ninety-fifth Commencement Day of the University of California. For twenty-seven of these ninety-five Commencement Days I have spoken at the exercises, in the beginning on the Berkeley campus alone, and latterly on from three to five campuses, from Davis in the north to Riverside in the south. On each of these previous occasions I have delivered a last message to those about to be graduated. Now the time has come for me to say the last words of all, for I am this year to be graduated along with the Class of 1958, which has already graciously conferred upon me an honorary membership in its distinguished company, and to have conferred upon me, by the authority vested in the Regents, a new title—President Emeritus.

These 1958 words of mine, however, will not be addressed by me to myself for I have not yet gotten to the point where I talk to myself. They will be spoken as in the past to those who are about to receive undergraduate, graduate, and professional academic degrees. Nor will they, except perhaps at the very end of this address be words of farewell. They will as usual be words of counsel as to how you who are about to begin the practice of life may make the most of the opportunities that your University has spread before you.

First I would remind you that the end and purpose of a university worthy of the name is neither to fill the heads of its graduates with more facts than they can hold, nor to improve their personalities and skills. One of its highest purposes, and the one I propose to talk about this afternoon, is to develop insight and understanding that will enable each of you, throughout your life, to foresee at least some of the possible results of your projected ideas and actions, and those of others. Lacking the capacity to discount and reject ideas of little merit, and to sense and act upon ideas that are good, most human beings must wait for events to overtake their ventures and experiments. They lack the powers of analysis and imagination that would enable them to anticipate what is likely to happen. I covet for each of you who is graduating today the God-like gifts of insight and understanding.

With these gifts, even in limited degree, you may face the future without anxiety as to your careers. I say this with full cognizance of the turmoil and uncertainty into which the political and economic affairs of our times have fallen the world around, and of the conclusion you may therefore draw that I am merely cheer-leading when the game is all but lost. My confidence is based upon a belief that the very insecurity of the age in which we live is a challenge to men and women with the capacity to think. The great advances of mankind, both social and biologically, have all come out of periods when wit and will had to make their way against unfriendly environments—and many of them periods when the struggle was to survive.

Whatever you personally may choose to do, your generation will have abundant opportunity to blaze new trails, to be creative, to salvage and revitalize traditions that have been thoughtlessly renounced, as well as to lay foundations for new and productive traditions, and for worthy personal careers. In the next twenty years, which will probably be the most telling years of your life, many of the formulas that now guide the thinking both of men and of nations will have to be adjusted to the new circumstances of an age of atomic science and universal technology. New kinds of leaders will have to be developed, new kinds of statesmen, new kinds of businessmen, new kinds of engineers, new kinds of labor leaders, new kinds of men—period.

This future, there is reason to believe, will be closed far more completely than is the present to men of undisciplined capacities, to business-as-usual routiners, to the mouthers of stale formulas, to the reactionaries who forget nothing and learn nothing, and to the radicals who sell themselves into slavery to rigid dogmas. The future of business, the future of education, the future of the professions then should be capturable and controllable by men who bring to their processes minds and characters that are free, disciplined, and realistic—three qualities of mind and character, I may add, that are even today far from incompatible.

I do not seek by these brave words to persuade you to believe that for each individual in the better tomorrow intelligence will be everything, and the nature of the social order in which he lives will be nothing. This would be absurd. But I do nail to my door the thesis that there is no substitute for individual thinking, individual character, and individual struggle. America has been converted by forces such as these from a wilderness inhabited by savages into a civilization of widely spread opportunity, freedom, and well-being. It will continue to make even faster progress in these directions if yours, the oncoming generation, cultivates and clings to these ancient virtues of self-reliance.

For there is no flaw in the social theories, political policies, or political organization of our society that steady and responsible intelligence of a high order cannot correct. America is not even seriously ill, let alone dying, as her chief and deluded rival in time will learn. Nor is the political or even the diplomatic genius of the nation bankrupt. There is still leadership to be found in groups such as this graduating class and others like it throughout the land, leadership that suffers neither from the *rigor mortis* of reaction nor the St. Vitus dance of irresponsible utopianism—leadership for labor and politics and industry and agriculture, as well as for the professions including the great profession of teaching. It is for each one of you to find that kind of leadership, and for the best of you to become a part of it.

The charge, then, that I would give you men and women upon whom the University of California confers degrees on this day of commencement, traditionally a day of memory and high resolve, is that you dedicate yourselves anew to the service of truth, of justice, and of the common life, and build your personal careers into the structure of your community, your state, and your nation. Thus and thus only can you hope to repay what you have been given on this campus in no carefully calculated fashion, but gladly, freely, and generously. And to this end, I hope that you will think of your Alma Mater always, not only as a fond mother, which she is and will continue to be, but also as a parent mindful of the public duty of her children and scornful of sons and daughters who seek only their own material success and illusory happiness.

So much for all of you to whom I have addressed myself thus far, and now for just a word for myself as I join with you in parting from my official connection with our University. My word is the word "Farewell," a word often uttered lightly and forgotten readily. But when this word marks the rounding off of a chapter in life, the severing of ties many and cherished, the parting all at once with many friends of the long years, and especially when it is spoken in a place of memories and sentiment, it somehow sticks in the throat. "Farewell" has been defined as "the word that makes us linger," yet it does not prompt me to many other words. Perhaps it is best expressed in few. Fortunately I am not being sent away alone. You who are being graduated this afternoon, and the one hundred and eighty-five thousand students upon whom I have conferred degrees in the past twenty-seven years, one hundred fifteen thousand of them from this Berkeley campus, will be my spiritual if not my corporal companions. Nor am I being sent away empty-handed. I go laden with happy memories, inexhaustible I am sure, for as long as I may live. And so I go willingly, if not gladly, even though I go with half my heart left behind. Good-by and good luck to all of you!

This book has been designed by
Adrian Wilson
and printed and bound by the
University of California Printing Department
under the supervision of
A. R. Tommasini

The type is University of California Old Style
designed during the administration of Robert Gordon Sproul
by Frederic W. Goudy
especially for the use of the University